THE BOARD OF TRADE AND THE FREE-TRADE MOVEMENT 1830–42

THE BOARD OF TRADE AND THE FREE-TRADE MOVEMENT 1830–42

BY

LUCY BROWN

OXFORD
AT THE CLARENDON PRESS
1958

Oxford University Press, Amen House, London E.C.4
GLASGOW NEW YORK TORONTO MELBOURNE WELLINGTON
BOMBAY CALCUTTA MADRAS KARACHI KUALA LUMPUR
CAPE TOWN IBADAN NAIROBI ACCRA

PRINTED IN GREAT BRITAIN

PREFACE

THIS study of the relationship of civil servants to the making of economic policy was first suggested to me by some years' work as a research assistant for the official history of the Board of Trade in the last war. I should like to take the opportunity of expressing my thanks for the help I have had from many sources in carrying it out. My deepest debts are to Professor T. S. Ashton and Mr. H. L. Beales, under whose guidance I worked, and to the Trustees of the Houblon-Norman Fund, whose grant of a research fellowship in the years 1950–2 gave me the opportunity of collecting most of the materials. I must also express my gratitude for the help I have had at various times from discussion with Professor A. Aspinall, Professor Asa Briggs, Mr. M. G. Brock, and Professor F. E. Hyde.

I would like to acknowledge the obligation which I owe, for the use of manuscript and other sources, to the Earl of Clarendon, for the Clarendon MSS., to Lady Salmond for the Melbourne MSS., to General Goulburn and the Surrey Record Office for the Goulburn MSS., to the Manchester Public Libraries for the J. B. Smith MSS., and to Messrs Longmans for the quotation from Beatrice Webb's *Our Partnership*, which appears on the next page.

Finally I would like to thank those friends, Miss B. F. Harvey, Miss R. E. Woolf, and Mr. P. A. Lane, who spent time and trouble in helping me to prepare the manuscript for publication.

LUCY BROWN

The University of Hull
28 April 1958

'There is no such thing as spontaneous public opinion; it all has to be manufactured from a centre of conviction and energy radiating through persons.'

BEATRICE WEBB, 1903

CONTENTS

PART I

THE POLITICAL ENVIRONMENT OF THE BOARD OF TRADE

PART II

THE BOARD OF TRADE AT WORK, 1830–40

PART III

THE BOARD OF TRADE AND THE ATTACK ON THE BRITISH TARIFF

PART I
THE POLITICAL ENVIRONMENT OF THE BOARD OF TRADE

1
PARLIAMENT AND ECONOMIC POLICY IN 1830

WHEN Huskisson died in September 1830, Greville wrote: 'It is probably true that there is no man in Parliament, or perhaps out of it, so well versed in Finance, commerce, trade, and Colonial matters, and that he is therefore a very great and irreparable loss. . . . It is equally true that all the ablest men in the country coincide with him, and that the mass of the community are persuaded that his plans are mischievous to the last degree.'[1] How far a careful analysis would show this to be a correct judgement is not for the moment to be discussed: Greville was a sensitive barometer of the political atmosphere, and this comment is valuable in the contrast it presents to his comments on Peel's Budget of 1842. Then he wrote: 'There is, however, a general disposition to accept the measure, and to acknowledge that Peel is entitled to a fair trial of what must be considered a great political and financial experiment.'[2] Three months later his opinion was unchanged: 'Peel's Government has been acquiring fresh power and solidity every day till now; there is hardly any opposition to it in Parliament or out. The whole country is prepared (if not content) to take his measures, and let him have his own way without let or hindrance.'[3] Between the entry in the Diary of 1830 and those

[1] C. C. F. Greville, *The Greville Memoirs, 1814–60* (edited by Lytton Strachey and Roger Fulford) (London, 1938), vol. ii, p. 47 (18 Sept. 1830).
[2] Ibid., vol. v, pp. 16–17 (14 Mar. 1842).
[3] Ibid., vol. v, p. 24 (5 June 1842).

of 1842 lies a substantial chapter in the history of the free-trade movement: it is the purpose of this narrative to discuss the part played in producing this change by technical advisers, and particularly by the permanent officials of the Board of Trade.

The economic policy with which Huskisson is associated had been closely related to problems created by the war, and had been carried out in the years of expanding trade between 1823 and 1825. It hinged on two requirements. There was the need to adjust commercial relations with other countries to take account of changes brought about by the war; the first changes in the Navigation Acts in 1822 had been designed to allow the former Spanish-American colonies to export goods to Britain in their own ships, as was done by European countries and by the United States. In 1823 the Reciprocity of Duties Act empowered the King in Council to extend to all countries, who were willing to act on the principle of reciprocity, equality of duties and drawbacks on goods imported in the ships of those countries into the United Kingdom. This reciprocity had been extracted from Britain under threat of retaliation, first by the United States in 1818, and then by Prussia in 1824. The second alteration in the Navigation Acts, that of 1825, opened the trade with the British colonies to the shipping of all countries which were prepared, if they possessed colonies, to offer similar concessions to British shipping. In all these measures, breaches were made with tradition, but they were probably less wide than they might have appeared to be at first sight. Alterations in the Navigation Acts were only of importance to those countries which possessed large merchant fleets, and much was still reserved to British shipping. There was still a considerable list of enumerated articles of European production which could only be imported in British ships, or in ships of the country of which they were the produce, or from which they had been exported. A similar restriction covered all goods which were the produce of Asia and Africa.[1] None of the changes had weakened the principle of imperial preference. Colonial tariffs gave a preference to British goods, and colonial produce—Canadian timber and wheat, East and West India sugar and coffee, wines from the Cape of Good Hope—all enjoyed a preference in the British tariff. The opening of the colonial trade to foreign shipping was a more drastic change, but here again the United States, the country which was chiefly

[1] Cf. p. 117 below.

affected, had, since 1794, been admitted to the trade with the West Indies.

The second aspect of Huskisson's policy was fiscal. During the war, and particularly before the introduction of the income tax in 1799, Customs and Excise duties had been raised steeply wherever it was possible. The abolition of the income tax in 1816 and the size of the national debt after the war had made it impossible to reduce the amount levied by indirect taxation. But in 1824 and 1825 the Government had surpluses at its disposal, and used them for reductions in the tariff. The duties on West India rum were reduced to the rates payable on British spirits; the import duties on raw wool were repealed and the export of raw wool permitted; the prohibition on the import of silk manufactures was removed and a 30 per cent. *ad valorem* duty substituted for it. All these were significant changes. Those of 1825 mostly consisted in the removal of obsolete protective duties, which sometimes ranged from 75 to 180 per cent. on goods such as cotton, iron, and earthenware, of which Britain was a considerable exporter, and in the reduction of duties on many raw materials.[1]

The present chapter will sketch the state of the free-trade movement in 1830. To express the situation in this way begs the question. Most traditional studies of commercial policy in this period, Buxton's *Finance and Politics*, for example, or Smart's *Economic Annals*, tend to be written in teleological terms. The removal of all restrictions on foreign trade, and the imposition of indirect taxes for revenue only, are conceived of as the necessary destination to which the country would arrive in time. Budgets or commercial arrangements tend to be judged by the extent to which they brought nearer this result. But to see things in this light does not do justice to the dangers and complexities of the situations which the Cabinets of 1815 to 1846 were periodically called upon to tackle. The situation in 1830 provides a good example of this.

In 1829 and 1830 debates in Parliament still showed the reaction against some of the work of Huskisson. Trade depression and a harvest failure in 1829 combined to stimulate discontent. Parliament was occupied with innumerable petitions and debates, all dealing with some aspect of the distress. According to Smart, 180

[1] The details of the legislative changes introduced by Huskisson and the Tories are given in W. Smart, *Economic Annals of the Nineteenth Century* (London, 1917), vol. ii.

petitions were presented on this subject during the session of 1829. There were complaints from agricultural districts of the working of the sliding scale of 1828. According to Charles Grant, Vice-President of the Board of Trade from 1823 to 1827 and President from 1827 to 1828, no industry could be considered to be suffering more than the rest.[1] Unemployment was general. Nevertheless, complaints came very loudly from those industries which believed themselves, rightly or wrongly, to have suffered from the work of Huskisson—from the silk industry, from the wool producers and manufacturers, and from the shipping interest, who were complaining of the effects of the opening of the colonial trade to foreign ships.

Thus far it would seem that economic distress was provoking a reaction against the economic liberalism of the Tory Government, and to some extent this is true. But it is also true that the distress spurred on a host of other people to make known their grievances. In the session of 1830 Parliament received many petitions for the restriction of the East India Company's monopoly. Sugar refiners and the West India planters joined in asking for reduction in the sugar and rum duties. Many agricultural districts joined to their complaints of distress an appeal for the reduction of the beer and malt duties. There were complaints, though not so many, of the assessed taxes and the stamp duties on newspapers, and complaints of a variety of other burdens—the tithe, the duty on beer, soap, and candles, the stamp duty on medicines.[2] Finally, overshadowing all these, was the demand for parliamentary reform.

It is important to emphasize this bewildering variety of grievances, and to remember, at the same time, the outbreak of agricultural rioting in the southern counties in the autumn of 1830. Parliament was not master of the situation. To the members of that period the economic problem was basically one of the maintenance of civil order.[3] Outside the metropolis there were no police forces in 1830; the maintenance of order lay in the hands of the

[1] Smart, op. cit., pp. 204, 423, 457, 467, 494.

[2] *Hansard*, 2nd ser., vols. 22–25.

[3] See, e.g., D. Le Marchant, *Memoir of Viscount Althorp* (London, 1876), p. 233. In Feb. 1830 the King's Speech had stated that the distress was confined to particular districts, while the Opposition had moved an amendment that the distress was general. Lord Althorp 'felt that, in voting for the Address, he should identify himself with them more closely than his sentiments warranted, besides sharing the unpopularity which in England may be observed always to attend the absence of sympathy with the grievances of the people'.

justices of the peace, of the existing and often inefficient watchmen, and in times of extraordinary tension of the military. The Government had no regular and impartial sources of information about the economic—or the political—state of the provinces. Many of the debates of the later eighteen-twenties, and of the eighteen-thirties, were concerned with questions of fact or of interpretation—how bad was the situation in fact in different parts of the country? Or how should the extent of the distress be measured?

There was no lack of suggestions for economic remedies. The disagreements about the nature of the economic problems of the country underlie much of the disputes about the extent of distress, and about the way in which the facts should be interpreted: the simplest and most frequently demanded remedies were tax relief for a particular section of the community, or protection against foreign competition. But there were also two general schools of thought which were at war in the Commons in this period: the followers of Attwood, and the followers of Henry Parnell, and ultimately of Ricardo. The relationship between the two groups in the Parliaments of the eighteen-thirties is left for a later chapter. Attwood claimed that the distress after 1815 had a monetary origin. He traced it to a 'deficiency of the circulating medium' and concentrated his political attack on the return to cash payments in 1821 and the fall in prices since the end of the war. The opposing school would have nothing to do with such a line of argument: a change in the supply of money would have no lasting effects on the consumption of goods; buyers and sellers would in time adjust themselves to the change.

The theoretical basis of the division between these schools is not under discussion here.[1] In practice, in Parliament, they concentrated on different sets of economic facts, and tended to be supported by different economic interests.[2] In a situation in which, on many questions, there was little authoritative information, their debates could not get very far. Attwood's followers among the landed interest talked of the farmers whose incomes had fallen and whose rents had remained the same. Their opponents could not affirm or deny this: the Select Committees of this period could not examine more than a handful of witnesses. Again, on the question

[1] See S. G. Checkland, 'The Birmingham Economists, 1815–1850', in *Economic History Review*, 2nd ser., vol. i, 1948.

[2] See pp. 40 ff. below.

of unemployment, there was no reliable information covering the country as a whole.

After the death of Ricardo the furtherance of his teaching in Parliament had fallen into the hands of a small group of politicians who were Whig supporters. Ricardo's most important disciples and friends, James Mill and McCulloch, were not at any stage in Parliament. The Ricardian point of view was put forward by Poulett Thomson, a young merchant who rapidly rose to political importance, and by Sir Henry Parnell, a Member of Parliament of long standing, but a somewhat unreliable person.

The basic doctrine which they were putting forward was that the comparative costs of production vary from country to country, and that it is to the advantage of each to concentrate on the production of those commodities in which it has a comparative advantage. Partly on these grounds, and partly on the grounds of political Radicalism, they were hostile to any kind of exclusive trading privilege, whether they were thinking of the Charter of the Bank of England, the Charter of the East India Company, colonial preferences, or protection to British industries. They showed no sympathy at all with the opposition to the resumption of cash payments in 1821. All these points of view had been demonstrated by them in the debates on economic policy of the eighteen-twenties: the views of the school appear to have been fully developed and applied while the Whigs were still in opposition.

Their views, to a considerable extent, were in harmony with those of Liverpool and Huskisson. They laid great stress on the need to free industry and commerce from restrictions, that is, in the present field of inquiry, from Customs and Excise duties. Where these conflicted with other objects of government policy, the cause of free trade should have priority. This showed itself in the later eighteen-twenties and the eighteen-thirties in two directions.

As far as alterations in the tariff were concerned, it was frequently argued that reductions should be made by tariff bargaining with other countries: silk goods, for example, should not be more freely imported from France, unless France gave Britain similar concessions in return. McCulloch had no use for such a line of argument:

Generally speaking, all treaties which determine what the duties on importation or exportation shall be, or which stipulate for preferences, are radically objectionable. Nations ought to regulate their tariffs in whatever mode they judge best for the promotion of their own interests, without being shackled by engagements with others. If foreign powers be all treated alike, none of them has just grounds of complaint; and it can never be for the interest of any people to show preferences to one over another.[1]

He admitted, however, that there might be occasions on which it would be useful to stipulate for reciprocal tariff concessions, but this kind of bargaining should be a temporary and exceptional expedient, rather than a general system of policy.

This might appear to show a difference from the views of Huskisson, one of whose major achievements had been the signing of reciprocity treaties with a great many European and American powers. Yet Huskisson himself subscribed to McCulloch's view in the Commons: Britain should act without reference to negotiations with foreign countries, and others would then follow her example.[2] On this issue, then, there was no difference of principle, but it was a principle which it was difficult to maintain in the Commons, if other nations showed no sign of following Britain's lead.

Secondly, there was scope for disagreement between the two groups in the relationship of public finance and commercial policy. In the first place, which was more important—the reduction of the national debt, or the removal of burdens on industry? The Tories had clearly held that the former was more important: until 1828 they had held on to the idea of Pitt's Sinking Fund, in the teeth of constant criticism from Parnell, and Joseph Hume, the Philosophic Radical. They criticized the Sinking Fund, not only because, in the actual circumstances of the eighteen-twenties, the sum paid regularly into the fund could be obtained only by further borrowing—this was described by Hume as a 'delusive fallacy'—but also because they held that any surplus could be more profitably used to repeal taxes which were burdensome on trade.[3] On this question then, the views of Parnell represent a breach with official Tory policy; Lord Liverpool himself had been a firm defender of the Sinking Fund. On the other hand, it appears that Huskisson, at the end of his life, was in agreement with them. The Finance Committee of 1828, of which Huskisson, Hume, and Parnell were all

[1] J. R. McCulloch, *Dictionary of Commerce* (ed. of 1835), p. 1170 (article, 'Treaties (Commercial)').

[2] W. Smart, *Economic Annals of the Nineteenth Century, 1821–30* (London, 1917), p. 282. (Speech of 25 Mar. 1825.)

[3] See pp. 43 ff. below.

members, was the body which recommended the abolition of Pitt's Sinking Fund, and the Government acted on their recommendations in the Budget of 1828.[1]

The attitudes of politicians to the income tax provides a further test of their willingness to make sacrifices for the sake of commercial reform. With the abolition of Pitt's income tax in 1816, the country had lost its biggest and most efficient source of direct taxation. The remaining direct taxes, the assessed taxes, were unpopular, and did not yield very much. About three-quarters of the national revenue was provided, in the eighteen-twenties, by the Customs and Excise: any policy which sought to reduce these duties drastically would be compelled to find alternative sources of revenue, and of these the most obvious and practicable was a new income or property tax. Such a tax had been criticized by Adam Smith; it had proved very unpopular when it was introduced during the Napoleonic wars, and was widely regarded as something which could only be tolerated in the necessities of war. To revive it in time of peace was therefore a drastic step.

Yet all through the eighteen-twenties there were pamphleteers who were arguing that it was a step which was worth taking if it would relieve the pressure of indirect taxation.[2] This was a point of view which increasingly became heard after the boom of 1825 had collapsed: the fullest and most influential expression of it is given in Parnell's *On Financial Reform*, which was published in February 1830. This was a considered summary of the opinions of his group, and combined theoretical arguments against the British tariff with administrative arguments which had been strengthened by the work of the Finance Committee of 1828. Most of the arguments, of these two kinds, put forward after 1830 by free-traders, both within the Board of Trade and outside it, are contained in *Financial Reform*.[3] The tariff was attacked on a variety of administrative grounds: a large number of duties on minor articles raised a very small revenue, and were expensive to collect: some of the major revenue duties were so high as to give encouragement to smugglers: others checked consumption to such an extent that reduction in the

[1] The machinery for the administration of the Sinking Fund was abolished in 1829 (10 Geo. IV, c. 27). See p. 12 below.

[2] F. Shehab, *Progressive Taxation, a Study in the Development of the Progressive Principle in the British Income Tax* (Oxford, 1953), chap. iv, describes the pamphlet literature of this period.

[3] See Part III below.

rate of duty would probably lead to an increase in revenue. A similar attack was made on the workings of the Excise, which gave encouragement to inefficient methods of production. In addition, *Financial Reform* analysed the uses to which public expenditure was being put, and recommended economies. It proposed drastic reductions in Customs and Excise duties, and suggested that any deficiency in the revenue resulting from this should be made good by the reintroduction of an income tax.

The revival of the income tax returned to the field of practical politics with the discussions on the Budget of 1830, when the Wellington ministry, in its anxiety to conciliate the most clamorous demands for tax relief, proposed to repeal the beer and leather duties and to reduce that on sugar, at an estimated cost to the revenue of about 4 millions.[1] A loss of revenue of this order inevitably raised again the question of new direct taxation, and the question was extensively discussed both by the Cabinet and by the Opposition. Opinions were divided: according to Ellenborough: 'The Duke, Rosslyn, and I were decidedly against income tax. Lord Bathurst and Lord Melville, as well as the Chancellor [Lyndhurst] less decidedly so. . . . Aberdeen said nothing neither did Sir G. Murray. . . . Herries seemed much in its favour.' The strongest supporters of the income tax were Goulburn, who was to become Chancellor of the Exchequer in Peel's Cabinet of 1841, and Peel himself. Peel's support is of importance, since he defended it with arguments which were remarkably close to those which he finally produced publicly in March 1842: 'He wished to reach such men as Baring, his father, Rothschild, and others, as well as absentees and Ireland. He thought too it was expedient to reconcile the lower with the higher classes, and to diminish the burthen of taxation on the poor man.' He supported, that is, a tax which would fall on manufacturing and commercial capital as well as on land, and he regarded it as a price worth paying if it would broaden and strengthen the support given to the party in the country. The plan produced by Goulburn, the Chancellor of the Exchequer, had, however, excluded the owners of manufacturing and commercial capital, as well as the occupiers of land, and it was largely on these grounds that the tax was finally rejected by the Cabinet: 'it would have led to an entire separation and hostility between the landed

[1] S. Dowell, *History of Taxation and Taxes in England* (London, 1888), vol. ii, pp. 288 ff.

proprietors and the united body of labourers and manufacturers'.[1] Wellington was above all anxious to avoid a further weakening of his ministry by a tax which would antagonize the country gentlemen.[2] In these discussions two things are noticeable. The income tax was not, as it was in 1842, to be introduced partly in order to make possible a reform of indirect taxation on consistent principles, such as those of Parnell. Secondly, the cry that the worst feature of the tax was its arbitrariness, which was raised so frequently in the House of Commons in the eighteen-thirties by Peel among others,[3] was not apparently raised within the Cabinet. The distribution of taxation between classes was the focus of discussion.[4]

The revival of the income tax was as extensively considered in the two main opposition groups in Parliament, the followers of Huskisson and those of Grey; and in both groups it was perhaps more definitely associated with the reform of commercial policy. In 1841 J. C. Herries, who had been Chancellor of the Exchequer under Goderich between September 1827 and January 1828, wrote that he had 'formed the determination, with the entire concurrence of Huskisson and Lord Ripon, to propose a Property Tax, by way of commutation for some of the other existing taxes which appeared to be most obstructive to the industry of the country. The change of Ministry put an end to these plans. . . .'[5]

Huskisson himself confessed to a 'reputed squeamishness' on the subject. He spoke in March 1830 very strongly on the need for tax relief for industry and commerce, and suggested the substitution of a tax on capital not so engaged.[6]

[1] Lord Ellenborough, *A Political Diary* (ed. Lord Colchester) (London, 1881), vol. ii, pp. 212–13. Ellenborough added a curiously prophetic comment, which foreshadows the fiscal ideas of Joseph Chamberlain and Lloyd George: 'These last would have joined on all occasions in urging a further and still a further increase of income tax, and would never have consented to a tax on consumption. The income tax would finally absorb all other taxes.'

[2] *The Journal of Mrs. Arbuthnot* (ed. by Francis Bamford and the Duke of Wellington) (London, 1950), vol. ii, pp. 335 (16 Feb. 1830) and 345 (15 and 16 Mar. 1830).

[3] Stafford Northcote, *Twenty Years of Financial Policy* (London, 1862), pp. 29–30.

[4] In this respect the Wellington Cabinet held rather more advanced ideas of social policy than writers such as Parnell. Cf. pp. 145 ff. below.

[5] C. S. Parker, *Sir Robert Peel from his Private Papers* (London, 1899), vol. ii, p. 506.

[6] Huskisson, *Speeches*, vol. iii, pp. 538, 545, 554. (Speeches of 16 and 25 Mar. 1830.)

Within the Whig opposition opinions were also divided: Parnell, Poulett Thomson, and Althorp were all unhesitating supporters of such a programme. But Grey, in Mrs. Arbuthnot's words, was 'furiously against it',[1] and Brougham had taken a leading part in securing the abolition of Pitt's tax in 1816. Palmerston, who joined the Whigs in Grey's Cabinet of 1830, was also hostile, and so was Spring-Rice, who became Chancellor of the Exchequer after 1835.[2]

But, in the years 1828 to 1830, as the Tory ministry became increasingly weak and increasingly divided, the chances of the Whigs' return to power were growing. It was therefore highly desirable for them to emerge with a policy to offer the country; and, leaving the major issue of parliamentary reform on one side, the economic and fiscal programme of Parnell provided such a policy. This programme became more closely associated with party politics in 1829 and 1830, when the sudden and unexpected complaints of industrial depression provided the occasion for a strong attack on the economic policies of the Tories.

There were sound reasons why the drive towards greater free trade should become associated with the Whigs rather than the Tories, in spite of the tradition of Pitt and Huskisson. On the Whig side, there is the fact that the leading free-traders, the 'theorists' as they were described by their enemies, were associated with the Benthamites, and were therefore strong supporters of parliamentary reform. On the Tory side, the backbone of opposition to parliamentary reform came from the borough-owners, who also, as a class, were those most concerned with the maintenance of agricultural protection.

There is a further reason why the views of Parnell should have been more acceptable to the Whigs than to the Tories. The main burden of Parnell's argument was the need to reduce as far as possible those taxes which were burdensome on industry and trade. The need to reduce taxation could easily and logically be allied to the need to reduce public expenditure. The attack on the scale of government expenditure, whether on pensions and places, or on the army and navy, had for a long time been one of the traditional themes of the Opposition. The point of view of Joseph Hume could easily be allied in Parliament with the point of view of Parnell and Poulett Thomson.

[1] *Journal*, vol. ii, p. 345 (15 Mar. 1830).

[2] Le Marchant, op. cit., pp. 238–9; Stafford Northcote, op. cit., p. 26.

Between 1828 and 1830, then, the Whig opposition became increasingly associated with the economic policy which derived ultimately from Ricardo, but which was voiced in the House of Commons by Parnell, Thomson, and Althorp. Three stages in this process can be noticed—the appointment of the Finance Committee of 1828; the publication of *Financial Reform* in the spring of 1830; and the debate, on a motion of Poulett Thomson, in March 1830, on 'injudicious taxation'.

The appointment of the Finance Committee of 1828 was not a party manœuvre, nor yet an exceptional occasion. Similar committees had been appointed since 1786 to review government expenditure, its control, and means of its reduction. The committee of 1828 was proposed by Peel, the Home Secretary, and contained members of both parties: among the Tories were Goulburn, the Chancellor of the Exchequer, and Huskisson; among the Whigs and Radicals were Hume, Althorp, and Parnell himself as chairman.[1] This committee issued a series of reports. The first, and most immediately important, was issued in 1828, examined the working of the Sinking Fund, and pointed out its weaknesses. It was on the advice given in this report that the decision to abolish the fund was taken in July 1828. Secondly, the committee initiated a series of measures which were carried out after 1830, and with which the officials of the Board of Trade were closely concerned. The committee of 1828 carried out investigations into the way in which public accounts were kept in England, and compared it with the way in which they were kept in Holland, France, and Belgium. These investigations were conducted by a nominee of Parnell's, the Benthamite Bowring, who was later very extensively employed on behalf of the Board of Trade. This was his first public employment. These comparative studies, carried out from 1828, were continued under the Whigs until 1832,[2] and they provided the basis for the remodelling of the Exchequer in 1834.

Thirdly, the committee of 1828 investigated the working of the Customs and Excise duties, collecting a large number of tables showing the amounts yielded by various duties, the expenses of

[1] Smart, op. cit., pp. 448–9. There is much material on this committee in the Huskisson papers, B.M. Add. MSS. 38,751–2.

[2] The committee's four reports were published in *Parliamentary Papers*, 1828, v. Bowring's reports are in *Parliamentary Papers*, 1831, xiv, and 1831–2, xxviii. Similar reports, on the keeping of public accounts in England, are to be found in *Parliamentary Papers*, 1829, vi; 1830, xxix; 1831, x and xiv.

collection, and so on. They did not use this information to make recommendations involving controversial issues of economic policy. On the other hand, they collected the material which was used for this purpose later.

It was a common custom in this period for the publication of projects of reform to be timed for the opening of a new session of Parliament,[1] and this is true of *Financial Reform*. Whether this book was Parnell's personal enterprise, or whether it was the manifesto of a group of the Opposition is not clear. It led, however, to an important debate in the House of Commons on 25 March 1830.[2] Poulett Thomson moved for the appointment of a Select Committee to inquire into the expediency of a revision of taxes. He supported this proposal with a powerful speech which outlined the faults of the existing system on exactly the lines laid down in Parnell's book. The motion was resisted by the Government: to put such a subject into the hands of a Select Committee would be to allow too much scope to manipulation and intrigue by interested parties, and would create too much uncertainty among those trades likely to be affected. The conventions that Budget proposals are prepared in secret, and that the initiative in financial questions rests with the ministry, were also for the public advantage. Nevertheless, despite the fact that Thomson's proposal was unrealistic, this debate gave opportunity for the Parnell group to put forward their case and test their strength. The motion was lost by 78 to 167 votes.[3]

It appears that by this stage the question of financial reform was being disputed along party lines. The minority of 78 all belonged to the Opposition. Their names may be compared with the division list of 15 November 1830 when Wellington was defeated on a motion to refer the Civil List to a Select Committee, and was forced to resign.[4] All those who had voted for a revision of taxes in March, if they were present on the second occasion, voted for the overthrow of Wellington.

It may be deduced from this complex situation that, as Greville had said,[5] 'all the ablest men in the country' were broadly agreed on the need for some reform of taxation and of commercial policy, but that, partly for reasons of parliamentary tactics, partly from

[1] See p. 18 below.
[2] Smart, op. cit., pp. 550–4.
[3] *Hansard*, 2nd ser., vol. 23, col. 857.
[4] Ibid., 3rd ser., vol. 1, col. 549.
[5] Cf. p. 1 above.

their fear of further exciting social antagonisms which were already dangerous, they could not put their ideas into practice. Essentially, however, Huskisson was not in agreement with Ricardian doctrines which held that the only import duties which were legitimate were 'countervailing' duties, which compensated industries for peculiar burdens which they were carrying, burdens, such as tithe, which were not related to their costs of production but to the legislation of the state.[1] Huskisson was not prepared to go as far as this. Where British industries were likely to suffer from foreign competition, he left them with substantial protection. Similarly, he did not press for a free trade in corn.[2] Parnell and Poulett Thomson were prepared to go very much further than this. Parnell criticized the Budgets of 1824 and 1825 on the grounds that they merely proposed half-measures; the import of silk manufactures and the export of raw wool should both as soon as was practicable be made entirely free.

How far this distinction should be pressed it is very difficult to say. Huskisson was in office and had to withstand the weight of public criticism if things went wrong: in theory it might be sound to talk of Britain's comparative advantage in the production of cotton goods, and France's comparative advantage in the production of silk, but the Government could not risk the disorder which would have been provoked had they deliberately left the silk industry to its fate. Secondly, it is possible that Huskisson's ideas might have developed further had he had the political opportunity: he was out of office after May 1828.

It remains to ask what happened to the Parnellite group when Grey formed his Cabinet in November. Althorp provided the link between them and the Whig Cabinet. He has already been mentioned as a firm supporter of Parnell's views, and during the summer of 1830 the leaders of the Whig opposition were concerting their tactics at meetings which were organized by him.[3] With his help Parnell's group won most of the positions in the Whig ministry in which they could influence effectively the formation of economic policy. Althorp became Chancellor of the Exchequer, and Poulett Thomson Vice-President of the Board of Trade. Parnell received no appointment, but he became Secretary at War in April 1831.

[1] Cf. pp. 179, 193 below.
[2] Smart, op. cit., chap. 37.
[3] Le Marchant, op. cit., pp. 243 ff.

All these appointments were received with criticism. Althorp was criticized for his lack of financial ability, but he came from a leading Whig family, and his claim to an important position in any Whig Government was not contested.

It is suggested that Parnell had had expectations of becoming himself Chancellor of the Exchequer. Alone of these three candidates, he had both a long experience of work in the House of Commons and an understanding of financial and commercial questions. He had been a member of the House of Commons since 1802, and had sat on many Select Committees, including the Bullion Committee of 1810 and the Select Committee of 1813 to inquire into the corn trade, of which he was chairman.[1] He had taken the lead in 1824–5 in pressing Huskisson to more drastic measures of free trade, and had been at the centre of the movement for financial reform.[2] But he had weaknesses as a politician, and never rose into political prominence after 1830. Le Marchant, who knew him, pointed out that none of the recommendations for economies in the army, which Parnell had made in *Financial Reform*, was furthered when he was Secretary at War from April 1831 till his dismissal in January 1832 for voting against the Government. Le Marchant added that,

> it is due to Lord Grey to state that Sir Henry Parnell was not overlooked in the formation of the Government: an appointment was offered to him, but he refused it as beneath his pretensions. Those seemed to many of the party rather extravagant. Though a perspicuous and effective writer, he was a tedious speaker, and, except on questions of finance, could seldom make any impression on the House. . . . His integrity, personal and political, was beyond question, and so was his industry, but he had not the qualifications for a leader.[3]

Poulett Thomson's appointment gave surprise because of his youth and the speed of his rise to power. 'There never was a more sudden rise than this; a young merchant, after two or three years of Parliament and two or three speeches, is made Vice-President of the Board of Trade.' Greville also stated the general opinion that 'Althorp put him in'.[4]

Poulett Thomson was Vice-President of the Board of Trade from 1830 to 1834. During these years the President was Lord

[1] *D.N.B.*

[2] Smart, op. cit., pp. 215–16, 284–7.

[3] Le Marchant, op. cit., p. 271.

[4] Greville, op. cit., vol. ii, p. 75 (1 Dec. 1830).

Auckland, whose effectiveness was limited by the fact that he sat in the House of Lords. Little emerges, either in the memoirs of this period or in the internal history of the Board, which throws much light on his character: the Auckland papers in the British Museum are an almost total blank for these years. The indications are that Poulett Thomson had considerable scope and power, even while he was Vice-President only. According to Le Marchant, Lord Auckland 'had good sense, honesty, and assiduity, and was highly esteemed, but the real business of the department was judiciously left to Mr. Poulett Thomson'.[1]

From 1834 until 1839, when he was appointed Governor-General of Canada, Thomson was President of the Board. He is therefore a key figure in this narrative. He had been born in 1799, the youngest son of J. P. Thomson, partner in the firm of Thomson, Bonar & Co., merchants trading with Russia. He had been brought up in the family business, and had been sent in 1815 to St. Petersburg to learn the Russian side of it. He returned in 1817 because of ill health, made a tour of France, Italy, and Switzerland, and returned again to England in 1819. Thereafter he settled down in London and became a partner in the firm. In 1826 he had entered Parliament as member for Dover.

Thomson's career was perhaps an unusual one. According to his brother, his biographer Poulett Scrope, he had 'entertained strong opinions of a liberal character on the more ordinary political questions of the age. These principles were entirely self-formed. Those of his family, of his father certainly, were rather of the opposite complexion.' When he contested the seat at Dover he was 'unsupported by the assistance, or even by the countenance and advice, of his family. His father and eldest brother remonstrated against the undertaking, as tending to withdraw his attention from the city business, to which it was desirable that he should devote himself.'[2] That is, he does not appear to have entered Parliament as the nominee of a recognized interest, nor did he enter it when he had reached mature years and financial independence. This perhaps provides a clue to his character, and suggests a reason for his unpopularity. He was extremely self-confident, and was con-

[1] Le Marchant, op. cit., p. 263, describes this as 'the only instance in which Lord Althorp actually interfered' with the formation of Grey's ministry.

[2] G. Poulett Scrope, *Memoir of the Life of Charles, Lord Sydenham* (London, 1843), pp. 6, 13–15.

temptuous of the people with whom he had to work. For example, he wrote to a friend in 1829 of his experiences in Parliament—'the majority of the House of Commons, ay, 600 out of the 650 senators, are opposed upon principle to any change, be it what it may; and a whole session could be readily spent by them in considering whether they had better consider'.[1] Or again, he met Greville in 1836 and 'descanted on the inefficiency of his subordinates; that Auckland did not like writing, that nobody else could, and consequently every paper had been written by himself since he first entered the office. To do him justice I believe he is very industrious.' Greville's opinion of him was that he was 'the greatest Coxcomb I ever saw, and the vainest dog, though his vanity is not offensive or arrogant'.[2]

But with this self-satisfaction went an equally obvious consciousness of dependence. He had already by 1825 become familiar with the Benthamite circle, in particular with Bowring, James Mill, Warburton, and Joseph Hume, and had learned economics from McCulloch. He entered Parliament with their advice and support.[3] Between 1825 and his appointment to the Board of Trade in 1830 he had spoken little in debates: his speeches had been marked by clear, but none the less dogmatic, statements of Ricardian theory. According to Le Marchant, 'there was often an ostentation of *doctrine* in his reasoning, which the practical and official experience of Mr. Huskisson successfully avoided'.[4] Littleton's description of him as 'the greatest of purists and political economists' tells the same story. With dependence on a body of dogma went also another characteristic which completed his unpopularity, namely his 'love of great society';[5] he had, on entering Parliament, attached himself to Althorp,[6] who supported his political ambitions.

In 1830, therefore, the Board of Trade fell under the guidance of one who was intelligent and energetic, who was a more consistent,

[1] Scrope, op. cit., p. 36.

[2] Greville, op. cit., vol. iii, p. 272 (30 Jan. 1836).

[3] Scrope, op. cit., p. 14. See also Bowring's *Autobiographical Recollections* (London, 1877), p. 301. 'I introduced him [Thomson] to Joseph Hume, and through him he was introduced to the electors of Dover, and returned by them to Parliament.'

[4] Le Marchant, op. cit., p. 237.

[5] A. Aspinall, *Three Early Nineteenth Century Diaries* (London, 1952), p. 6.

[6] It is interesting to see that Sir John Shaw-Lefevre also appears to have owed his start in political life to Althorp. He was auditor to the Spencer family (Le Marchant, op. cit., p. 542).

or at least a more explicit, free-trader than Huskisson had been, but who lacked Huskisson's political experience and his standing, both in Parliament and in the country. His appointment gave impetus to the development of the Board of Trade along Benthamite and Ricardian lines.

The alliance between the Whigs and the Ricardians in the House of Commons did not immediately dissolve, although it was obvious that once the Whigs were in office it would be subjected to new strains. The policy laid down in *Financial Reform* was not politically an easy one to introduce. McCulloch, the great exponent of Ricardianism after the death of Ricardo, was in close touch with the Whigs in the early years of their ministry: he acted as their interpreter and apologist. During the period from 1825 to 1830 he had at some time been giving lessons in economics to 'several young men of influence', among them George Villiers (who was later to be employed by the Whigs on commercial negotiations) and Poulett Thomson.[1] After 1830 McCulloch, in close association with Thomson, wrote a considerable amount in exposition of Whig policy. In November 1831, for example, he sent an article to the *Edinburgh Review* on the colonial question, remarking, 'What I have stated *accords entirely with the views of Lord Althorp*, Parnell, and Thomson. . . .' A year later he sent an article on the Bank: 'Thomson says it is of the utmost consequence that there should be such an article and that also is Lord Althorp's opinion. It will appear shortly before the meeting of Parliament and just at the right time. My views exactly correspond with those of Thomson, as his do with those of the government.' In the spring of 1833 he composed an article on taxation, after discussion with Thomson on the intentions of the Government—which almost suggests that he was given inside information about the next Budget. It was 'at the suggestion of Thomson that I added the paragraphs about the assessed taxes. . . . I am very anxious that it should appear as soon as possible. Thomson is particularly anxious as to this.'[2]

There is evidence that Althorp also leant heavily on expert advisers. As will be shown in a later chapter, he acknowledged his debt to Parnell in his first Budget of 1831. J. L. Mallet, who kept a

[1] J. S. Mill, *Autobiography* (World's Classics ed.), p. 106.

[2] McVey Napier papers, B.M. Add. MSS. 34,615, ff. 215, 447; 34,616, f. 60. See pp. 47, 92 below for further examples of this kind.

diary of the meetings of the Political Economy Club, has left an account of the way in which this expert advice was given:

> Sir Henry Parnell, Mr. Tooke, and Norman mentioned having twice dined lately at Lord Althorp's, who has the good sense to ask men of talent and practical information to his house, and to put them on the discussion of subjects that they understand; so that without committing himself or the Government, he obtains valuable information and assistance with a view to measures of commerce and finance.[1]

He added that the two Radicals Joseph Hume and Henry Warburton had also dined with Althorp in this way.

Altogether then, the Whigs of 1830 were more closely associated with a definite economic policy than the Tories of the twenties had been, or than Peel was to be in 1841. The same principles were already firmly established in the Board of Trade.

[1] *Proceedings of the Political Economy Club* (London, 1921), vol. vi, Diary of J. L. Mallet, p. 220. (The entry in the diary is dated Jan. 1831.)

2

THE BOARD OF TRADE

IN 1830 the Board of Trade was a small department, with two joint assistant-secretaries, a comptroller of corn returns, and about a dozen clerks on its establishment. It had a political President and Vice-President. It was still, as it had been in the eighteenth century, a Committee of the Privy Council for Trade, and the Board still included a number of great officers of state, who had no immediate concern with the problems of trade.[1]

In this period the whole Board never met. The President and Vice-President met about twice a week; all papers which had come in to the Board in the meantime were read at these meetings and action was decided. But the original character of the Board had not wholly disappeared: in 1830 Greville, as Clerk of the Privy Council, alarmed by talk of financial retrenchment, suggested that he should work there: 'I . . . proposed that we Clerks of the Council should be called upon to act really at the Board of Trade, as we are, in fact, bound to do; . . . My predecessors Cottrell and Fawkener always acted. . . .'[2]

The functions of the Board of Trade at this date were mainly advisory. The administration of the Customs was in the hands of a Board of Commissioners, with a very large executive staff, and this Board was responsible to the Treasury. There were, similarly, Commissioners for the Excise. The Board of Trade could be consulted, and was in fact frequently consulted, by the Treasury on

[1] The membership of the Board at the beginning of 1830 (under the Tories) was as follows:

President: W. V. FitzGerald.

Vice-President: T. P. Courtenay.

Members: Lord Chancellor; Archbishop of Canterbury; First Lord of the Treasury; the principal Secretaries of State; Chancellor and Under-Treasurer of the Exchequer; Speaker of the House of Commons; Chancellor of the Duchy of Lancaster; Paymaster of the Forces; Treasurer of the Navy; Master of the Mint; such officers of state in Ireland as were Privy Councillors in England; Sir John Nicholl; Lord Redesdale; Rt. Hon. Charles Arbuthnot.

Secretaries: James Buller; C. C. F. Greville.

(*Royal Kalendar*, 1830.)

[2] Greville, op. cit., vol. ii, p. 84 (12 Dec. 1830).

questions of Customs policy, but its position was advisory only. Secondly, the Board was interested in the organization of commercial relations with foreign countries. This was the responsibility of the Foreign Office, which appointed consuls, and received their reports, and which conducted commercial negotiations with foreign governments. Here again, the Board of Trade had influence, but how great that influence was at any particular time was necessarily dependent on the relations between the Ministers at the head of each department. Palmerston and Poulett Thomson were both anxious to open markets abroad for British exports, but they differed radically in their general point of view, and in their notions of what constituted a good commercial treaty.[1]

The development of central administration between 1830 and 1841 did not do much to enlarge the Board's field of activity: factory legislation was the province of the Home Office. Responsibility for railways and the merchant navy became vested in the Board of Trade, but not until 1840 and 1850 respectively. An important branch of commercial regulation came within the sphere of the Board in this period, however, when the Registry of Designs was established in 1839. (The Registry of Companies was not established until 1844.[2])

It is easy to see that for the intellectuals of the free-trade movement, who were being driven by protectionist reaction into the paths of research and propaganda, this department provided a congenial home. Civil Service conditions were, in any case, considered to be generally light and easy: John Stuart Mill, for example, chose a Civil Service career as the one which would give him the best opportunity to pursue his own speculative inquiries.[3] In the Board of Trade, in particular, the Ministers and their officials were not burdened with a great mass of daily executive decisions, and the subjects on which they were consulted were precisely those which they found interesting, and on which they had something valuable to say. Above all, the Board of Trade still followed in the tradition of Huskisson, who had 'made the business a science'. In the eighteen-twenties the Board of Trade had led the movement for commercial liberalism: in the later twenties, after

[1] See p. 95 below.

[2] H. Llewellyn Smith, *The Board of Trade* (London, 1928), pp. 126, 105, 201, 165.

[3] J. S. Mill, *Autobiography* (World's Classics ed.), p. 69.

Huskisson had left it,[1] his successors had had to defend his policy against the complaints of the industries affected, notably of the silk and shipping industries. There was, in short, an anti-protectionist tradition in the Board of Trade, which tended to be strengthened in this period by the general conditions of employment in the department.

The staffing arrangements of the Board of Trade appear to have been those which were fairly general in the Civil Service at this time. Senior officials were chosen by Ministers: in 1836 Poulett Thomson told Greville that, having superannuated the existing secretary, Thomas Lack, he was 'going to appoint the best man he can find'.[2] It is plain that in making these appointments political considerations played a part: two joint-secretaries, Le Marchant and McGregor, were undeniably Whig adherents. Le Marchant, before his arrival in the Board of Trade, had been secretary to Brougham,[3] and he was a political correspondent, in the later eighteen-thirties, of Russell and Ellice.[4] He was to be elected Member of Parliament for Worcester in 1846, in the Whig interest. McGregor showed his Whig sympathies most plainly during Russell's attempt to form a Government in December 1845, when he wrote to Russell offering to resign his paid appointment at the Board of Trade if he could be assured of the Vice-Presidency of the Board in a Whig Government.[5]

But while their political views were probably a qualification for their appointment, these officials were not usually changed when a new ministry took office: there were no alterations in the department either in 1830 or during Peel's 'hundred days' in 1834–5; Le Marchant, on the other hand, resigned from the Board in 1841, and returned to it in 1848, and this may perhaps be explained by his politics. Appointments below the rank of Vice-President were considered incompatible with a seat in Parliament.

[1] Huskisson left the Board of Trade in Sept. 1827 after the death of Canning.

[2] Greville, op. cit., vol. iii, p. 273 (30 Jan. 1836). Cf. the description of methods of selection given in E. Hughes, 'Civil Service Reform, 1853–5', in *History*, N.S., vol. xxvii, 1942. C. K. Webster, *The Foreign Policy of Palmerston, 1830–41* (London, 1951), describes the system of appointment at work in the Foreign Office in the eighteen-thirties (chap. 1).

[3] A. Aspinall, *Three Early Nineteenth Century Diaries* (London, 1952). See Introduction.

[4] Russell papers, P.R.O. 30/22/4; Ellice papers, National Library of Scotland.

[5] Russell papers, P.R.O. 30/22/4.

There is no evidence of the method of recruitment of clerks, but it may be guessed that in the Board of Trade, as in other departments, family connexions were of value in getting appointments to clerkships. In the Board there was a strong connexion with a family named Lack. Thomas Lack joined the Board between 1785 and 1790: he remained there, rising in the end to be joint-secretary, until he was superannuated in the spring of 1836.[1] In the Board were three clerks of the same name, Edward, Richard, and Frederick Lack. Once made, these appointments appear to have been permanent; there is little change in the list of clerks from year to year. They rose in the service by strict seniority—there is nothing to suggest that politics affected their tenure or promotion.

Two officials who were already at the Board in 1830 were fairly well-known people. The comptroller of corn returns was William Jacob. Jacob had been born about 1762, and had entered the Board of Trade in 1822, after ten years' life as a farmer. He had, however, both before and during his time at the Board, become known as an expert on the working of the corn trade—his earliest publication is dated 1814.[2] In 1826, and again in 1828, he had been sent by the Government to carry out a survey of the corn trade of northern Europe. These surveys were published; they discussed both the methods of agriculture of northern Europe, and the way in which grain was marketed; and they became accepted as authoritative.[3]

The second, and more important, was the joint-secretary, James Deacon Hume. Like the Lacks, he came of a Civil Service family. His father had been first a commissioner and then secretary of the Customs under the younger Pitt: he himself joined the Customs as a clerk in 1791.[4] From 1822 to 1825 he had been engaged in the work of codifying the many Acts of the Customs. This work had brought him fame, and had been praised in the House by Huskisson. How far Huskisson had relied on

[1] *Royal Kalendar*; Greville, loc. cit.

[2] *Considerations on the Protection required by British Agriculture* (London, 1814). Jacob's other published works on the corn trade are listed in the bibliography. See p. 234.

[3] McCulloch wrote to Napier of Jacob: 'His reports on the Corn trade have always astonished me. They are so much better than anything else that ever came from him that I confess I doubt their filiation' (B.M. Add. MSS. 34,615, f. 276, letter dated 22 Feb. 1832).

[4] C. Badham, *The Life of James Deacon Hume, Secretary of the Board of Trade* (London, 1859), pp. 1–10, 24.

Deacon Hume's advice is uncertain; the Huskisson papers in the British Museum contain few references to him.[1] On the other hand, John McGregor, who later succeeded him as joint-secretary, was given Deacon Hume's political and administrative papers as a parting present, and declared that they contained evidence of the dependence of Huskisson on his judgement and advice.[2] These papers are now lost, and McGregor, as will be shown, was not reliable in his statements. But it is certainly true that Deacon Hume regarded himself as the man who was carrying on the tradition of Huskisson, whom he patently admired,[3] and that he was considered a man of great influence by contemporaries. Greville, who was familiar with events in the Board of Trade in the course of his own work, wrote of Deacon Hume's position in the following terms:

> Huskisson and Hume, his Director, made the business a science; new Presidents and Vice-Presidents succeeded one another in different Ministerial revolutions; they and Lack were incompetent, and Hume was made Assistant-Secretary, and it is he who advises, directs, legislates. I believe he is one of the ablest practical men who has ever served, more like an American statesman than an English official. I am anxious to begin my Trade education under him.[4]

In 1830 Deacon Hume had not yet published very much on economic subjects. He had produced an anonymous book in 1801,[5] and in 1815 a protectionist tract on the corn laws.[6] During the war he had worked a farm at Pinner, but he gave it up in 1822, having lost much money with the post-war collapse of agricultural prices.[7] Whether as the result of this experience or not, he emerged between 1830 and 1840 as a champion of free trade: he became

[1] B.M. Add. MSS. 38,283, f. 261; 38,766, f. 124.

[2] J. McGregor, *Commercial Statistics of all Nations* (London, 1843), vol. i, p. vii.

[3] C. R. Fay, *Huskisson and his Age* (London, 1951), pp. 276–86, 290–6, summarizes the facts of Deacon Hume's career. He describes how 'Deacon Hume constituted himself the keeper of the Huskissonian conscience, and soft-pedalling all that side that was dearest to Huskisson, advertised him as the Great Free Trader' (p. 291).

[4] Greville, op. cit., vol. ii, p. 84 (12 Dec. 1830). See also the entries for 8 Aug. 1829 (vol. i, p. 306) and 18 Sept. 1830 (vol. ii, p. 48).

[5] *Thoughts on the Best Modes of Carrying into Effect the System of Economy Recommended in His Majesty's Proclamation.* (This work has been identified and described by C. R. Fay, op. cit., p. 281.)

[6] *Thoughts on the Corn Laws as Connected with Agriculture, Commerce and Finance* (London, 1815).

[7] Badham, op. cit., p. 17.

hostile to protection for agriculture, silk, and shipping, to the prohibition of the export of machinery, and to the idea that the British tariff should be reduced by international tariff bargaining.[1] He was elected to the Political Economy Club in 1834, and thereafter faithfully attended its meetings. J. L. Mallet thus described the impression made by Deacon Hume:

Mr. Hume is a man of sense and talent; and who disavows any opinions in common with the Schools of Godwin or Owen, but whose abhorrence of the aristocracy and landlords and monopolisers of property often brings him on the confines of those wild regions. He is a strenuous advocate for a free trade in corn, and has written an able disquisition on the subject.[2]

His known publications in the eighteen-thirties consisted of a series of letters to the *Morning Chronicle*, written in 1834,[3] and of various articles in the quarterlies. Two of these can be identified, one on the corn laws in no. III of the *British and Foreign Review*, and another on the timber duties, which developed further the evidence he had given to the Select Committee of 1835, in no. IV of the same journal. Both were published in 1836. He may well have written more; Badham, his son-in-law, suggests that this was so, but no more than these two have been identified.[4]

His influence on politicians after the death of Huskisson is difficult to assess; Badham tended to exalt it, saying that many statesmen were in the habit of consulting him privately. Greville, in the passage quoted above, believed him to be the directing mind of the Board of Trade. Sir James Graham, after Deacon Hume's death in 1842, described him as 'the life and soul of that department'.[5] Yet, in spite of this testimony, and in curious contrast to it, there are very few references to him in the manuscript collections of this period. And, unlike his more showy colleagues, he was little known on the Continent. He probably exerted the greatest influence in his evidence before Select Committees on economic policy. He gave evidence on silk in 1832, on timber in 1835, on fresh fruit in 1839, on import duties generally in 1840, and on the export of machinery in 1841.[6] In all these his evidence

[1] See Part III below.

[2] *Proceedings of the Political Economy Club* (London, 1921), vol. vi, p. 266.

[3] These letters were afterwards published in book form, *Letters on the Corn Laws*, by H. B. T. (London, 1834).

[4] Badham, op. cit., p. 330.

[5] Ibid., p. 337.

[6] *Parliamentary Papers*, 1831–2, xix; 1835, xix; 1839, viii; 1840, v; 1841, vii.

stood out for its clarity and for its demonstration of long administrative experience. It was published and discussed, and was quoted as authoritative by Peel and other politicians. His reputation, unlike that of his colleagues, was unconnected with party politics. J. B. Smith, a leading figure of the Anti-Corn Law League, who knew him, described him in 1841 as a Tory. His interests were not confined to commercial policy: he was, at the end of his life, chairman of the Atlas Insurance Company, and perhaps his most original project was one of introducing the principle of national insurance to supplement the poor law. (He suggested a scheme of contributory old-age pensions, but it does not seem that he pushed the idea forward, except among his friends.[1])

It is not difficult to detect the principles which governed the other senior appointments made in the Board of Trade in this period, nor to describe the characters of the officials appointed. In 1831 John Bowring, described by Greville as a 'creature' of Poulett Thomson, was appointed to accompany George Villiers to Paris to conduct inquiries, which are the subject of a later chapter.[2] Bowring was perhaps the best-known character in the circle of the Board of Trade: throughout his long career, until his death in 1872, he was prominent in an astonishing variety of activities. He had been born in 1792, and was therefore still a young man, but he had already had an eventful career in Radical politics. In 1822 he had been arrested at Calais while he was carrying a message to the Portuguese of the Bourbons' intention to invade the Peninsula. He was imprisoned in France, and on his release was exiled from the country until the revolution of 1830. It was as a result of the publicity gained by this adventure that he was first brought into contact with Benthamite and Radical circles. During the eighteen-twenties he was deeply involved in the work of the committee organized in London to support the Greek nationalists.[3] Bentham, during the last years of his life, leant heavily on him as secretary and confidant, to the annoyance of the Mills, who mistrusted Bowring. When the *Westminster Review* was founded in 1824, Bowring became joint editor with Henry Southern, being responsible for the political side of the journal. In this capacity he

[1] *Manchester Guardian*, 10 Feb. 1841 (speech of Smith to the Manchester Chamber of Commerce); ibid., 9 Feb. 1842 (obituary notice of Deacon Hume).

[2] Greville, op. cit., vol. ii, p. 222 (28 Nov. 1831). See Part II, chap. 7 below.

[3] The Broughton papers, B.M. Add. MSS. 36,460–2, illustrate Bowring's activities in this connexion.

was strongly criticized in Mill's *Autobiography*.[1] His employment in the public service from time to time dated from 1828, when he was secretary to Parnell, the chairman of the Finance Committee of 1828, and carried out investigations for the committee on the Continent, which gave him some qualification for the work he was to do in Paris. He was a man who made a strong impression on contemporaries with his strange mixture of qualities: enthusiasm for the good causes which he supported, enormous energy, a linguistic ability and passion for foreign travel which gave him the status of an expert on the customs and literature—as well as the economic organization—of many remote corners of Europe; and in contrast to all these an air of unreliability and self-advertisement, both in his actions and in his researches, which has tended to exclude him from the gallery of eminent Victorians. Greville's description of him as a 'theorist and jobber' seems accurate.[2]

When in the following year the post of head of the Statistical Department was to be filled, a person of similar background was chosen. The establishment of the department was of considerable importance in the history of the Board of Trade, and it will be discussed in a later chapter. But it is also important in a discussion of the Board's policy of appointment, for it is the only occasion for which there is some evidence of the processes by which appointments were made. Lord Auckland, the President of the Board, first approached Charles Knight, who at that date was engaged in producing the *Cabinet Cyclopaedia*, and offered him the appointment. Knight refused, and recommended G. R. Porter in his place.[3] Porter was not known at that date, except as the author of an article on life assurance in Knight's *Companion to the Almanac*, and of a technical work on the management of a sugar estate, the *Nature and Properties of the Sugar Cane*.[4] He had been in business as a sugar-broker, but this business had failed in the slump of 1830. He was married to a sister of Ricardo, but there are no other

[1] World's Classics ed., pp. 77–81.

[2] Greville, loc. cit. George L. Nesbitt, *Benthamite Reviewing: the First Twelve Years of the Westminster Review, 1824–36* (New York, 1934), pp. 29–32, has collected a number of descriptions, mostly unfavourable, of Bowring at this period of his life. His doctorate, a title which he used constantly until he was knighted in 1854, was an honorary LL.D. of the University of Groningen, and he was constantly referred to by his friends as 'the Doctor'.

[3] *D.N.B.*; Charles Knight, *Passages of a Working Life* (London, 1864), vol. ii, pp. 178–9.

[4] London, 1830.

indications that he moved in the circles of McCulloch or Bentham.[1] The dedication of his book 'to the most honourable Richard Plantagenet Grenville, Marquess of Chandos, chairman, and to the gentlemen comprising the standing committee of West India planters and merchants', suggests a different environment.[2]

Once inside the Board of Trade, Porter emerged as a free-trader. This is clear from the judgements expressed on controversial topics in the *Progress of the Nation*, the first section of which was published in 1836. He was active in the formation of the London Statistical Society, but was not elected to the Political Economy Club until 1841.[3]

The Statistical Department was not put on a regular and permanent footing until November 1833, and it was then that two further candidates appeared. One, McCulloch, had an unofficial connexion with the Board of Trade which has already been mentioned. Thomson was his old pupil, and gave him semi-official support in his search for facts and figures for his *Dictionary*, support which is eloquently acknowledged in the preface to the second edition of the work.[4] According to McCulloch, Thomson had promised to make the connexion an official one by appointing him to the Statistical Department, but told him 'that he had done all he could to carry the project but that *he had been over-ruled*. . . . He said that he was extremely vexed at the thing.'[5]

The third candidate was John Marshall, who had anticipated some of the work of the department by the production in 1833 of his *Digest of all the Accounts*.[6] He was of similar background. He was the protégé of Joseph Hume, and, according to some, a paid employee. Hume made many efforts to help him. He tried to persuade the Treasury to subsidize his book;[7] then he got the House of Commons to agree to the purchase of copies for the use of members.[8] In 1836 he again came forward to back Marshall for a

[1] There are occasional references to Sarah Porter in Ricardo's *Letters*, but nothing which throws any light on Porter's early career.

[2] Chandos was a noted protectionist member of the House of Commons.

[3] *Proceedings of the Political Economy Club* (London, 1921), vol. vi, p. 361. See p. 81 below.

[4] J. R. McCulloch, *Dictionary of Commerce* (London, ed. of 1835), p. vi.

[5] McVey Napier papers, B.M. Add. MSS. 34,616, f. 224, McCulloch to Napier, 7 Dec. 1833.

[6] London, 1833.

[7] *Select Committee on Public Documents*, *Parliamentary Papers*, 1833, xii, p. 38, appendix 2.

[8] *Hansard*, 3rd ser., vol. 17, col. 744, 29 Apr. 1833.

post in the new department of the Registrar-General of Births and Deaths, of which the first occupant was T. H. Lister, brother-in-law of George Villiers. Joseph Hume wrote in September 1836 to Russell, the Home Secretary, saying that the latter had promised Marshall a post in the department. Francis Baring, a Lord of the Treasury,[1] opposed his candidature, assuring Russell: 'I should have hesitated very long before I could have selected a gentleman whose judgement I have no reliance upon—whose tables were proverbially inaccurate and whose conduct at the Treasury has been anything but satisfactory'.[2] Hume defended his follower very strongly, writing: 'I have seen with great regret a degree of Jealousy of Mr. Marshall in persons in the Treasury and in the Board of Trade which do them little credit but which have done Mr. Marshall much injury. I have seen words and acts to discredit Mr. Marshall whilst they were borrowing his labours and proceeding in the work he had the credit of commencing. . . .'[3]

By the end of the period under discussion, there was no senior official in the Board of Trade who was a neutral in the controversial problems of economic policy. It remains to discuss how far this can be ascribed to the effects of their environment in the Board of Trade, and how far to a policy of selection, or to a prevalence of Radical free-traders among the suitable candidates. All three explanations have some truth. Deacon Hume became a free-trader in the course of his administrative career, and no doubt he would have said that it was experience which had altered his economic policies. He had been an advocate of agricultural protection in 1815, and of retaliation against the Zollverein in 1829:[4] in 1840 both these policies stood condemned by him. Possibly Porter's views crystallized into the usual shape while he was in the Board of Trade: there is no clear evidence on this. Le Marchant, who was rather more of a politician and rather less of an 'economist' than the others, commented on the regularity with which the Board of Trade made converts to free trade of its successive Presidents. He said, of Alexander Baring's qualifications for the post in 1834: 'The distrust he occasionally showed of Free Trade would soon have yielded to the influences which of late years have imperceptibly

[1] Baring became Chancellor of the Exchequer in 1839.

[2] Russell papers, P.R.O. 30/22/2, Baring to Russell, 3 Sept. 1836.

[3] Ibid., Hume to Russell, 9 Sept. 1836.

[4] See p. 100 below.

brought all holders of office in that Board to support Free Trade.'[1] But Bowring and McGregor were undoubtedly free-traders before they entered the Board of Trade.

It cannot be denied that Poulett Thomson had a natural preference for those who thought along the same lines as himself. It is more important to ask what alternatives he could have found. It might well have been true that there were a group of writers of conservative and mercantilist sympathies at that date, whose works disappeared into obscurity with the triumph of free trade. There were many politicians in England who would have used and supported them, and there were then many such writers in Germany and in France. A search[2] has, however, failed to discover any such group in England. The rivals for the control of the Statistical Department were, all three, followers of Ricardo, and in the eighteen-thirties the Ricardians were thought to be becoming increasingly uncompromising in their views on economic policy.[3] It seems probable that for the kind of work needed in the Board of Trade it was in fact necessary to go to Benthamites and Ricardians.

With the exceptions of Deacon Hume, the professional civil servant, and Le Marchant, the orthodox politician, all these men were of a type who were prominent in almost every administrative development in this period. The men who filled the Board of Trade were of a kind who found difficulty in fitting into any of the more usual walks of life in the early nineteenth century, when the opportunities of professional employment were so much more limited than they were later to become. Often they were self-made and self-educated; this is true of Bowring, McGregor, and Porter.[4] Le Marchant ascribed Poulett Thomson's aggressive and unpopular manner in the House of Commons to the fact that he had had the wrong kind of education to feel at ease there.[5] But in any case, whatever their education, they were too opinionated and too heterodox to have found the existing professions agreeable; they

[1] D. Le Marchant, *Memoir of John Charles Viscount Althorp* (London, 1876), p. 263 n. (Alexander Baring was President of the Board of Trade during Peel's ministry of 1834–5.)

[2] The catalogues of the library of the Board of Trade (1866) and the London Bibliography of the Social Sciences have been used, and the books written between 1815 and 1845 classified as being on 'commerce' or 'statistics' have been examined. Only one author of these statistical compilations, Montgomery Martin, has been discovered who had protectionist leanings.

[3] *Proceedings of the Political Economy Club*, pp. 262 ff.

[4] *D.N.B.*

[5] Le Marchant, op. cit., p. 237.

would hardly have found scope for their interests in Oxford or Cambridge, and they would have found the army or the navy intolerable. The only possible professional alternative to these which they could have found congenial was the Law, which was the profession of a fair number of Benthamite politicians and administrators. At the same time they were too restless, too intellectual, to succeed in industry or trade. It is noticeable that Poulett Thomson, Porter, and Bowring had all been intended for business careers: none had succeeded in them. Thomson quarrelled with his family when he went into politics in 1825, and left the business altogether when he entered the Whig ministry in 1830.[1] Porter's sugar business collapsed in 1830.[2] Bowring abandoned the merchant's business in Exeter, in which he had been placed, and came to London in 1811, at the age of nineteen.[3] Jacob had been originally a farmer, but had been driven out of business by the depression after 1815.[4] It has already been stated that Deacon Hume lost money in agriculture in 1822. Ill luck continued to pursue the financial and business enterprises of these men in later life. In 1825 Hume was awarded £6,000 by the Government in grateful recognition of his work in the codification of the Customs laws, and he promptly lost it by unwise investment.[5] After 1841 Bowring went into the City and became interested in railway promotion and in the iron-works of Glamorgan. He lost much of the money he had invested in this way in the depression of 1847, and was again compelled to look for public employment.[6]

A further common characteristic of the officials of the Board was that they were not of aristocratic stock. Under the prevailing system of nomination to Civil Service appointments there was considerable variety in the kind of people who were to be found there. In the Foreign Office, where in any case Palmerston had a firm control of his subordinates, the officials who were appointed tended to be younger sons or relatives of political families.[7] Greville at the Privy Council was wholly aristocratic in his origins, friendships,

[1] Scrope, op. cit., pp. 15, 42. [2] *D.N.B.*

[3] J. Bowring, *Autobiographical Recollections* (London, 1877), p. 4.

[4] *Parliamentary Papers*, 1836, viii, question 292, evidence of W. Jacob. (He had farmed from 1812 to 1822.) [5] Badham, op. cit., pp. 17, 28.

[6] *D.N.B.* See also *The City or the Physiology of London Business* (Anon., London, 1845), pp. 187–8, for an account of Bowring's City reputation at this date.

[7] Sir Charles Webster, *The Foreign Policy of Palmerston, 1830–1841* (London, 1951), vol. i, p. 65.

and general point of view. But at the Board of Trade the officials, chosen for more strictly professional qualifications, had neither personal links nor political sympathies with the dominant aristocracy. Hence, like Thomson,[1] they showed a resentful hostility to the claims of the landed aristocracy, which emerged clearly in their attitude to the corn-law question. Deacon Hume's 'abhorrence of the aristocracy and landlords and monopolisers of property' lies behind the arguments of his H. B. T. *Letters*.[2]

It is clear that, at this date, the public service was conceived of in terms very different from those which we would today accept as a classical description of the executive in the British constitution. Bagehot, in 1865–6, describes the Civil Service in terms which are familiar today: he writes at length on the evils of bureaucracy—addiction to routine, timidity in action, love of power. He defends the anonymity of the Civil Service and the doctrine of ministerial responsibility on the grounds that most civil servants are not of the calibre which can stand up to direct questioning. He could only write like this on the assumption that the Civil Service was non-political and that its sphere of influence was limited to the tactics rather than the strategy of government. These assumptions are incorrect for the Board of Trade in the eighteen-thirties: its list of publications shows that it was neither anonymous nor neutral in controversial issues of economic policy. 'Protection', according to Bagehot, 'is the natural inborn creed of every official body; free trade is an extrinsic idea alien to its notions.'[3] This seems at least arguable, and it is interesting to notice that the course of action on which Deacon Hume and his colleagues embarked was one which would lead to the abandonment of much of their official routine. How far this change of temper can be associated with the change in methods of appointment, and how far Bagehot may in fact have exaggerated it, are open questions. In the Board of Trade the tradition of dogmatic free-traders continued into the second half of the century with such men as Giffen and T. H. Farrer. At the beginning of the century the initiative taken by the officials of the Board was not unique, as is proved by the careers of Sir James Stephen, or Edwin Chadwick, or the early factory inspectors.[4]

[1] Cf. p. 17 above. [2] Cf. p. 25 above.

[3] W. Bagehot, *The English Constitution* (London, ed. of 1878), chap. vi, pp. 194–5.

[4] A further example of official influence is provided by the history of the emigration commissioners. (See O. MacDonagh, 'Emigration and the State,

While it is fairly easy to explain the general conditions which governed the appointment of officials to the Board of Trade and to similar departments, it is more difficult to define the conventions which governed official behaviour. The kind of influence which Deacon Hume was supposed to have possessed was exercised under a certain cover of discretion; the advice he gave to politicians was unofficial, his articles in the quarterlies appeared anonymously, and the letters to the *Morning Chronicle* were signed 'H. B. T.'. One or two indications, relating to other departments, suggest that discretion was more rigidly observed between members of opposing parties. For example, in March 1841 Gladstone received a cold reply to an inquiry about churches abroad from Backhouse of the Foreign Office:

. . . the arrangements themselves cannot be communicated on a private application to a subordinate Member of the office.

. . . I could not bring the enclosed before Lord Palmerston without risk of his drawing from it very inconvenient conclusions.[1]

A rather similar example occurred at the Treasury in 1843, during Peel's ministry. Graham wrote to Peel:[2]

Have you seen in the Morning Chronicle today a letter about Ireland containing all Mr. Trevelyan's Information in the very words, which he used to us?

Surely it is highly improper that a Secretary of the Treasury should thus communicate to an Opposition Paper intelligence which he made known to the Government as of official importance.

Think of that Blockhead Trevelyan boasting to Fremantle of his letter to the Morning Chronicle as a great public service!!

Yet, in the eighteen-thirties the officials of the Board of Trade behaved again and again in this way. The explanation may lie in greater laxity, among the Whigs, in standards of official etiquette, or it may lie in political sympathy between the officials and the Ministers to whom they were responsible. In any case, the result was to give them a greater influence.

1833–55: an Essay in Administrative History', in *Transactions of the Royal Historical Society*, 5th ser., vol. v, 1955.)

[1] Gladstone papers, B.M. Add. MSS. 44,357, f. 310, Backhouse to Gladstone, 21 Mar. 1841.

[2] Peel papers, B.M. Add. MSS. 40,449, ff. 84–85, Graham to Peel, 14 Oct. 1843.

3

PARLIAMENT AND ECONOMIC POLICY 1830–6

IN 1830 there was broad agreement among many political leaders on economic policy: some kind of income or property tax, some reductions of indirect taxation, further encouragement of the reciprocity system, were all measures which had influential support among the followers of both Huskisson and Wellington, and among the Whigs. In Grey's ministry key positions were given to those who took their ideas from *Financial Reform*. Yet in the years 1830 to 1841 there was no definitive change in the structure of taxation, and little extension of the reciprocity system. This situation, the background for the work of the Board of Trade, requires some discussion and explanation.

Down to about 1837 or 1838 political circumstances were, on the whole, unfavourable to change. The diplomatic difficulties which were encountered in attempting to extend the reciprocity system and to negotiate tariff agreements with foreign countries are discussed in later chapters.[1] In Parliament the Whigs, had they had greater determination, would still have been subject to peculiar difficulties. Their first two years of office were spent in an atmosphere of threatened revolution, in which the political aristocracy, as their memoirs show, could not forget that they were the target of public attack. The Whigs were embarked on a formidable programme of reform; not merely the reform of Parliament, but that of the English and Irish churches, and of the municipal corporations, were questions which deeply divided opinion in the House of Commons. In these circumstances they tended, after the failure of the Budget of 1831,[2] to avoid questions which unnecessarily divided opinion; and the question of financial reform could be avoided because, until 1837, it was not necessary to find ways of increasing the revenue.

The legislative programme of the Whigs was also affected by their relationship with the country at large. Between November

[1] See Part II below.

[2] See pp. 47–50 below.

1830 and the general election of May 1831 their majority was tenuous, but the elections of 1831 and 1832 both left them with substantial majorities. These majorities had, however, been produced through an almost revolutionary agitation in which the Whigs found themselves forced to appear as leaders of a popular movement. They were therefore peculiarly sensitive to the demands of the electorate, and at times these demands would have made it very difficult to introduce a consistent economic programme: they could not deal with colonial preferences if they were at the same time abolishing slavery,[1] nor could they reduce indirect taxes if they were being compelled to give way to the attack on the assessed taxes. There was no movement in the country, like the Anti-Corn Law League ten years later, to drive them on.

A third reason why they made little progress lies in the relative strength of protectionist interests in Parliament. From 1826 until about 1834 the policies initiated by Huskisson were steadily under attack in the Commons, and the most effective Whig leaders were not to be found either at the Exchequer or at the Board of Trade. Thomson's speeches read well in *Hansard*, yet there is plenty of contemporary evidence that they did more to annoy than to persuade.[2] Althorp was popular, but was not respected as a Chancellor. Spring-Rice was a nonentity. Certainly none of them had the impact on the House of Huskisson, Peel, or Cobden. They were not able, as Huskisson had been, to resist the pressure for Select Committees into protectionist grievances.

It is difficult to assess the parliamentary strength of these interests: sometimes, but not very often, the opposition to the ministry ran along party lines, as in the attack on the Budget of 1831; sometimes it came from definite economic interests which felt themselves aggrieved; and sometimes the opposition ranged round general theories of economic policy, support for which might cut across all other groupings. Further to this, of course, it does not necessarily follow that the Commons faithfully reflected the balance of opinion in the country.[3]

[1] It is perhaps significant that Joseph Hume, who held doctrinaire views on free trade, had doubts about the wisdom of abolishing slavery (*Hansard*, 3rd ser., vol. 18, col. 459).

[2] Cf. p. 17 above.

[3] See pp. 53–54 below.

The economic interests in Parliament which were discontented are easily defined. One of the most important, the West India planters, had been given a reduction of duty on West India sugar relative to other sugars in the Budget of 1830;[1] they had therefore no grounds for complaint against the tariff, and they were fully occupied with the anti-slavery agitation. In the years 1830 to 1836 complaints came from the landed interest, from the shipping interest, and from the silk and glove manufacturers. In addition there were general complaints of 'distress' from retail traders. It is noticeable that in these years no similar complaints were heard from the cotton or woollen industries, from iron and steel manufacturers, or from the manufacturers of pottery, that is from those industries which in 1840 were said to be disclaiming protection for themselves.[2]

The course of agitation by the landed interest follows very closely the course of the harvests. Little was heard from them in 1831 when the harvests were below average, or in 1832, although prices of corn fell during this year.[3] In June 1832, on the contrary, a Bill for the repeal of the corn laws was introduced by Lord Milton in the Commons.[4] It was withdrawn after a short discussion.

In the session of 1833, the agitation of the landed interest began to gather momentum; in the second half of 1832 the price of wheat had fallen from 63*s*. a quarter in July to 54*s*. in December.[5] In February, at the opening of the session, the Marquess of Chandos, the leader of the agricultural protectionists, asked if the Government had included an alteration in the corn laws in their programme, and received the reply from Lord Althorp that other matters were more pressing.[6] The campaign of the landed interest was then switched to an attack on the manner in which the tithe was levied, and in April and May there were further lengthy debates on the question of the corn laws. A motion by Wolryche Whitmore for the introduction of a fixed duty was defeated on 17 May by an overwhelming majority of 305 to 106. In June

[1] It was a reduction of 3*s*. a hundredweight.

[2] See p. 181 below.

[3] T. Tooke, *History of Prices* (London, 1838), vol. ii, pp. 201–4.

[4] *Hansard*, 3rd ser., vol. 13, col. 300.

[5] A. D. Gayer, Rostow, and Schwartz, *The Growth and Fluctuation of the British Economy* (Oxford, 1953), vol. i, p. 245. Statements of wheat prices in this chapter are taken from this source.

[6] *Hansard*, 3rd ser., vol. 15, cols. 139 ff.

another motion, for the total repeal of the corn laws, was defeated in a fairly empty House by 73 to 47.[1]

In May 1833 Lord Althorp had proposed the appointment of a Select Committee to inquire into agricultural distress.[2] This committee was later said by Poulett Thomson to have been 'composed wholly of landowners' and to have been diligently attended by 'Peel and all the great Tory landowners, by Graham and the Whigs';[3] nevertheless, they were unable to prove that foreign competition was the cause of agricultural distress. They drew attention in their report to the fiscal burdens which bore unduly heavily on agriculture.

In the session of 1834 the situation continued in much the same way; by the end of 1833 the price of wheat had fallen to 49·4*s*. There were petitions from industrial towns against the corn laws, and there were complaints from Chandos and his group. In February a motion introduced by Chandos, that the House should further consider the state of agriculture, was lost, but only by 206 votes to 202.[4] Petitions from Glasgow and London in March led to a general debate on Hume's motion that a fixed and moderate duty should be substituted for the sliding scale of 1828. This motion was lost by 312 votes to 155.

In the sessions of 1835 and 1836 the complaints against the corn laws dwindled, and the anxieties of the landed interest increased. The harvests of 1835 and 1836 had both been good, and prices fell to their lowest point, 36·5*s*., at the end of 1835.

In these circumstances it was difficult for the landed interest to press their attack on the corn laws since very little foreign grain was being imported. They therefore tended to say more about the burden of highway and county rates, and about the malt duties. Or they joined those sections of parliamentary opinion who were still in 1835 pressing for an alteration of the standard established by Peel's Act in 1819.[5] At the beginning of the session of 1836 the ministry were forced to allow a further inquiry: a Select Committee of the Commons was appointed on 8 February, and of the

[1] Ibid., vol. 15, cols. 1133–42 (House of Lords) and 1159 (House of Commons); vol. 17, cols. 752, 1161–92, 1378; vol. 18, col. 976.

[2] Ibid., vol. 17, col. 958.

[3] Lord Melbourne's letters, Hertford County Record Office, Thomson to Melbourne, 30 Jan. 1836.

[4] *Hansard*, vol. 21, cols. 649 ff., 1195 ff., 1266 ff.

[5] Ibid., vols. 26–28, 32–33 *passim*.

Lords on 18 February, although it seemed that no useful purpose could be served by them. The committees were evenly divided between supporters and opponents of the standard, and were unable to agree on a report.[1] Howick expressed the Government's disappointment that in a committee of twenty-five members, eighteen of whom were county members, no one had been able to bring forward concrete proposals for discussion.

It is clear then that, whatever the views of the ministry, there was no prospect whatever of an alteration in the corn laws so long as the low prices of grain persisted. In any case, the views of Ministers were divided. Melbourne himself defended them: within his Cabinet, the question appears all along to have been treated as an open one. On one occasion the corn laws were attacked in debate by Poulett Thomson and defended by Graham, the First Lord of the Admiralty.[2] The Tories, as a party, were supporters of the corn laws; nevertheless, their leaders did not support the agriculturists all the way. Of the committee of 1836, Thomson had written: 'There is but one point into which the Committee ought not to go—the Standard—and only one recommendation which is to be avoided—the repeal of the Malt Tax—upon both points Peel is with us.'[3]

The remaining discontented groups within the House of Commons, the shipping interest, the silk and glove manufacturers, were less important numerically and were heard less often. Nevertheless, like the landed interest, they could impose an effective brake on the plans of the ministry: in 1831 the shipping interest, as will be shown later, succeeded in defeating their proposal to reduce the protection given to Canadian timber.[4] Thereafter they were constantly alert to stifle any further attempts of the same kind.

The complaints of the silk and glove manufacturers were persistently heard in Parliament in 1832. The years 1830 to 1832 were a time of unemployment and high food prices. Basically the complaints of the operatives were of reduced wages, while those of the employers were of reduced profit margins.[5] But Huskisson had removed the prohibition on the import of French silks and French gloves in 1824 and 1825: thereafter any difficulties experienced by

[1] *Hansard*, vol. 31, cols. 147, 520; vol. 35, col. 382.

[2] S. Buxton, *Finance and Politics* (London, 1888), vol. i, p. 41.

[3] Lord Melbourne's letters, loc. cit.

[4] See pp. 48–49 below.

[5] Gayer, op. cit., pp. 226 ff.

either industry were always attributed to French competition. In the winter of 1831–2 both industries were complaining of distress. In December 1831 petitions were presented from the glove operatives of Worcester and Yeovil, in January from those of Milborne Port in Somerset, from Ludlow, and from 'two thousand of the clergy, gentry, and other inhabitants of the first respectability of Worcester', who claimed to describe the distress without any interested motives. In February similar petitions were presented in the House of Lords from Worcester and London.

The protests from the silk industry ran an exactly similar course; an isolated complaint was received in January, and full-scale petitions from the employers and employees of the Spitalfields silk industry in February.[1]

The parliamentary champions of these two interests were both aiming at the same thing: like the landed interest, they were hoping to use the complaints of distress to secure the appointment of a Select Committee to consider these complaints and to suggest remedies. Colonel Davies's motion of 31 January 1832, for a committee to inquire into the glove industry, was strenuously resisted by the ministry, and was unsuccessful: it was defeated by 223 to 168.[2] Poulett Thomson and Althorp, speaking against it, denied that French competition was the cause of the distress, and blamed 'over-trading' instead: no legislative alterations could alter this basic fact. Lord Grosvenor's motion for inquiry into the distress of the silk industry was more successful: it was, for reasons of their own, and to the annoyance of the glove-makers, supported by Poulett Thomson and Althorp. Here again they did not blame French competition which arrived in England through legitimate channels, but they did, by implication, blame the quantities of goods imported by smugglers. They had had evidence of the scale of smuggling, and were glad to take the opportunity of a Select Committee to investigate it further.[3]

The work of this committee, and the problems raised by the glove trade, are discussed in a later section of this work. The Silk Committee, under the chairmanship of Lord Grosvenor, sat for five months and examined about seventy witnesses, but made no

[1] These protests are all contained in *Hansard*, 3rd ser., vols. 9 and 10.

[2] Ibid., vol. 10, col. 992.

[3] An important firm of wholesale drapers, William Leaf & Co., had just been fined £25,000 for smuggling of silk (ibid., vol. 10, col. 585). (Leaf later gave evidence before the Select Committee on Import Duties.) See pp. 73–74 below.

recommendations.[1] Further petitions expressing 'grief and disappointment' of the silk trade were received in the House, but after that date the agitation died down; except for an isolated debate on the Coventry ribbon trade of June 1834 there were no more debates on the subject.[2] Similarly nothing more was heard of the glove trade.

These sections of parliamentary opinion were all distinct from one another, and in each case they claimed that the industry they represented was, for one reason or another, in a peculiarly disadvantageous position. The proper place for dealing with their claims, therefore, was a Select Committee of the House of Commons, and it is in the work of such committees that the influence of the Board of Trade is most clearly seen. But they also provided the backbone of support to the general criticisms of economic policy which were being made in this period, that is, to the attacks on the currency and on the structure of taxation.

Attwood attacked the corn laws, and thought of himself as a free-trader, but his currency theories provided a rallying-point for protectionists. And the fact that he placed his greatest emphasis on a monetary theory of which Thomson violently disapproved, meant that the attitude of each school to the other was at least distrustful, even in fields where their views might be similar.

Thomas Attwood entered Parliament as member for Birmingham at the general election of 1832, and the following twelve months were the period of his greatest parliamentary influence.[3] If distress could not justifiably be ascribed to increased foreign competition, the fall in prices since 1815 was an attractive alternative reason; and both shipowners and the landed interest could reasonably claim to have been particularly hard hit by it. In the spring of 1833 two motions for an inquiry into public distress were introduced. The first, introduced by Thomas Attwood on 21 March, was lost by 192 votes to 158;[4] the second, introduced by his brother Mathias on 22 April, proposed in addition an inquiry into the monetary system. It led to a three-day debate.

[1] The findings of this committee are discussed on pp. 165 ff. below.

[2] *Hansard*, 3rd ser., vol. 24, cols. 479, 570.

[3] C. M. Wakefield, *Life of Thomas Attwood* (privately printed, 1885), pp. 260 ff., considers that Attwood's parliamentary career was an anti-climax. A. Briggs, 'Thomas Attwood and the Economic Background of the Birmingham Political Union' (*Cambridge Historical Journal*, vol. ix, 1947–9), describes his election at Birmingham.

[4] *Hansard*, vol. 16, cols. 918 ff.

Poulett Thomson denied that there had been an increase in distress: to prove this he leant heavily on the statistics of raw materials imported; if these quantities were increasing it could not be true, he said, that industry was stagnating.[1] This was an argument which failed to convince Attwood's followers. Silk and glove manufacturers could produce reasons, sometimes apparently specious, why increased raw material imports could be compatible with industrial depression and increased foreign competition. The weakness of the Board of Trade in handling such arguments lay in their lack of first-hand knowledge of industrial conditions, especially outside London: Poulett Thomson had no effective way of countering the concrete evidence provided by increasing poor-rates in the areas concerned.[2] It seems probable that it was a consciousness of this weakness which underlay the Board's anxiety in 1833 to establish its Statistical Department on a permanent footing, and to make its main purpose the collection of regular and impartial information on the state of the manufacturing districts.

The debate of 22–24 April showed that Attwood could command considerable support: his motion which had included inquiry into the monetary system was lost on a division, but by 271 to 134 only. A fortnight later the Government gave in to the agitation by itself proposing a committee to investigate the condition of manufactures, shipping, and commerce.[3] By this course of action it could appoint a committee on its own terms: the terms of reference excluded any discussion of monetary policy, and the ministry could exert a greater control over the membership of the committee and the choice of witnesses. The Government's handling of the agitation of 1833 is in striking contrast to its handling of the corn-law agitation and the import duties committee in 1840.[4]

The Select Committee on Manufactures, Commerce, and Shipping heard evidence from a large variety of merchants, retail traders, shipowners, and manufacturers; and, in general, they tended to confirm the accounts of reduced profits in a number of trades. The committee submitted the evidence to Parliament in August 1833 but made no report.[5]

After 1833 Attwoodism was a declining cause in the House of

[1] Ibid., vol. 17, cols. 384 ff., 444.

[2] These figures were used by the spokesmen of the silk and glove manufacturers. See p. 77 below.

[3] *Hansard*, vol. 17, col. 958.

[4] See pp. 67 ff. below.

[5] *Parliamentary Papers*, 1833, vi.

Commons: as the complaints of the silk, glove, and shipping interests died away, the support for Attwood dwindled. In February 1834 a motion was introduced by Ruthven, member for Dublin, for a parliamentary inquiry into the state of the currency and national debt, but it was negatived without a division.[1] A further motion on the same subject, introduced by Attwood himself, was counted out.[2] Thereafter nothing further was heard in Parliament on the question.

During these years there were still many people in Parliament who were persuaded that the work of Huskisson had been 'mischievous to the last degree'. This is shown by the kind of support given to Chandos or Attwood. They were sufficiently strong to discourage further attempts at the reform of economic policy; but they did not succeed in making economic policy a party question, because on the main points at issue there was a broad agreement between Peel and the ministry. This was shown in Peel's attitude to the committee on agriculture of 1836, and more explicitly in a letter written to Goulburn in 1831 on the future of the Tory party: 'I would not abandon any one opinion I entertain in order to conciliate Ultra Tory support—I positively as I told Sir R. Vyvyan would not advance—so far as abandonment of opinion is concerned on such a question as the Currency Question for instance—one single yard to gain over a whole party.'[3]

On silk and gloves, T. P. Courtenay, who had been Vice-President of the Board of Trade in the Wellington administration, spoke in the debate in complete support of Poulett Thomson and Althorp.[4] On Attwood's motion of April 1833, the division cut across party lines: Peel and Gladstone, Alexander Baring, C. and R. Grant, voted against Attwood. But Attwood had the support of Chandos and Cayley and Lord George Bentinck, the leaders of the

[1] *Hansard*, vol. 21, col. 959.

[2] Ibid., vol. 24, col. 1116.

[3] Goulburn MSS., Peel to Goulburn, 5 June 1831. A second letter of 3 Jan. 1833, written shortly before the first of Attwood's debates on the currency, maintains exactly the same point of view. Cf. p. 38 above.

[4] *Hansard*, vol. 9, col. 1086; see also p. 49 below. Cf. Aspinall, *Three Early Nineteenth Century Diaries* (London, 1952), p. 207, Ellenborough diary, 9 Mar. 1832: 'Ld. Strangford moved for a Committee on the glove trade. Auckland . . . showed the distress which he admitted did not arise from Parliamentary enactment, but from change of fashion, & causes over which Parliament had no controul . . . & . . . *very properly* resisted the motion.

'I was obliged to support it, & therefore spoke . . . to distinguish my vote from that of Strangford, who talked against Free Trade, &c.'

landed interest in the Commons, of G. F. Young and Aaron Chapman of the shipping interest, Colonel Davies, the spokesman of the glove manufacturers, Brocklehurst, the silk manufacturer. But the ultimate defeat of the protectionists was perhaps foreshadowed by their inability to produce an alternative policy: none of these committees succeeded in producing a report.

The ministry were also attacked by the critics of the existing structure of taxation, and here, since the preparation of the Budget is the essential function of any ministry, they were more likely to encounter an organized party opposition. The critics were probably most active in the years 1830 to 1834, when they had the greatest opportunities. From 1831 to 1836, with the exception of the year 1832, the Budget produced a surplus every year. It was not achieved by increased taxation, but either by reductions in expenditure, or by the increasing yield of existing duties and taxes. The Chancellor's estimates fell in 1832, 1833, 1834, and 1835.[1] In spite of the new administrative enterprises undertaken by the Whigs, public expenditure was falling. Some of this may be accounted for by the reductions in places, pensions, and sinecures, but it can mostly be ascribed to the fact that the country was at peace, and that the estimates for the Services were being reduced.[2] Joseph Hume continued to attack the scale of public expenditure in these fields,[3] but nevertheless the course of events was such as he should have approved.

The chance of tax reductions offered by these surpluses stimulated bitter discussion in the House of Commons. In the first place there was the question whether the prime object of government policy should be to use any surplus for the reduction of the national debt, or whether it should be to reduce taxes. It was the view of leading members of the Tory party that a surplus should be used for the reduction of the national debt: Peel and Goulburn were

[1] The estimates of expenditure were as follows:

	£ million
1831–2	46·9
1832–3	45·7
1833–4	44·9
1834–5	44·8
1835–6	44·7

[2] Considerable reductions in Service estimates were made in 1832 and 1833. After 1835 they began to rise again.

[3] *Hansard*, vol. 21, col. 379.

insistent on this point.[1] During Peel's short ministry of 1834–5 no Budget was introduced, so that there is no means of knowing if they would have adhered to this view in practice: by the time that the Tories were secure in office after 1841, both the financial situation, and Peel's views on it, had radically changed.

The view that reduction of the national debt should have priority over reductions in taxation was not generally popular in the House of Commons after the abolition of the Sinking Fund in 1829. Althorp expressed a common point of view when he used the words: 'If parliament had been sluggishly inattentive to the general interests of the country,—if it had contended for a large sinking fund. . . .'[2] His declaration of 1830 summarizes the Whigs' general point of view:

He always looked on the debt, not as capital to be liquidated, but rather as a perpetual annuity chargeable upon the country; and he was convinced that if, as he believed, by repealing taxes the general wealth of the country would be more increased than the debt would be diminished by their continuance, good policy dictated that the amount of the taxes should be left in the pockets of the people.[3]

The only group which showed a concern with the national debt, other, that is, than the Tory leaders already mentioned, were the people who were preoccupied with the 'question of the standard'. On 2 July 1833 there was a motion introduced by James Silk Buckingham, for a Select Committee to consider ways of reducing the national debt, but it was lost by 57 to 38 votes.[4] It was supported by people of the same views as those who had supported Attwood's motion for an inquiry into the currency, Colonel Davies, Sir J. Guest, and G. F. Young. Cobbett also supported the motion. (But it would hardly be fair to judge this question on the strength of a single debate held in a half-empty House.)

But, granted that money should 'fructify in the pockets of the people', there were many interpretations which could be given to this doctrine: it did not necessarily make easier the reduction of import duties. During the first half of the decade there was steady pressure on Ministers to reduce the Excise duties: part of the agitation about commercial distress was deflected into this channel.

[1] Peel, *Speeches*, vol. ii, pp. 188, 456–7, 662, 685, 761; vol. iii, pp. 40, 657; *Hansard*, vol. 33, col. 673.

[2] Ibid., vol. 32, col. 564.

[3] Ibid., 2nd ser., vol. 23, cols. 337–8.

[4] Ibid., vol. 19, col. 4.

There were repeated demands from the landed interest for the reduction or abolition of the malt duties.[1] G. R. Robinson, a persistent enemy of Poulett Thomson, in March 1833 placed near the head of the list of his desired reforms the abolition of the Excise on bricks, tiles, glass, hops, malt, paper, soap, starch, and stone bottles.[2] Many of these reforms had been suggested by Parnell, and had been recommended by Poulett Thomson in his speech on injudicious taxation of 25 March 1830.[3] Taken together, these duties brought in a considerable revenue: Parnell estimated their yield for the year 1827 in the following way:

	£
Bricks and tiles	368,000
Hides and skins	386,000
Soap	1,199,000
Starch	85,000
Glass	614,000
Paper	650,000
Printed calicoes	662,000

The abolition of these duties did not raise controversial issues of free trade and protection, and they were, therefore, likely to prove a popular form of tax reduction. In the sessions of 1832 and 1833 there were repeated demands for alteration of the soap duties.[4]

But the strongest demand for the reduction of taxation came, in this period, from an entirely different quarter. Judging by the volume of complaint in *Hansard*, the most generally unpopular taxes were the assessed taxes. The landed interest complained of the tax on farm carts, retail traders complained of the tax on shopmen, and there was very general complaint of the house and window taxes.[5] This was particularly marked in the session of 1833. 1833 was the year in which Attwood had been able to muster 134 votes against the Government, and in which the Select Committee on Manufactures, Commerce, and Shipping had been appointed. The manufacturing and commercial interests whose complaints were heard by this committee were drawn into the attack on

[1] This was particularly true of the sessions of 1833 and 1834.

[2] *Hansard*, 3rd ser., vol. 16, col. 1072; he introduced a similar motion in Mar. 1836 (ibid., vol. 32, col. 552). See also p. 101 below.

[3] *Financial Reform*, chaps. ii and iii; *Hansard*, 2nd ser., vol. 23, col. 857.

[4] Ibid., 3rd ser., vol. 10, col. 898; vol. 12, col. 1402; vol. 15, col. 1098; vol. 16, col. 725.

[5] Ibid., vols. 15–19 *passim*.

the assessed taxes: it was claimed that commercial premises were over-assessed in comparison with the country mansions of the aristocracy.[1]

There were therefore many proposals for the use of available funds, and most of them appear to have been more generally popular, and less controversial, than those for a reduction of the import duties. There was therefore little scope for a continuation of Huskisson's work.

This is best illustrated by a summary of the Budgets introduced between 1831 and 1836. These illustrate better than anything else the relative weight of the various claims for tax relief.

In 1831, when their enthusiasm for the doctrines of Parnell was still fresh, the Whigs made their first attempt to introduce changes in commercial policy by means of the Budget. It was a disastrous attempt, and thereafter Budgets appear to have been designed primarily to offer concessions to those who asked for them most loudly. When the Budget of 1831 was introduced in the House, Althorp declared that it had been framed on the recommendations of Parnell: 'It was but justice to his rt. hon. friend to declare, that the general views of finance which Ministers had adopted, were those laid down in his admirable work on *Financial Reform*.'[2] To some extent the Budget could be said to show this influence: the duties on tobacco, newspapers, and newspaper advertisements were to be reduced; those on sea-borne coals, slates, candles, glass, printed calicoes, and cottons were to be repealed.[3] As well as this it was proposed to make an attack on colonial preference: the duties on the wines of France, Portugal, and the Cape were to be equalized[4] and new duties of 50*s*. and 20*s*. for Baltic and colonial timber respectively were to be substituted for the existing rates of 55*s*. and 10*s*. To offset any loss in revenue it was proposed to introduce two new taxes, both of which were potentially controversial. There was to be a tax of ½ per cent. on the transfer of landed and funded property, and also a new tax on the import of raw cotton. This last tax was in direct opposition to the teachings of Parnell.

These Budget proposals, and particularly the transfer tax, were

[1] S. Maccoby, *English Radicalism, 1832–1852* (London, 1935), p. 84.

[2] *Hansard*, 3rd ser., vol. 2, col. 407.

[3] Altogether 263 articles were to be made free of duty.

[4] Cape wines enjoyed a preference, and Portuguese wines, since the Methuen treaty of 1703, paid a duty one-third less than that paid by any other country.

generally ascribed to the influence of Poulett Thomson over the Chancellor, Althorp.[1] There were accusations of jobbery: Ellenborough believed that the repeal of the duty on candles was a 'job for Tallow Thomson' and that the repeal of the coal duty was one for Lord Durham 'which according to his own calculation, will put £36,000 into his pocket, & the same into Lord Londonderry's'.[2] Behind Poulett Thomson there was in fact the intellectual influence of McCulloch: on 3 February, ten days before the Budget was introduced, he had written to McVey Napier of the *Edinburgh Review*: 'My coal pamphlet[3] has been thoroughly successful, more so than any pamphlet published for a long time—There have been 7,000 copies dispersed, and the repeal of the tax is certain.' Later, when most of the provisions of the Budget had been abandoned, he wrote again, '. . . the Budget has been a most unfortunate matter. . . . Poulett Thomson is I apprehend much vexed up with the affair. I pressed upon him the repeal of the coal duty and the modification of the timber duties, and in this latter measure he is quite right.'[4]

The Budget was a doctrinaire piece of work, and its innovations were badly mistimed. Many of its proposals were genuinely unpopular. It was believed that an income tax had been discussed in the Cabinet, but that it had been rejected, largely as a result of Brougham's opposition, as too controversial a measure.[5] But its substitute, the transfer tax, which was in effect a tax on the fundholders, roused violent feelings. The Acts raising loans during the Napoleonic Wars had specified that these loans should be exempt from stamp duty. It was on the grounds that it was a breach of faith with the fundholders that the new tax was attacked in the Commons, in particular by Peel and Goulburn.[6] In the City there was alarm.

The uproar in the City [wrote Le Marchant] was not to be described. Andrew Thompson said of Powlett, 'Brother or no brother, we are foes

[1] Greville, op. cit., vol. ii, p. 116 (15 Feb. 1831); Aspinall, op. cit., p. 9 (Le Marchant's diary, undated).

[2] Aspinall, op. cit., pp. 49–50.

[3] *Observations on the Duty on Sea-borne Coal and on the Peculiar Duties and Charges on Coal in the Port of London, founded on the Reports of Parliamentary Committees and other Official Documents* (London, 1831).

[4] McVey Napier papers, B.M. Add. MSS. 34,615, ff. 17, 37.

[5] Le Marchant, op. cit., pp. 273–4; cf. Aspinall, op. cit., p. 52 (Ellenborough diary, 14 Feb.).

[6] *Hansard*, 3rd ser., vol. 2, cols. 407 ff.

in future.' The sons of Sir Thomas Baring, who are in business, sided with the trade against their father and brother. . . . Lord Althorpe made matters worse by an incautious remark. Someone said to him, 'Your Budget does not please the monied interest.' 'That,' he answered, 'is its best recommendation.'[1]

On the other hand it may be noticed that unlike the income-tax proposals of 1830[2] the transfer tax could not be construed as an attack on the landed interest, whose goodwill, as far as it could be obtained, was important at the time when the Reform Bill was about to be introduced.

The various tariff changes encountered equally strong hostility. The proposed tax on raw cotton would, as Peel argued, penalize British goods in competition abroad.[3] Ellenborough recorded that 'A cotton broker of London called on Ld. Althorpe yesterday & was shown into a room where he found 40 other cotton brokers and manufacturers, most of whom had put themselves into chaises at Manchester the instant they heard of the Budget.'[4] The opposition to the changes in colonial preference was more serious. The equalization of the wine duties could, like the transfer tax, be represented as a breach of political faith: the Methuen treaty could not be altered without the consent of Portugal. Petitions against change were received from Oporto in July 1831, and from the Cape in September.[5] The timber duties roused the greatest volume of protest, for their rates had once before, in 1820–1, been under review.[6] To reduce the protection given to the Canadian timber trade involved an important colonial interest, and, which was more important from the present point of view, threatened also the carrying trade of the powerfully organized shipping interest. In the House of Commons petitions were received from merchants in the City of London, Glasgow, and Dublin. The shipowners, Canadian timber interests, and the Tory opposition quickly got in touch with one another.[7]

[1] Aspinall, op. cit., p. 9. A similar account is given in Le Marchant's *Memoir of Viscount Althorp*, pp. 283–4.

[2] Cf. pp. 9–10 above.

[3] *Hansard*, 3rd ser., vol. 2, cols. 643, 784.

[4] Aspinall, op. cit., p. 52 (14 Feb.).

[5] *Hansard*, vol. 4, col. 1091; vol. 6, cols. 1022, 1218.

[6] See pp. 186 ff. below.

[7] *Hansard*, vol. 2, col. 455; Aspinall, op. cit., p. 55 (Ellenborough, 21 Feb.) and p. 66 (13 Mar.): 'There were 310 people at the dinner of the colonial and shipping interests yesterday. . . . They have exerted all their influence to obtain Petitions against the Budget from the outports. All these Petitions are to say of

It is clear, therefore, that the Budget proposals would in any case have been unpopular. But they were also doomed for tactical reasons. Until the general election of 1831, the Whigs' majority was insecure, and their intention to introduce a Reform Bill was known: any controversial measure which could bring additional numbers into the Opposition would be used for a trial of strength by the Tories, and most of these proposals were of this class.[1] The Whigs, therefore, had the choice of withdrawal of their measures or defeat in the House. The transfer tax was abandoned immediately. The duty on raw cotton, the only proposal about which sound theoretical objections could be made, was accepted, but the mode of collection was altered in response to the wishes of the Manchester Chamber of Commerce. The question of Cape wines was postponed until 1834, and, in the event, nothing more was heard of it.[2] The equalization of the duty on French and Portuguese wines was treated separately, and on this the ministry held firm. The Bill finally became law at the end of September 1831, although complaints against it continued to be heard for the next few years. It is interesting, as a further example of continuity between the Tories and Whigs, that Courtenay stated that he approved the Bill as a 'financier and political economist' and opposed it as a 'man of honour'.[3]

The trial of strength came on the timber duties, on which there was a division in which

> Government was beat by forty-three, all the Saints, West Indians, and anti-Free-traders voting with the great body of Opposition. Their satisfaction was tumultuous. They have long been desirous of bringing Ministers to a trial of strength, and they did not care much upon what; they wanted to let the world see the weakness of Government, and besides on this occasion they hoped that a defeat might be prejudicial to the Reform Bill, so that this matter of commercial and fiscal policy is not decided on its own merits, but is influenced by passion, violence, party tactics, and its remote bearing upon another question with which it has no immediate relation.

And this was in spite of the fact that according to Le Marchant he

Reform is that if the proposed Bill should pass they must have colonial representatives.'

[1] Wellington resigned in Nov. 1830 after he had been defeated in the Commons by 29 votes. The Reform Bill was introduced on 1 Mar.

[2] *Hansard*, vol. 2, col. 1048; vol. 6, col. 981.

[3] Ibid., vol. 6, col. 425.

had been 'assured by Poulett Thomson that he had ascertained from information in the department that a similar remission of duty had been contemplated by the late government'.[1]

After the general election of May 1831 the Whigs had an overwhelming majority. It was reduced by the election of 1835, but remained adequate until that of 1837. But, whether from lack of determination or from a recognition of the strength of protectionist interests in the country, the Whigs did not again attempt an ambitious Budget until the end of the decade. The Budget of 1831 was considered to have destroyed the Whigs' popularity in the City.[2]

The Budget of 1832 was not introduced until July because Parliament was preoccupied with the passage of the Reform Bill. When it came, it introduced no alterations in taxation: the financial year 1831–2, unlike its successors, had ended with a deficit.[3] In 1833, however, Althorp could report a surplus of £1·5 million and make a number of tax reductions. He was faced with complaints of agricultural and industrial distress, and with petitions against the assessed taxes, and his Budget was designed to conciliate these claims. He resisted change in the malt duties, but repealed the tax on carts. He offered commercial interests a considerable reduction of the taxes on newspaper advertisements, shopmen, and commercial clerks, and of the house and window taxes as they affected shops. The duty on marine insurance was halved,[4] and the additional duty on raw cotton imposed in 1831, and the Excise duty on tiles were both repealed. He resisted the demands of the Radicals for reduction or repeal of the taxes on newspapers: the aim of his Budget, he said, was to reduce taxes which could be shown to be pressing on industry.[5] This he had done, but (with one exception) he had done it without any alteration in the scale of import duties.

In 1834 Althorp reported a surplus of £1·5 million. On this occasion, again as the result of repeated public demand, the main change was to repeal the house tax. In 1835 there was a surplus of

[1] Greville, op. cit., vol. ii, p. 131 (20 Mar. 1831); Le Marchant, *Memoir of Viscount Althorp*, p. 286.

[2] Aspinall, op. cit., p. 263 (Le Marchant, 17 May 1832).

[3] *Hansard*, vol. 14, col. 854.

[4] This was a demand of the Radicals (see Joseph Hume's speech in *Hansard*, vol. 17, col. 339), and probably of the shipowners (see memorial from Lloyds' Committee of Management, dated Dec. 1838, in B.T. 1/348).

[5] *Hansard*, vol. 17, col. 332.

£1·2 million, but the new Chancellor, Spring-Rice, made no major alterations in taxation. In 1836 there was again a surplus of £1·8 million, and, as in earlier years, the Government found alterations in the stamp duties or the Excise to be the safest and most popular course of action. Duties on paper and glass and the tax on newspapers were reduced.[1]

1836 was the last year in which the reduction of taxation was a practicable programme: after that year there began the series of mounting deficits which contributed to the Whigs' electoral defeat in 1841. In 1837 there was still a small surplus, but there was no question of repealing further taxes.

Against this account of, from a Parnellite point of view, frustration, various things can be quoted on the other side, which suggest that the Whigs, had they been able, were still anxious to carry out the recommendations of Parnell, and that they were still opposed to the giving of state support to commercial privilege. In 1834 the East India Company's trading monopoly with China was abolished. In 1835 the rates of duty on coffee imported from the British West Indies and from British India were equalized. Previously a higher rate of duty had been charged on East India coffee.[2] But at the same time the Government resisted prolonged pressure for a similar equalization of the sugar duties. In 1835 a Select Committee on the timber duties was appointed, on which opponents of the existing imperial preference were strongly represented, but once again strong opposition from shipowners and the Canadian timber interests prevented any action by the Government.

Between 1830 and 1840 a fair amount of unobtrusive and non-controversial work was carried out by the Board of Trade. In August 1833 a series of Acts consolidating existing commercial regulations was introduced.[3] These dealt with navigation regulations, with the registry of British vessels, with the prevention of smuggling, and with the organization of the Commissioners of Customs. They do not appear to have introduced anything new in policy. Similarly, the tariff which was enacted in 1833 appears to have been merely a consolidation of existing statutes.

[1] Ibid., vol. 21, col. 360; vol. 30, col. 514; vol. 33, col. 635.

[2] See p. 150 below.

[3] 3 & 4 Will. IV, caps. 50–61. A series of reforms of Excise administration was also carried out at this time.

The tariff changes which were introduced during these ten years were directed towards lower duties and smaller imperial preferences, but they were not fundamental. In 1831 a reduction of the duties on barilla, which had originally been proposed by the Tories, was finally passed, as were the Customs changes associated with the Budget of 1831. In August 1832 the duties were reduced on various kinds of foods and drugs, on cordage, on bark for tanning, on dye-stuffs, paints, gums, and varnishes, and other miscellaneous articles. Altogether they merely represented a loss to the revenue of £110,000 to £120,000 a year.[1]

In introducing the Bill, Poulett Thomson explained the choice of articles:

> The objects he had had in view . . . had been first to relieve from oppressive duties articles which largely entered into the manufactures of this country, such as dyes; secondly to relieve from oppressive duties a number of articles consumed by the poor—medicines, drugs, and other articles of that description; which duties, in consequence of successive alterations in the Customs had, without its being so intended, been raised to a scale extremely burthensom; and thirdly to classify articles which, being of a similar description, ought to be subject to the same rate of duties, but which had hitherto been classed under separate heads, and subjected to separate duties, to the great trouble of the officers, and the inconvenience of the trade.[2]

Similar Acts were passed in 1833, 1834, 1836, and 1838.[3] The Act of 1833 dealt with another miscellaneous collection of items, of little revenue importance: canes of all kinds, coco-nut, madder, ginger, and pickles, among others. Apart from these, the most important classes of goods tackled in 1835 were hides and skins—import duties on undressed furs, of all kinds from cat to ermine, were reduced to sums varying between one-third and one-twelfth of the previous rates. Undressed hides were reduced from 40 to 30 per cent. *ad valorem.* The Act of 1834 covered a much longer list of goods, in which dried fruits were prominent, and the same Act repealed the export duty on coal and slates. In 1836 the duties on various hardwoods were reduced, and imperial preferences,

[1] *Hansard,* vol. 13, col. 757. The revision included 51 articles producing less than £100 each in duty, 48 which yielded from £100 to £1,000, and 43 which yielded between £1,000 and £10,000.

[2] Ibid., loc. cit.

[3] 3 & 4 Will. IV, cap. 56; 4 & 5 Will. IV, cap. 89; 6 & 7 Will. IV, cap. 60; 1 & 2 Vict., cap. 113.

where these existed, were abolished. In short, the kind of reorganizing work for which Huskisson and later Peel drew much credit was also carried out by the Whigs.

It remains to be asked whether there was evidence, in the years 1830–6, of public support for a reduction of the tariff, or for an attack on imperial preference. Were there, for example, petitions presented to the House of Commons asking for a more liberal importing policy? There is no record of this: the Government did not receive petitions from the importers and consumers of French wines or Baltic timber, who stood to gain by the changes which were so bitterly opposed. It might be argued that petitions are not a fair indication of feeling in the country as a whole: before 1832 Parliament might have been indifferent to the views of the manufacturing districts, and after 1832 the same tradition might have continued. Small towns were still over-represented in relation to their population, and industrial towns under-represented. There was little, if any, increase in the numbers of merchants and manufacturers who sat in the first reformed Parliament. A series of detailed local studies would be necessary to establish definitely whether opinion in the country was faithfully reflected by the course of events in Parliament: in their absence it is necessary to use the records of the Board of Trade.

These appear to contain all the communications received from the public, and copies of the Board's replies. (Notes and memoranda circulated within the department, giving the unvarnished views of particular officials, are very rare.) It is surprising to find how exactly the records of the Board reflect the picture of public opinion given in *Hansard*. In 1831 there were protests about the soap and timber duties; in 1832 there was much complaint from the silk trade.[1] But there were no complaints of the duties on imported raw materials, nor, with one exception, of the preferences given to British colonial products. The exception was provided by the traders to Brazil, particularly in Liverpool, who complained, both to Parliament and to the Board, of the effects of the sugar duties. These complaints, however, were not frequent.[2] During the years when trade was good and bread was cheap, it seems that the commercial public was largely indifferent to tariff questions; it will be suggested in a later section of this narrative that even in the

[1] Public Record Office, IND 14103.

[2] *Hansard*, 3rd ser., vol. 28, col. 960; vol. 48, cols. 164, 1021 ff.

years 1838 to 1841, when the corn-law question was again an important matter of national politics, there were considerable sections of opinion, who, to judge from their actions or lack of them, remained apathetic.[1]

A final point concerns the attitude of the Philosophic Radicals. It is suggested that, in the years immediately after 1832, protectionist interests were efficiently organized in Parliament, and that, when the Whigs after the failure of their Budget proposals of 1831 made no further attempt to introduce sweeping tariff changes, they were not seriously out of touch with public opinion. But, on the other hand, the years between 1832 and 1835 were a period in which Radicalism in Parliament was a stronger force than it was to be for many years after: four of the most prominent Philosophic Radicals—Grote, Buller, Molesworth, and Roebuck—entered Parliament in the general election of 1832, and many of the new constituencies returned members who claimed to hold Radical opinions. The legislation of the first reformed Parliament on slavery, on the East India Company, on the Bank, and on the poor law, and the attack on the assessed taxes, all bear a close resemblance to the pledges which Radicals had given to their constituents. It might be expected that the Radicals would have given valuable support to the policy summarized in *Financial Reform*.

It is not easy to say how their presence affected the development of policy. Many of them would have described themselves as opposed to restrictions on trade, though this could mean different things: Attwood was a Radical, and an opponent of the corn laws, but deeply divided from the Benthamites on the currency question. Most of the Radicals of the eighteen-thirties were marked individualists, who defeated attempts to weld them into a party. In any case they did not have the kind of backing, either from their constituencies, or from the machinery of 'influence', which would have forced them to agree on a common programme and concert their tactics in Parliament. They had been driven forward by the campaign for parliamentary reform, and once that had been achieved they began to lose their hold in the country, being weakened by the general election of 1835 and even more by that of 1837. In this period, when the corn-law question was dormant, Radical activities in Parliament were directed to questions other than free trade.

Within the narrower Benthamite circle, opinions on economic

[1] See pp. 180 ff. and 224 below.

policy were more uniform than among the general body of Radicals. But the Benthamites had individual specialized interests; and they did not contribute very effectively to debates on economic policy. After Joseph Hume, Roebuck was perhaps the most forceful of them, and was member for Bath from 1832 until he was ejected in the general election of 1837. Although he was a member of the London Anti-Corn Law Association of 1836 and active in the House, he had comparatively little to say on economic policy, most of his speeches being on political questions—the ballot, the conduct of elections, the taxes on knowledge, the Canadian question, and so on. A series of cheap and widely circulated *Pamphlets for the People*, which he edited in 1835, shows the same range of interests.[1] Molesworth and Buller spoke rarely, and from their first entry into Parliament concentrated on colonial policy—a subject in which there was a latent risk of conflict between the colonial reformers and those who held a Cobdenite view of colonies. Grote and Warburton, belonging to a rather older generation, had in the twenties been friends of Tooke, Ricardo, and James Mill, and had been original members of the Political Economy Club. Grote, as a banker and as a member for the City of London, spoke in defence of orthodoxy against Attwood in 1833, and was a member of the Select Committee on Manufactures, Commerce, and Shipping of that year, and of the Select Committee on Banks of Issue of 1840; yet an examination of his work in Parliament shows clearly that his main interests were political. In particular he was working for the introduction of the ballot. Warburton, a timber merchant, worked hard for the alteration of the timber duties in 1835, but apart from this he was interested in postal reform.

The kind of people who were commonly returned for the northern industrial and commercial constituencies in the eighteen-thirties, and who would describe themselves as 'Reformers', were probably in the long run a greater source of strength to the free-trade movement. People like John Marshall, member for Leeds from 1832 to 1835, William Ewart, member for Liverpool from 1830 until 1837, or Joseph Brotherton, member for Salford from 1832 to 1857, came from families of great wealth and local influence. A few years later they subscribed heavily to the funds of the Anti-Corn Law League, and in the House of Commons they

[1] 2 vols., London, 1835. Mrs. Grote (*Personal Life of George Grote*, London, 1873, p. 104) says that 10,000 copies a week were sold.

were always able to speak with the moral authority of representatives of large and economically powerful constituencies. But, while they had much in common with the Benthamites, they were more pragmatic in their approach to economic policy: they were not inclined to agitate in advance of public opinion, nor to become deeply involved in questions which were not of immediate importance to their constituencies. In the debates on the currency of 1833 the members for Lancashire constituencies were prominent, but apart from this they did not make a striking contribution to parliamentary discussions on tariff policy until the revival of the anti-corn-law movement in 1838.

The Radicals, efficient and influential as they were in their handling of many questions, were lacking political cohesion. This is the basis of Joseph Hume's claim to fame. He did not develop a particular sphere of interest: any index to *Hansard* bears witness to the fact that he was much the most frequent and persistent speaker among the Radicals, and much the most comprehensive in the range of his activities. Of equal importance with this—for he was known as a boring speaker—was his liaison work between different Radical groups. He formed links with a working-class expert like Place, with anti-corn-law agitators in the north, such as Prentice or J. B. Smith, with Benthamites like Grote, and with officials such as Deacon Hume.[1] He provided in himself the nearest equivalent they possessed to a party machine.

[1] See p. 71 below, and Part III, Chap. 13 below.

4

PARLIAMENT AND ECONOMIC POLICY 1837–40

THE year 1837 marks a dividing line in the history of the Whig Government: in the House of Commons they were seriously weakened after 1837, and in the country they had very much more serious problems with which to contend. At the general election of 1835 the Whigs had lost seats to the Conservatives, but had still retained a substantial working majority. The general election of 1837, held on the death of William IV, reduced the Whigs' majority to a handful: between 1837 and 1839 they could usually, with Radical and Irish support, count on a majority of about twenty, though at times it might be very much smaller.[1] In the counties the Conservatives had reasserted their position in 1835, and maintained it in 1837.[2] The important difference between the two elections lay, however, in the position of the Radicals. The results in 1837 were generally interpreted as evidence of the decline of Radicalism in the country: Bowring was unseated in the Clyde Burghs, Ewart in Liverpool, Perronet Thompson in Hull, and Roebuck in Bath. A particularly striking defeat was that of Joseph Hume in Middlesex. All these men except Bowring and Roebuck quickly found seats elsewhere. In the City of London, Grote, who had made the ballot the centre of his programme, escaped defeat by two votes only. 'There cannot, however,' wrote Greville, 'be a doubt that questions of organic change are not at present in any degree of public favor.'[3] But, while Radicalism might be out of public favour in the country, it held a dominant position in the Commons: to lose the support, not necessarily of the sixty-odd Radicals as a whole, but of ten or twenty of them, would mean defeat for the Whig Government.[4] The return of the Conservatives

[1] Greville, op. cit., vol. iv, p. 136 (25 Mar. 1839).

[2] Ibid., vol. iii, p. 146 (23 Jan. 1835) and p. 391 (25 Aug. 1837).

[3] Ibid., p. 391.

[4] In the division on the Jamaica Bill of 6 May 1839, after which Melbourne resigned, 'ten of the Radicals voted against them, and ten or a dozen staid away' (Greville, op. cit., vol. iv, p. 160, 10 May 1839).

to power was foreshadowed by the election result of 1837, and, had it not been for the Bedchamber incident, would have taken place in 1839. Thus, while the ministry was weakening and losing its grip on economic policy, the Radicals, whose views were clear-cut, were gaining an influence out of proportion to their numbers and to their popularity in the country; and after 1839 they had exceptionally good political opportunities.[1]

This situation was reflected in the policies of the Whigs. The Radicals placed the Ballot at the head of their demands, and the Whigs were forced to make it an open question. Two motions were introduced by Grote, on 15 February 1838 and on 18 June 1839. On both occasions the Ballot found surprisingly wide support, the first motion being lost by 198 votes to 315, and the second by 216 votes to 333. In June 1839 Poulett Thomson and Macaulay voted against the rest of the Cabinet. Russell, the most powerful politician among the Whigs, had declared his opposition to the Ballot in May 1839.[2] In colonial policy, the decision to send Durham to Canada, and, later, to act on his report, provides further evidence of Radical pressure. In fiscal policy, the Penny Post was also a Radical demand. With the corn-law agitation after 1838, Melbourne, though he personally was bitterly opposed to repeal, was obliged to allow the question to be treated as an open one.

While this was happening, the Whigs were also becoming confronted with economic problems very much more intractable than any which they had previously been called upon to handle. After 1837 they began to run into the fiscal problems which contributed largely to the Government's defeat in 1841. The policy adopted between 1831 and 1836 had never been very securely based. It had been possible to reduce unpopular taxes so long as it had been possible to reduce expenditure, and so long as trade continued to expand.[3] The attack on the assessed taxes of 1833 to 1834 had increased the country's dependence on indirect taxation. A depression of trade, or an increase in public expenditure, both of which

[1] There is, for example, a letter among Lord Melbourne's letters (Hertford County Record Office) from Palmerston, of 21 July, on the subject of Bowring. It was proposed to send him back to France: 'Employing him conciliates some of our extreme Left in the House of Commons, and in that way it is useful.'

[2] L. C. Sanders, *Lord Melbourne's Papers* (London, 1889), p. 399; *Hansard*, vol. 48, col. 504; Spencer Walpole, *Life of Lord John Russell* (London, 1889), vol. i, pp. 318–19.

[3] See table on p. 75 below.

occurred after 1837, found the ministry without any reliable way of increasing the revenue. After 1836 expenditure rose, for two unavoidable reasons. In 1838 the army and navy estimates rose, and in addition a sum was voted for the suppression of the rising in Canada. As well as this, the grant of £20 million in compensation to the West India sugar planters had made necessary an increase in the national debt, and had increased the interest charges payable every year. Altogether, then, the estimates rose from £44·7 million in 1835 to £45·2 million in 1836, and £47·5 million in 1838.

At the same time the revenue fell, in a way which had not been foreseen, and for which the Whig politicians were not to blame. When Peel attacked the Whigs' management of the national finances in the great debate on the sugar duties of May 1841, he could point with great effect to the mounting deficits of these years. When the same problem had recurred regularly for some years, the Whig ministry could be blamed for avoiding any attempt to impose satisfactory new taxes. But in the early stages of the question, the reason for the deficits was largely a technical one, namely the inability of the Chancellor or of his advisers to find a satisfactory way of estimating the future yield of Customs and Excise duties. In this period the yield of the assessed taxes, of the stamp duties, and of the Post Office varied little from year to year, and could be predicted with sufficient accuracy for the Chancellor of the Exchequer's purposes. But, as was made clear after 1837, the total yield of the Customs and Excise showed itself to be extremely sensitive to trade fluctuations. In the first half of the decade, in a period of expanding trade, it had been possible to reduce a considerable amount of indirect taxation without reducing the total yield to anything which approached the same extent. After 1836 the effects of changes in Customs and Excise duties became unpredictable. In 1835 Customs and Excise duties to the value of £160,000 had been removed, yet the total revenue from indirect taxation rose by £300,000. In 1836 the same thing occurred: Customs and Excise duties which had in the previous year brought in £680,000 were repealed, but the total Customs and Excise revenue rose by £2,100,000. This was far above the estimated increase (£1,194,000 above). In 1837 no changes were made in taxation, but in this year the yield of the duties fell below the Chancellor's estimate, and the financial year 1837–8 ended with a deficit of £1,428,000.[1] This was the first year in which politicians became fully conscious of the problems involved in making these estimates. Spring-Rice in his Budget speech of 1838 held that the failure of his calculations could be explained by the fact that manufacturers and retailers import or hold bigger stocks during a boom in anticipation of rising prices. No alterations were made in taxation, as it was hoped that the deficit would show itself to be the result of abnormal trading conditions, and would not be repeated. This seems to have been accepted as satisfactory by the Opposition; no general attack on the Whigs' handling of the finances was developed though no one would have regarded it as desirable to budget deliberately for a deficit. In 1839 the Customs and Excise revenue had risen by £500,000; nevertheless, there was again a deficit, of £786,000.[2] This would not appear to have been a suitable occasion on which to introduce a major change in taxation.

It was in the Budget of 1839 that the political weakness of the Whigs was first clearly seen. It was not introduced until 5 July 1839, after Peel's unsuccessful attempt to form a government, and it shows the power which the Radicals had acquired. The Penny Post was introduced, but no provision was made to cover the loss to the revenue which this might entail, beyond a vague and general statement that Parliament would pledge itself to make good any loss in the future. Since early in the eighteen-thirties, the Philosophic Radicals had wished to reform both postage rates and the administration of the Post Office. In 1835 Wallace, the leading postal reformer in the Commons, had secured the appointment of Commissioners to inquire into its management. In 1837 Rowland Hill published his *Post Office Reform*, and in the same year a Select Committee of the Commons, under the chairmanship of Wallace, was appointed. It was heavily weighted with postal reformers and in its report, which was well publicized, it recommended a uniform postal rate of twopence.[3] In the session of 1837–8, 320 petitions in favour of a Penny Post were presented to Parliament. There was thus considerable pressure on the Government to introduce it.

[1] *Hansard*, vol. 33, col. 638; vol. 38, col. 1718; vol. 42, cols. 1366, 1374.

[2] Ibid., vol. 48, cols. 1343–5.

[3] *Select Committee on Rates of Postage, Parliamentary Papers*, 1837–8, xx. See Croker's article in the *Quarterly Review*, vol. lxiv (Oct. 1839). There is a letter in the Place papers (B.M. Add. MSS. 35,151, f. 291) which shows the way in which the findings of the committee were publicized.

Parliament had had abundant and recent proof of the difficulty of forecasting the effects which changes in indirect taxation would have on demand, and therefore on the yield to the revenue. The introduction of a uniform Penny Post in place of the varied and often very high postage rates which were being currently charged would have effects which could not be predicted. The postal reformers pointed out convincingly that the number of letters going through the post would increase greatly if the Penny Post were introduced: many more business circulars would be sent, soldiers might write home to their relations, the incentive to use private and unofficial postal arrangements—which were very extensively employed—would be removed.[1] But no one could guess approximately to what extent any of these possible increases would actually take place. The estimates of the postal reformers had been very optimistic: Rowland Hill had estimated that the loss to the income of the Post Office would be about one-eighth, but that there would be no loss to the national revenue.[2] (He believed that the introduction of a uniform rate and of prepayment would greatly reduce administrative expenses.[3])

The Cabinet, however, was not convinced of the financial soundness of the scheme. The three official members of the Select Committee on Rates of Postage appointed in 1837, Poulett Thomson, Lord Seymour,[4] and John Parker,[5] all, according to Rowland Hill, opposed it, and opposed it for reasons of government policy.[6] Both Spring-Rice and his successor, F. T. Baring, were hostile to the scheme. Spring-Rice wrote to Melbourne in the following terms in September 1839: 'I am sorry to read Warburton's missive.' (Warburton was a prominent Radical and postal reformer.) 'It will be impossible for me to undertake a bill in the present session. I can never be a party to the reduction of the postage by law without the contemporaneous imposition of an equivalent tax.' He described it as 'a measure of reckless daring—for which I confess I have not courage. I do not think it would be honest.'[7] After

[1] *Select Committee on Rates of Postage, Parliamentary Papers*, 1837–8, xx.

[2] Howard Robinson, *The British Post Office, a History* (Princeton, 1948), p. 286.

[3] G. B. Hill, *Life of Sir Rowland Hill* (London, 1880), book ii, chap. iii.

[4] Member for Totnes, and a Lord of the Treasury.

[5] Member for Sheffield, and junior Lord of the Treasury.

[6] Hill, op. cit., p. 287.

[7] Lord Melbourne's letters, Hertford County Record Office.

the Penny Post had been passed, Baring wrote to Melbourne in December that there was 'no going back on the penny rate . . . the whole game must be played out'.[1]

It is surprising that, in spite of these misgivings, the scheme was officially adopted. It was announced in Spring Rice's Budget speech of 5 July 1839. The new postal rates came into force in January 1840. The fears expressed about a possible loss in revenue were fully justified: the revenue from the Post Office dropped from £1,626,000 in 1839 to £448,000 in 1840.[2]

The fiscal weakness of the Whigs did most, in the long run, to undermine their prestige, and contributed powerfully to their defeat at the polls in 1841. The introduction of the Penny Post was the first occasion on which the leaders of the party gave their support to measures about which they had secret misgivings, because they had fallen to attacks by a well-organized pressure-group, and because they could not run the risk of losing even a few Radical votes. It was also the first occasion on which the leaders of the Opposition began to express serious criticism of their abilities: Peel supported the reform of the postal system, but he made it clear that it was wrong to introduce it without at the same time introducing new taxation to cover a loss in revenue.[3]

How did the fiscal problem affect the prospects of the free-traders in Parliament or in the Board of Trade? In one way it imposed a limitation on their activities. Any measure which reduced import duties could be opposed on the ground that the financial situation would not permit it at the time. It was necessary to prove that the proposed reduction would in some way benefit the revenue in order to capture the attention of politicians. As the discussions on the postage question showed, the amount of proof required was not very great. On the other hand, the prospects for a successful attack on some of the major protective duties were improved by

[1] Lord Melbourne's letters. Neither of these letters, as far as I know, has been printed. Generally speaking, the biographers of the Whig politicians of this period omitted the letters on financial questions, particularly those which show that they were being driven into measures in which they had no confidence. There is a fair amount of financial correspondence among the papers of Melbourne and Russell. Yet Russell afterwards held that the Cabinet had been unanimous for the measure, as conferring great benefits on the public (*Recollections and Suggestions* (London, 1875), pp. 231–2).

[2] Porter, *Progress of the Nation*, 1847 ed., p. 506.

[3] *Hansard*, vol. 48, cols. 1387 ff.

this situation. Where foreign goods were kept out by very high rates of duty, it could be plausibly argued that lower duties would increase the consumption of foreign goods and therefore increase the revenue.

But apart from the fiscal problem, the harvest failures and the trade depression of the later eighteen-thirties would have involved the party in renewed difficulties. The harvest of 1837 was less abundant than that of previous years, while that of 1838 was, in Tooke's words, 'the most deficient crop of any since 1816'. At the end of 1837 the price of wheat had risen to 53*s.* and by August it had risen to 74*s.* For the first time for many years large quantities of grain were imported, from wherever it could be obtained, at the lowest duties.[1] In the following year the harvest was again very poor.

These failures were accompanied by the depression of trade of 1837, a particular feature of which was a slump in exports of cotton manufactures, which dropped from 637 million yards in 1837 to 531 million in 1838.[2] In their search for alternative export markets, manufacturers were brought sharply up against the facts of contemporary European tariffs, and in particular of the tariff of the Zollverein.

Thus, the situation was ripe for a renewed attack on the corn laws. Little more was heard of the distress of the landowners in Parliament. They were concerned to defend themselves against attack: they resisted C. P. Villiers's annual corn-law motions and in May 1838 resisted a proposal to allow the grinding of foreign corn in bond—according to Chandos, 'the agricultural interest was now enjoying some little respite from the distress of past years, and all it asked was for peace and quietness, and that it should not be inconvenienced by legislative enactments of any kind'.[3] But Chandos and his associates abandoned their attacks on the county rates or the malt tax.

On the other hand, all the elements of a cogent economic case were present to the hands of the free-traders. They could show that when the price of provisions was unusually high, the home consumption of goods other than food was bound to suffer; they could

[1] Tooke, op. cit., vol. ii, p. 262; vol. iii, p. 11; Porter, *The Effect of Restrictions on the Importation of Corn* (London, 1839).

[2] Porter, op. cit., p. 371.

[3] A. Prentice, *History of the Anti-Corn Law League* (London, 1853), vol. i, p. 61, quoted this with disapproval: 'Peace and quietness to the robber who retires to enjoy himself on the produce of his adroitness.'

point to the growth of hostile tariffs, and suggest that the maintenance of agricultural protection had at least contributed to their growth. And they could speak of the risk of a banking crisis, from the drain of bullion to meet the cost of grain imported from northern Europe. Were the imports of grain less irregular, as they would be under free trade or under a fixed duty, there would be a chance of establishing regular trading relations with these countries, and the imports of grain would be paid for in goods and not in gold.

All these arguments were put forward in the years 1838 to 1841, in pamphlets, books, and parliamentary debates. In some of them, notably the argument that British protectionism had provoked retaliation abroad, the opinions and experience of the Board of Trade carried a great deal of weight.

The movement against the corn laws developed rapidly after 1838. In Parliament, Villiers introduced the first of his annual motions for inquiry into the workings of the corn laws on 15 March 1838. It was defeated by 300 votes to 95, after a short debate. Poulett Thomson voted with the minority, but did not speak, to the dissatisfaction of some of his Manchester constituents.[1]

The Anti-Corn Law League came into being in the winter of 1838–9. The first step towards this had been the founding of an Anti-Corn Law Association in London towards the end of 1836. The committee had been composed partly of Radical Members of Parliament of various kinds, including Grote and Roebuck, Richard Potter, Brotherton, Perronet Thompson, and T. S. Duncombe, who later came to be regarded as the champion of the Chartists in the Commons. It also included a number of provincial representatives. This early committee had failed to achieve much because, in Prentice's words, 'the body was not representative; it had not the support of a numerous constituency; and there was no arrangement for united action'.[2] Or, in other words, it had been founded at an unpropitious time; in the conditions of 1838 there was a greater chance of success.

On 10 September Dr. Bowring was travelling through Manchester on his return from Egypt, and he addressed a meeting of manufacturers which had been hurriedly summoned together by Prentice.[3] His speech, as Prentice has recorded it, dealt exclusively with the threat of foreign retaliation, and with the benefits which

[1] *Hansard*, vol. 41, col. 909; Prentice, op. cit., vol. i, p. 60.

[2] Ibid., p. 50.

[3] Ibid., pp. 64 ff.

other countries had enjoyed when they had allowed freer economic competition. The most potent arguments he could produce were ones which were derived from his official experience. At this meeting it was agreed that Manchester, which had as yet no Anti-Corn Law Association, should form one. The association, once established, grew very rapidly in numbers. In December its members demanded a special general meeting of the Chamber of Commerce to consider a petition to Parliament for the repeal of the corn laws. At this meeting they won a striking success: largely through a compelling speech by Cobden, the chamber carried by a large majority a motion which called for a petition which would demand total repeal of all duties on imported foodstuffs, and the abandonment of industrial as well as agricultural protection. This represented a defeat for the gradualist, and in practice passive, attitude of the officers of the chamber.

In the opening months of 1839 the Manchester Association made contact with similar groups in other towns, and in March, at a meeting of delegates in London, the Anti-Corn Law League was officially established. Compared with its work in the forties, the league's activities in 1839 were on a modest scale, but the first tracts were printed almost immediately, and from April 1839 the *Anti-Corn Law Circular* was appearing every fortnight. Whether as a direct result of pressure from the league or not, a great number of petitions were presented to Parliament in the spring of 1839[1] (in preparation for Villiers's debate). In March 1839 Villiers again brought forward his motion, and it caused considerably more excitement than it had caused the year before. The debate lasted for four days, and the motion was finally lost by 342 votes to 195. A considerable number of leading Whigs, including Russell, Hobhouse, Palmerston, and Ellice, voted with the minority. On this occasion Thomson supported the motion with a powerful speech, which, like Bowring's speech in Manchester, placed great emphasis on the threat of retaliation.[2]

This agitation presented a difficult tactical problem to the ministry. The strength of the movement in the country could not be estimated from the number of petitions to Parliament, nor from the scale of the league's activities: the agitation against the corn laws, like the agitation in favour of the Penny Post, showed every sign of extremely skilful management. Melbourne was not convinced of

[1] *Hansard*, vols. 45, 46. [2] Ibid., vol. 46, col. 418.

the strength of the movement.[1] It is curious that, in spite of this pressure of organized opinion, Parliament did not show the same preoccupation with economic problems and remedies in the years 1838 to 1841 as it had shown ten years before. There was one very long debate on the corn laws in March 1839, but it was not accompanied by the constant debates on the causes and extent of distress, which had occurred so frequently in years such as 1826, 1829–30, or 1832–3. There seems to be no very obvious reason for this change, though various tentative explanations can be offered. It is possible that the agitation against the corn laws was driving all other explanations of economic distress to one side; manufacturers no longer blamed the state of the currency or foreign competition, but concentrated their hostility on the corn laws. Attwood himself had left Parliament and had become involved with the Chartists. But if this is the sole explanation, it is surprising that the corn-law question was not more frequently raised. It is also possible that Parliament had begun to accept the wide trade fluctuations of this period as a normal feature of economic life: Spring-Rice in his Budget speeches of 1838 and 1839 emphasized that the trade depression would not last. Again it is also true that in the years 1839–40 there was much discussion and criticism of the Bank's actions in relation to the foreign exchanges, which culminated in the appointment of the Select Committee on Banks of Issue in 1840. Or again, the difference in atmosphere between the later twenties and the later thirties may be traceable to political circumstances. The civil disturbances of 1839 were not so widespread and not so unnerving in their effects on parliamentary opinion; the crisis of the Reform Act had been safely passed.

It is certainly true that little more was heard from the industrial protectionists in the House of Commons; nothing more was heard of the injustice of Huskisson's alteration of the navigation laws or of the silk and glove duties.

The change in the political environment of economic policy between the beginning and the end of this decade cannot be described without further research. In particular, research into the development of the old protectionist industries is necessary. Dis-

[1] L. C. Sanders, *Lord Melbourne's Papers* (London, 1889), p. 389: 'The present outcry is raised evidently by the master manufacturers, taking advantage of the present dearness of corn, and with the object of lowering wages. It is not at present very strong . . .' (Melbourne to Russell, 20 Jan. 1839).

cussion in Parliament was bound to take a simplified view of the problem, particularly in a period when only a few members had first-hand knowledge of industry and commerce, and when the statistical resources of the Government were still rudimentary. It is clear that different features of the economic landscape attracted discussion at different dates. In the later eighteen-twenties the focus of discussion was the fall in prices of agricultural produce and of manufactured goods. Where this fall could plausibly be ascribed to foreign competition, this led to a demand for protection, or if it could not be connected with foreign competition, it could add to the support given to Attwood. In the later eighteen-thirties emphasis in discussion was laid on retaliatory tariffs, and on foreign competition in export markets, which led to a demand for alteration in the corn laws. To some extent the industrial interests most affected were different in the two periods.

The Whigs were more concerned with their immediate political prospects than with the development of these industries. Their majority was tenuous, and on two current issues, the Penny Post and the Ballot, they had gone as far as was possible to conciliate the Radicals. On the question of the corn laws, the Cabinet was divided, and the question was treated as an open one. Melbourne himself was strongly hostile: 'I own I dread it very much', he wrote to Russell, 'not so much from either the difficulty or danger of the question itself . . . as from the conviction that it will not be settled either one way or the other without a very severe struggle. . . . Nothing is so bad in my mind as abuse and condemnation of classes of society, and this question naturally produces it.' He was willing to allow inquiry into their working, but 'I am not prepared, on account of the present high prices, to put myself at the head of this Corn Law movement'. That is, he was not prepared to pledge the Government to the introduction of a fixed duty. (Thomson himself appears at this date to have been talking of a fixed duty rather than of the total repeal of the corn laws.)

This represented a check for Poulett Thomson, although it was still possible for him to push for the repeal of the corn laws on his own initiative. 'I do not see', wrote Melbourne, 'why P. Thomson should not move upon the question as member for Manchester, just as Plunket, when Irish Attorney-General in 1825, moved the Roman Catholic question, whilst Lord Liverpool was against it.'

[1] Sanders, op. cit., pp. 387–90.

It is not easy to form a fair assessment of Poulett Thomson's work in this situation. It is clear that he was discontented, but it is not clear whether he could have done more than he did. There is a curious letter among Melbourne's papers, from his brother, Lord Beauvale, British Ambassador at Vienna. McGregor was in Vienna in 1838 working on the Anglo-Austrian Commercial Treaty, and made a very strong impression on Beauvale. Beauvale wrote on 25 June 1838: 'MacGregor tells me that the secret of Paulet Thomson's indolence lies in the lowness of the Salary to which Auckland had the office reduced. Nothing so dear as cheap labour, every thousand saved to the Country in this way has cost to demonstration furnished by MacGregor hundreds of thousands to the Country in another.' Two months later he wrote: 'Are you aware that there is among Merchants and Manufacturers a great clamour that the material interests of the country are neglected? It is aimed chiefly at Thomson—I hear much of it.'[1]

It is not necessary to believe all that McGregor had to say about his master, but these letters show that there was dissatisfaction of some kind. Thomson was an ambitious man, and not a very patient one. In the summer of 1839 he was anxious to move from the Board of Trade. Spring-Rice was raised to the peerage as Lord Monteagle in September 1839, and the Chancellorship of the Exchequer fell vacant. Thomson was the obvious candidate for the post, and his claims had been canvassed for some time. On 20 December 1837 Spencer, his former patron, had written: 'Thompson has turned his mind more to financial science than any of them, and his ability is very great; there can therefore be no doubt that he will look very much to being Chancellor of the Exchequer on a vacancy and is likely to be very angry if he does not get it.'[2] In a letter to Russell of October 1838 Melbourne supported his claims, again on the ground of his particular ability in finance.[3] According to his brother's biography of him the Chancellorship was offered to him in August 1839.[4]

Yet he turned it down, and this suggests that the real cause of his discontent was the Cabinet's unwillingness to support his policy rather than the frustration of his personal ambitions. In preference to the Exchequer, Thomson accepted appointment as Governor-

[1] Lord Melbourne's letters. [2] Ibid. [3] Sanders, op. cit., p. 383.

[4] G. Poulett Scrope, *Memoir of the Life of Charles, Lord Sydenham* (London, 1843), p. 98.

General of Canada, and set sail in August 1839. In Canada, where he was sent to put the proposals of the Durham Report into effect, he showed his abilities to the full, and when he died, after a riding accident in September 1841, the comments of his political colleagues and acquaintances showed none of the criticism and rancour with which he tended to be regarded while he was in the Cabinet.[1]

The Cabinet reorganization of 1839 produced a stronger Chancellor of the Exchequer in F. T. Baring, who continued in office until the Dissolution of 1841. At the Board of Trade, Thomson was replaced by Henry Labouchère, who had been Vice-President of the Board since 1835. The new Vice-President was Richard Lalor Sheil, a follower of O'Connell. Neither of these appears to have carried much weight in politics nor to have left any mark on the history of the department.

Between 1830 and 1840 the original momentum of the Whigs' financial and commercial policy slackened and finally disappeared. The traditional account of their paralysis in the face of economic problems appears to be entirely correct. Thomson himself was glad to go to Canada, as he recognized that the immediate political future lay with the Conservatives. He wrote of his new appointment in his journal:

> . . . if I had not taken it then, as I could not well have got out of the government, I should have shared in the disgrace next session. It is a *great field*, too, if I bring about the union, and stay for a year to meet the United Assembly, and set them to work. On the other hand, in England there is little to be done by me. At the Exchequer all that can be hoped is to get through some BAD tax. There is no chance of carrying the House with one for any great commercial reforms, *timber*, *corn*, *sugar*, &c.; party and private interests will prevent it. If Peel were in, he might do this, as he could muzzle or keep away his Tory allies, and we should support him.[2]

But while the ministry weakened, the power of the parliamentary Radicals became yet greater, after the political crisis of 1839. In the session of 1840 they concentrated their offensive on the questions of free trade and the corn laws. On the Ballot, and on further parliamentary reform generally, it was clear from the determined opposition of some of the Whigs that they could not

[1] Greville, op. cit., vol. v, pp. 46–47 (29 Oct. 1842).
[2] Scrope, op. cit., pp. 101–2.

expect to make progress in the existing parliament.[1] It had also been clear from the election results of 1837 that they could not count on much support in the country. In the two years since then, Chartism had emerged as a political force with more extreme demands, and more violent tactics, than could be approved by the great majority of parliamentary Radicals and their supporters in the constituencies. The winter of 1839–40, when the Newport Rising took place, was a time of public alarm, during which people, such as Samuel Smiles in Leeds, or Ebenezer Elliott in Sheffield, withdrew their earlier support for Chartism. The fear that the Ballot would lead to political disorder was more widespread. In these circumstances, an agitation against the sugar, timber, and corn laws offered greater prospects of success in the Commons, particularly as the growth of the Anti-Corn Law League was evidence that this agitation had increasing support in the constituencies. And in the agitation for free trade, the officials of the Board of Trade were ready to form an alliance with the parliamentary Radicals.

On 1 April 1840 C. P. Villiers again brought forward his annual anti-corn-law motion, and a three-day debate followed.[2] Speakers of both parties concentrated on one main line of argument, which is discussed at length in a later chapter, that Britain could not expand her export trade unless she were willing to take foreign goods in exchange.[3] Little was said about the price of bread, but there was much reference to Bowring's *Report on the Prussian Commercial Union* which had just been published. The effect of the corn laws on international trade was a subject which the officials of the Board had made peculiarly their own, and to which their reports and articles had drawn public attention: this debate is one of the occasions on which their influence is most clearly shown. After prolonged discussion the motion was lost by 129–245.

This debate provided the reason for the appointment of the Select Committee on Import Duties a month later. If the House would not allow an inquiry into the corn laws, they might be willing to allow inquiry into the working of import duties generally. With careful management, an inquiry into the tariff could also be made into an indictment of the corn laws. According to Badham,

[1] Cf. p. 58 above.

[2] *Hansard*, 3rd ser., vol. 53, cols. 315–97, 432–78, 481–544.

[3] See Part III, Chap. 12 below.

Deacon Hume's biographer, the opportunity was seized by Deacon Hume in the first place:

As a last, and, as it proved, a crowning effort, he took an opportunity of suggesting to an experienced and influential member of Parliament . . . to whom, however, he was not allied or even intimately known, Mr. Joseph Hume, the expediency of moving for a Select Committee . . . intimating at the same time that he would be able to give important evidence if he were examined. This suggestion was energetically seconded by Mr. MacGregor. They thought that it would be for the public interest if those who were, or who had been in office at the Board of Trade could be transferred for a short time from their homes, or from their private offices in Whitehall, into a committee room of the House of Commons, for then, not only would their evidence be given publicly, but it would be ordered to be printed, and circulated through the country. Mr. Joseph Hume was much too sensible of the great results which might be expected from such a course, not to give it due consideration.[1]

There is no evidence to confirm this account of the part played by Deacon Hume, but, equally, there is no reason to disbelieve it: he had had long experience of handling this kind of committee, and later events certainly suggest clearly a close partnership between the officials of the Board and the free-trading Members of Parliament who supported the venture. On 5 May 1840, shortly before the end of the session (and before F. T. Baring had announced his Budget),[2] Joseph Hume moved, successfully, for the appointment of a Select Committee, 'To enquire into the several duties levied on imports into the United Kingdom: how far those duties are for protection to similar articles, the produce of this country or of the British possessions abroad, or whether the duties are for the purposes of revenue alone.'[3]

The membership of this committee bore every mark of its propagandist origin. It consisted, as all Select Committees at this date consisted, of fifteen members. Joseph Hume, as the proposer of the motion, had the chief share in the nomination of members, and he received suggestions from the Conservative side from Sir George Clerk, the member for Stamford. Clerk was a prominent Tory, and a friend of Peel: he is stated to have been an 'earlier convert to the principles of free trade than most'.[4] His papers,

[1] Badham, op. cit., p. 241.
[2] The Budget was introduced on 15 May.
[3] *Hansard*, vol. 53, cols. 1308–9.
[4] *D.N.B.*

preserved in the Register House in Edinburgh, show that he worked with Peel on the tariff revision of 1845, and on the agricultural measures of January 1846. He was, therefore, someone with more than the average interest in economic matters. The papers say little, however, about his career before 1841, and nothing about the work of this committee. In addition, there were five Conservative members: two, William Duncombe and William Ormsby Gore, were of landowning families, and both had spoken strongly against C. P. Villiers's motion the month before.[1] Sir Charles Douglas, another landowner, and Sir George Sinclair, a moderate Conservative who was known to be in favour of the Ballot, were also members. The remaining Conservative was Aaron Chapman, the member for Whitby, a spokesman for the shipping interest in the Commons.

On the other side were nine Whigs and Radicals. In addition to Joseph Hume, the chairman, there were the two members for Wolverhampton, C. P. Villiers, and Thomas Thornely, a Liverpool merchant. Villiers (the brother of Lord Clarendon) had already made a name for himself in the debates on the corn laws which he had opened: Thornely was a spokesman of the sugar merchants opposed to the prohibitive duties on foreign sugar. A second opponent of the sugar duties was William Ewart, formerly member for Liverpool, and since 1837 member for Wigan. Two other members, W. J. Blake and William Williams, were both Radicals. Finally, there were three official members, Labouchère, President of the Board of Trade, Henry Parnell, Paymaster-General of the Forces, and Henry Tufnell, a Lord of the Treasury.[2]

Thus this committee, like its predecessors on the silk duties, on the timber duties, or on rates of postage, was heavily weighted, more markedly so, perhaps, than any of these. Joseph Hume is said to have 'observed exultingly . . . that "the battle for free trade was about to be *won*" '.[3] This lack of balance was accentuated in practice. Whether by accident or design, the hearings of the committee took place during the summer recess, at a time inconvenient to some members: Sir Charles Douglas later complained that 'the Committee did not meet for two months, viz. not until the 6th

[1] *Hansard*, vol. 53, cols. 465, 497.

[2] The information about these members is derived partly from the *Dictionary of National Biography* and partly from Dod's *Parliamentary Companion* for 1839.

[3] Badham, op. cit., p. 243.

of July, and it was too much to expect that Members, whose residence was not in London, should remain in town to enter on the labour of a committee at that late period of the Session'.[1] The result was that the free-traders, who were in earnest, succeeded in circumventing opposition. The committee drafted its report after meeting fourteen times only: from the beginning, the number of members which attended was small, and as the summer wore on it dropped further and further. Labouchère and Sinclair never attended at all. This suggests that the Whigs thought that the inquiry was of no political significance:[2] later, when the full consequences of the committee's work began to be known, Labouchère was much criticized for this.[3] Clerk, Duncombe, Blake, Ormsby Gore, Tufnell, and Williams attended a few times and then stopped coming. Chapman and Douglas, who were not free-traders, and Parnell, who was, attended irregularly, but were present when the report was drafted. But Hume, and his friends Villiers, Thornely, and Ewart, never missed a hearing and formed, with Parnell, a solid voting majority of the seven members who drafted the report.

The same kind of management can be seen in the choice and handling of witnesses. The Select Committee on Rates of Postage had already shown the way: witnesses before both committees were not so much examined as invited to give prepared propaganda lectures.[4] The Select Committee on Import Duties was the child of the Board of Trade and of the Anti-Corn Law League, and nearly all the witnesses whom they summoned can be shown to have been connected with one or other of these parent bodies. On the iron industry they heard Sir John Guest, Whig member for Merthyr Tydfil, the great ironmaster and a free-trader.[5] J. B. Smith, president of the Manchester Chamber of Commerce, and a prominent member of the Anti-Corn Law League, gave evidence on cotton.[6] In addition they heard a number of merchants who were well known in other connexions: William Leaf, who had given

[1] *Hansard*, vol. 58, col. 435.

[2] Cf. p. 41 above.

[3] *Hansard*, vol. 58, col. 499. See p. 224 below.

[4] See, for example, the evidence of Henry Warburton before the Select Committee on Rates of Postage.

[5] His career is described in *Lady Charlotte Guest, Extracts from her Journal, 1833–52*, ed. by the Earl of Bessborough (London, 1950).

[6] Smith was president of the Anti-Corn Law Association in 1838. Prentice, *History of the Anti-Corn Law League* (London, 1853), vol. i, p. 105.

evidence before the silk committee of 1832, John Mitchell, who had given evidence on timber before the committee of 1835, and Alexander Johnston, an active member of the Anti-Corn Law League, and a man whose signature appears on memorials submitted to the Board of Trade in this period.[1]

Apart from William Leaf,[2] three other witnesses from the silk industry were heard. Henry Hilton was a Manchester silk manufacturer, T. F. Gibson a Spitalfields manufacturer; both had appeared before the 1832 committee, and both were keen supporters of the league.[3] The third was John Dillon, who seems to have been a professional witness; on previous occasions, before the 1832 silk committee, and before the Select Committee on Rates of Postage, he had always said exactly what his questioners wanted him to say. Apart from this, he was a partner in the very large and well-known retail and wholesale drapery business of James Morrison. (Morrison was later to become closely involved in the campaign to publicize the findings of this committee.[4])

The remaining witnesses were all, in some way or other, connected with sugar and coffee. The sugar and coffee duties became, next to the corn laws, the main preoccupation of the committee: this is hardly surprising in the circumstances of 1840, and in view of the fact that both Thornely and Ewart were connected with Liverpool. Four Liverpool merchants trading with Central and South America were examined—Richard Shiel, J. B. Moore, Charles Saunders, James Cockshott.

Their evidence was supported from a different quarter: 'It was part of Mr. Deacon Hume's suggestion, and it was adopted, that . . . some individuals of a very different class of life should be called in, and questioned as to the moral effects of high duties in the articles of coffee, tea, and sugar.'[5] In pursuit of this aim five London coffee-house keepers, whose places of business ranged from the Haymarket to St. Giles' High Street, were called in and gave evidence. They had much to say on the moral value of the coffee-houses, which were providing mid-day meals, unaccompanied by alcohol, in rapidly increasing numbers. This habit, and the older habit of using coffee-houses for business negotiation and for the

[1] B.T. 3/28.

[2] Cf. p. 39 above on the smuggling activities of Leaf's firm.

[3] Prentice, op. cit., vol. i, pp. 49, 93.

[4] See p. 216 below.

[5] Badham, op. cit., p. 270.

reading of the daily newspapers, were threatened by the high duties on tea and coffee.

By far the greatest part of the evidence, and the most important part, came from Deacon Hume, McGregor, Bowring, and Porter. It covers nearly half the pages of printed evidence, was widely quoted afterwards, and discussed nearly every aspect of the question as it had emerged in the previous ten years.

This body of evidence provides, therefore, the most convenient starting-point for studying the policy of the Board, and it is discussed at length in a subsequent section of this narrative.[1] For the present, however, the organization of this committee deserves to be described in some detail, for in it the political and propagandist skill of Deacon Hume, and of Joseph Hume, is clearly shown. The officials of the Board could speak, over the heads of Parliament, to the general public. While their articles and pamphlets, in spite of the easy-going conventions of the eighteen-thirties, appeared under a cover of semi-anonymity, their evidence before this committee appeared plainly under their own names, and with full emphasis on their professional experience in the matter. And, by the use of such witnesses as the coffee-house keepers, they ensured that the findings of this committee would be presented in a form interesting to the public.

APPENDIX

Public Revenue and Expenditure, 1830–42[2]

	£ million Revenue	Expenditure
1830	50·1	49·1
1831	46·4	49·8
1832	47·0	46·4
1833	46·3	45·8
1834	46·4	46·7
1835	45·9	45·7
1836	48·6	48·1
1837	46·5	49·1
1838	47·3	47·7
1839	47·8	49·4
1840	47·6	49·2
1841	48·1	50·2
1842	47·0	51·0

[1] See Part III below.

[2] Porter, *Progress of the Nation*, 1847 ed., p. 483.

PART II

THE BOARD OF TRADE AT WORK 1830–40

5

THE STATISTICAL ACTIVITIES OF THE BOARD OF TRADE

THE establishment of the Statistical Department in 1833 was, until the creation of the Railway Department in 1840, the most important expansion of the Board's activities. It had a predecessor in the same field of work, the Comptroller of Corn Returns and his assistants, but the Comptroller's work was limited to the working out of average corn prices made necessary by the corn laws. The new department was given wide terms of reference: it was suggested 'that a distinct Branch for this Purpose obtaining Returns from other Departments and concentrating the Information already in their Possession, might be of great public Utility',[1] and to this end parliamentary returns, consular reports, colonial and Indian statistics, and the records held by government departments should all be collected. The appointment of the first head of the department, Porter, has been described in a previous chapter.[2] By 1840, when he had a staff of about half a dozen clerks working under him, the expenses of the Statistical Department accounted for a substantial proportion of the whole expenditure on the Board of Trade.

This, in a decade in which there was constant and severe pressure in Parliament to reduce the estimates, is significant: the department would not have come into existence had there not been strong reasons and substantial support for it.

[1] B.T. 24/1, Thomas Lack to the Treasury, 31 Mar. 1832.
[2] See pp. 27 ff. above.

Of these reasons, the first, and the most obvious, was the administrative one: an economic crisis, or a major debate on economic policy, tended to produce a crop of demands for papers in Parliament, each couched in a slightly different form, and each requiring considerable clerical labour in its compilation. If the main series of government statistics were readily available in print, and were regularly brought up to date in standard form, there would be, as the Assistant-Secretary to the Board, Thomas Lack, argued in the original proposal to the Treasury, a 'saving to the Public upon the costly and desultory Returns which are occasionally called for'.[1] The volumes of Parliamentary Accounts and Papers of these years bear witness to the quantity of statistical information which was constantly demanded. The Statistical Department of the Board of Trade can then first be seen as a piece of administrative rationalization comparable with the reorganization of the public accounts which was going on at this time.

Beyond this, there was the need to establish satisfactory sources of information on the state of trade and manufactures, or even perhaps of morale, in the English provinces. Unlike, for example, the French administration, the government at the centre had no professional paid servants in the provinces on whose reports it could rely, nor yet an organized system of consultative bodies, like the French chambers of commerce.[2] The debates on economic distress of 1829 and 1830 showed wide disagreement on the extent of the distress, on the reasons for it, and on the remedies. Again, in 1833, the debates on Attwood's currency proposals, which have been discussed in the previous chapter, made the weakness of the Board's position obvious: Thomson had no first-hand information with which he could counter the arguments produced by Attwood, and by supporters in various industries who complained of distress, but whose complaints he believed to be unjustifiable.[3]

The inadequacy of the existing channels of information (which again became obvious when Porter began his work) was well illustrated by Sir Henry Parnell at a meeting of the Political Economy Club: 'Sir Henry Parnell, who spent a fortnight lately in Kent, the district first disturbed, and saw there many Country gentlemen and Magistrates, said that their ignorance and prejudices on subjects of population, wages, Tythes, Free Trade and

[1] B.T. 24/1, loc. cit. [2] See pp. 120, n. 1, below.
[3] See p. 41 above.

Taxes, exceeded all belief and that he could not make any impression on them.' Parnell's views on these questions were not those of everyone, but he was a member of the Government. He went on to say that 'Mr. Philips, the Under Secretary of State for the Home Department, told Whishaw yesterday that the correspondence of his Department with Magistrates during the disturbance shewed a profound ignorance of the causes of the distress, and of the proper remedies.'[1] The same difficulty was illustrated in a letter from Peel to Goulburn of 1829: 'Can you make any enquiry through the Excise, as to the operation of the acts in England? Forty-nine out of fifty magistrates would tell me if I wrote to them that they knew nothing about the matter.' In another letter, of 1828, suggesting that in view of a threatened shortage of wheat, information about stocks in England and abroad should be collected, Peel wrote of the political value of accurate knowledge: '... it may be of importance to shew that the attention of Government was at an early period called to the subject. It can probably do very little—but I can conceive circumstances that are not impossible, under which it might be of great advantage to shew that it had done all that it could—at least that it had not altogether overlooked the subject.'[2]

The same need explains the course of events leading to the establishment of the Statistical Department. At the end of 1831 Deacon Hume wrote to a friend that he was about to undertake some 'long journeys through the manufacturing districts. On Monday I set off, making Birmingham my first point. . . . The object is, not only to acquire, for present use, as much knowledge as may be of the state of manufactures, but also, if possible, to lay the foundation for obtaining such knowledge at all times.'[3]

In 1833 the question of putting the Statistical Department on a permanent footing was discussed by a Select Committee, which included Peel and Goulburn, as well as a fair number of Radicals. The ways in which regular information from the provinces could be obtained was one of the principal subjects which it investigated. McCulloch in evidence suggested that informal personal contact

[1] Political Economy Club, *Minutes of Proceedings* (London, 1921), vol. vi, pp. 221–2 (Diary of J. L. Mallet, 13 Jan. 1831).

[2] Goulburn MSS., Surrey County Record Office, Peel to Goulburn, 16 July 1829 and 18 Aug. 1828.

[3] Badham, op. cit., p. 132. See *Hansard*, vol. 10, col. 999, for comment on this expedition.

with statistical observers in the big industrial towns was all that was needed to keep the Government in touch with local conditions, but some at least of the committee thought this an inadequate scale of inquiry. Bowring, considerably more ambitious, proposed to have a statistical agent in every parish. As a true Benthamite, he was critical of the parish as a unit of administration, but he believed that in this case, as it was the traditional and social unit, it was the best. (He may perhaps have wished to enlist the country clergy as statistical agents, but he did not say this.[1]) The department was then, from the beginning, expected to be, not merely a repository of official statistics, but also a unit devoted to economic and social research.

It is easy to see how the establishment of such a department would be acceptable to the Philosophic Radicals, who were the people who were most relentless, in the eighteen-thirties, in their attacks on the scale of government expenditure. The codification of public statistics by a central body with suitably chosen local agents was something which held obvious attractions to the orthodox Benthamite. In addition, Joseph Hume and his circle always favoured schemes for the wider diffusion of knowledge. Sometimes, like London University or the Society for the Diffusion of Useful Knowledge, they were private ventures or financially independent. But where it was necessary, the Radicals did not grudge public money for such purposes, and considered that it was a proper function of the State to provide directly the framework of a civilized life. In 1824 Hume had said that the lack of a National Gallery was a 'disgrace', and he fought a long battle to open the resources of the British Museum to the general public.[2] Apart, therefore, from the narrow considerations of finding work for such people as Marshall, the new department could expect Radical support. Such opposition as there was came from the Tory Opposition, who wished to show 'how well the economists could, when they had the opportunity, take care of their friends'.[3]

[1] *Select Committee on Public Documents, Parliamentary Papers*, 1833, xii, questions 223–8, 512–13. McCulloch published an interesting article on the 'State and Defect of British Statistics' in vol. lxi of the *Edinburgh Review* (Apr. 1835), in which he discussed at length the topics on which information would be desirable.

[2] W. Smart, op. cit., p. 194; *Hansard*, 3rd ser., vol. 10, col. 977; vol. 31, col. 310; vol. 53, cols. 1186–7.

[3] Ibid., vol. 10, col. 474; cf. pp. 28–29 above.

A department of this kind was not an administrative novelty: many countries of western Europe had had statistical departments for some time. In Prussia, a central statistical bureau had been set up in 1805, but had had an interrupted history since that time. In 1833 a Central Bureau for the Zollverein was established, which in the eighteen-forties and fifties produced compilations closely analogous to Porter's *Progress of the Nation.* Bavaria had had something of the kind in 1808, Württemberg in 1820, Austria in 1829. In France there had been central departments both at the end of the eighteenth century and under Napoleon, but neither had survived. A new department, inspired by the example of England, was opened in the French Ministry of Commerce in 1833.[1]

But, while England may have been slow to introduce a central organization, there can be no doubt that, within England, the officials of the Board played a leading part in what might almost be described as the statistical movement of the eighteen-thirties. In setting up the department the Board, or more probably Poulett Thomson himself, was moving along in the full stream of a contemporary intellectual current. A series of statistical societies was formed at about this time, all having as their object economic and social investigations, and Thomson and Porter entered at once into close relations with them. It is noticeable, in a period in which so many social or administrative reforms were forced upon the Government by various pressure groups, that on this occasion the official consideration of the subject, which goes back to 1830, considerably antedates the formation of private statistical societies. The Manchester Statistical Society did not meet until September 1833, and, when it did, it was given precise advice by Poulett Thomson, the member for Manchester, on the lines of inquiry it was most desirable to pursue:

> Dr. Kay read a report of a conversation which had taken place between Poulett Thomson and the members of the Society. . . . Poulett Thomson had announced that there was no prospect of the Government's adopting any extensive scheme for collecting statistical information throughout the country, but had made valuable suggestions as to the type of investigations to which a body of amateur statisticians like

[1] *Handwörterbuch der Staatswissenschaften* (4th ed., Jena, 1926), article, 'Statistik'; P. G. Marietti, *La Statistique générale en France* (Paris, 1949), pp. 21–24. C. F. W. Dieterici, author of *Statistische Übersicht der wichtigsten Gegenstände des Verkehrs und Verbrauchs im preussischen Staate und im deutschen Zollverbande* (Berlin, 1838–57), was the head of the statistical bureau of the Zollverein.

the Manchester Society might turn their attention. Their first task might well be to make a classification of the people of Manchester and to ascertain 'the command which in a right state of moral feeling the working classes have over the necessaries of life'.[1]

The rest of his recommendations detailed the particular social investigations necessary to this end.

The London Statistical Society first met in March 1834: Porter was active in its formation, and introduced Poulett Thomson and Deacon Hume to it. On this occasion also, it was suggested that the society should specialize in those fields of inquiry which the Board did not propose to enter.[2]

At this date, statistics was a much-discussed subject, the scope of which was not fully agreed, but which was certainly different from that of statistics at the present day. It was defined as the 'science of the state'. What this meant was not entirely clear: it was possible to interpret it as a calculation of the power of states.[3] More generally it was taken to mean the collection of facts descriptive of a state: its geographical features, climate, population, resources, scale of trade, and habits. It is clear from this that statistics as they understood it was not restricted in its scope to quantitative information—a 'statistical' account of Hanover, for example, included an appraisal of the work of the opera-house there.[4] Still less was the body of mathematical theory used in the handling of quantitative information describable as statistics: according to one writer it was correctly termed political arithmetic. Nor was it a study of the 'causes of wealth or fluctuations': that was then, as now, described as economics.

The Statistical Department of the Board of Trade therefore began its career with very wide terms of reference, and with few resources. The local societies on which they would have to depend were themselves in their infancy. The subject itself was only

[1] T. S. Ashton, *Economic and Social Investigations in Manchester, 1833–1933* (London, 1934), p. 16. A similar investigation was carried out by the Statistical Committee of the Leeds Town Council in 1838–40. It was chiefly aimed at housing and sanitary conditions in the town. Its results were published in 1841 and circulated, among others, to the Manchester Statistical Society, in the hope of gaining support for a local Act of Parliament.

[2] The papers contributed by Porter to the proceedings of the Royal Statistical Society were mostly concerned with social conditions in London.

[3] *O.E.D.*

[4] F. v. Reden, *Das Königreich Hannover statistisch beschrieben* (Hanover, 1839).

beginning to pass from the stage of compiling public information to the stage where definite questions were solved by certain recognized methods. In setting off to discover the true state of the English provinces, Porter needed both local contacts and tried and tested techniques of inquiry.

The first letter-book of the Statistical Department is preserved among the papers of the Board in the Public Record Office, and gives a clear picture of the way in which Porter set to work, and of the objectives he had particularly in mind. The collecting of information from other public offices presented no difficulty, and, on a smaller scale, such collections had been made for the previous three or four years. In July 1833 Porter circulated the first set of his published tables.[1]

The attempt to obtain regular economic information from provincial centres ran, as it might have been expected to do, into greater difficulties, but the persistence and ingenuity with which Porter pursued it were remarkable. He began by approaching chambers of commerce, asking for a quantity of information which could only be available locally—principal local industries, the number of factories, the size and kind of labour force they employed, information about local rents, prices, and wage-rates since the end of the war, whether there was an 'increase or diminution in the means of employment'.[2] In the summer of 1832 he approached a number of Irish chambers and those of Manchester and Birmingham. Of all these, the only places from which he received returns were Londonderry and Manchester.[3] He thereupon turned to individuals who might be expected to be sympathetic to the aims of the department. In this way he approached Dr. Cleland of Glasgow, author of the *Annals of Glasgow* and other 'statistical' works, 'in order to obtain more frequent but less formal returns, as to the condition of the Trading and Manufacturing classes: whether they are fully employed or otherwise—and to be made acquainted with the causes which apparently operate to produce those results, and to alter the relative position of different interests'.[4] He wrote similarly to Charles Pope, a Customs official in Bristol, and author of the *Import and Export Guide*, and to the Collector of Customs in

[1] B.T. 24/1. The tables are to be found in *Parliamentary Papers*, 1833, xli.

[2] B.T. 24/1.

[3] Ibid. The Chamber of Commerce of Birmingham was in a dormant condition at this time. Cf. p. 182 below.

[4] B.T. 24/1.

Liverpool, in each case asking particularly about the volume of Anglo-Irish trade: since 1825 no official records of this had been kept.[1]

Finally he tackled personal acquaintances, and a variety of sources which show his resourcefulness. To the Clerk of the Peace in Anglesey he wrote: 'The means of obtaining statistical information . . . are principally defective as regards the past and present condition of the rural districts of the kingdom. . . . I believe that in some if not all the Counties of the Kingdom it has been the practice during a long series of years for the Grand Jury at Quarter Sessions to make a presentment of the price of grain. . . .' He wrote to W. J. Smith, a shipowner of Belfast, asking to use the records of his firm to make good the deficiency of official records of Anglo-Irish trade; and he wrote to Benjamin Gott and James Marshall, the two notable Leeds manufacturers, for information from their business records. To Marshall, he again spoke of the need for local information: 'Lord Auckland and Mr. Thomson are very urgent with me in regard to such matters and the Committee which sat during last Session upon Public Documents and of which you were a Member attached so much importance justly I think to the possession of such information.' To W. Vaughan, a canal proprietor in the Potteries, he wrote asking for figures of the quantity of earthenware transported by him over a series of years.[2]

Porter's correspondence has been described at some length to show that if he failed to establish contact between the Board and the manufacturing districts, it was through no lack of persistence or resourcefulness. Yet it is clear that he failed to achieve solid results. The work of the department was published in a series of reports, known as *Porter's Tables*, from 1833 until his death in 1852. These show that the Board was getting, to some extent, the kind of information it was looking for: the tables contain figures, usually covering the years since 1815, of wage-rates, retail prices, and sometimes of the volume of production of the most important manufactures of London, Glasgow, Manchester, Sheffield, Londonderry, Waterford, Limerick, Leicester, Bradford, and Newcastle upon Tyne. They also include similar information from

[1] This question is discussed in Porter, *Progress of the Nation*, sect. iii, chap. 7.

[2] B.T. 24/1. These letters are dated between Sept. 1832 and Apr. 1834. There appear to be no further letter-books of the Statistical Department after 1834 which have survived.

Bethlehem, St. Thomas's, and Greenwich Hospitals.[1] Some of these sources are used in the *Progress of the Nation*. But it is clear that the underlying purposes of the inquiry were not achieved, and perhaps in the circumstances could not have been achieved. Porter, in the chapter in the *Progress of the Nation* on wages, laid great emphasis on the difficulty of obtaining adequate and comparable statistics on the relationship of wages and prices. He inclined to the view, which was widely held, that the standard of living of most sections of the working class, who were in employment, had improved since 1815.[2] But he could not examine the question on a scale which would prove the point one way or the other. This was one of the points at which the Statistical Department, had it had the means, could have contributed decisively to the formation of national trade policy. The question whether repeal of the corn laws would lower money wages or would increase or decrease real wages underlay the discussions on the subject: and the Statistical Department had nothing authoritative to say.

Nor were they able to get information on an adequate scale on production. The effects of the corn laws on the acreage growing wheat, the increase or decrease in the production or consumption of meat or dairy produce, the proportion of the total consumption of grain which was supplied, in different years, by imports, were all unknown, and the *Progress of the Nation* confessed its failure to advance knowledge on these questions. The same kind of situation existed with many manufactures. In some cases it was possible to know the total volume of production, or, more important, changes in the volume of production. This could be done where there was an Excise (as with glass or bricks), or where the raw material was wholly imported and used for one kind of manufacture only (as with silk or cotton), or where figures of the amounts distributed by canal, railway, or sea could be obtained (as with coal). Such industries as the woollen or hardware industries presented more intractable problems. Still less could the department hope to provide the Government with reliable forecasts of business fluctuations in provincial centres.[3]

The campaign to improve the handling and collection of com-

[1] These local and private returns are printed in *Parliamentary Papers*, 1833, xli; 1835, xlix; and 1839, xlv.

[2] *Progress of the Nation* (1847 ed.), p. 459.

[3] Cf. p. 82 above.

mercial information extended to inquiries abroad. Here the initial impulse seems to have come from McCulloch, who was already at work on his *Dictionary of Commerce* when the Whigs took office in 1830. He greeted the news of Poulett Thomson's appointment to the Board of Trade significantly: 'I shall get from him early and *accurate* information on all commercial and financial subjects and as far as I am concerned that is the entire difference the change will make.'[1] In August 1832 this prophecy was proved correct, when the Board sent the Foreign Office a series of questions for transmission abroad.

> We drew up [wrote McCulloch in the Preface to the second edition of the *Dictionary*] a series of queries, embracing an investigation of imports and exports, commercial shipping regulations, port charges, duties etc., that might be transmitted to any port in any part of the world. There would, however, in many instances, have been much difficulty in getting them answered with the requisite care and attention by private individuals; and the scheme would have had but a very partial success, had it not been for the friendly and effectual interference of Mr. Poulett Thomson. Alive to the importance of having the queries properly answered, he voluntarily undertook to use his influence with Lord Palmerston to get them transmitted to the Consuls. This the Noble Lord most readily did. . . .[2]

The problems connected with the collection of economic information from abroad were discussed before two Select Committees, that on Public Documents, which has already been mentioned, and that on Consular Establishments of 1834. The latter was appointed in June 1834, after a debate in which Hesketh Fleetwood, member for Preston, who became chairman of the committee, criticized the lack of useful trade information in the consular reports.[3] The committee did not conduct a full-scale inquiry into the working of the consular service: nothing was said or done about the routine work of the consuls in dealing with British merchant shipping or commercial interests abroad. It concentrated on two questions, whether consuls should be allowed to trade[4] and

[1] McVey Napier papers, B.M. Add. MSS. 34,614, f. 434.

[2] F.O. 83/63; *Dictionary of Commerce*, 2nd ed., p. iv of Preface. (He singled out the consuls at Hamburg, Trieste and Venice, Naples, Danzig, Bordeaux, Christiania, Amsterdam, Elsinore, NewYork, and Charleston for especial praise.)

[3] *Hansard*, vol. 24, cols. 883–91. The committee's report is in *Parliamentary Papers*, 1835, vi.

[4] This had been permitted by Canning, and was considered by critics to be the cause of consular inefficiency.

whether the existing system of reporting was efficient. On the second question, no very clear evidence was received. The only criticism of serious importance came from the Consul-General at Bogota, James Henderson, who said that reports from South America gave an inaccurate account of British exports in that they excluded exports in foreign vessels. As well as this, there were complaints, not of the reports, but of the fact that they were inaccessible to the commercial public. There was a suggestion that a government-sponsored trade journal should be established, but, as far as the writer knows, nothing of this kind was produced until the establishment of the *Board of Trade Journal* in 1886.[1]

Other questions concerned the efficiency of the consular administration, a subject about which the committee showed the greatest interest. Witnesses were repeatedly asked whether the returns sent to the Foreign Office were transmitted to the Board of Trade, whether there were delays in dealing with commercial correspondence at the Foreign Office, and finally, which suggests rivalry between departments, whether it would not be better for the consular service to be directly under the control of the Board of Trade. The implication of these questions is that the Board was not satisfied, and wished to extend its operations.[2]

The support given by the Board to *ad hoc* commercial investigations in foreign countries strengthens this impression. In 1832, before either of these committees, John McGregor, who later became joint-secretary to the Board, went to France on a commercial investigation. In the following year the scope of his work was greatly enlarged; according to himself he travelled in other European countries between 1833 and 1836, and from 1837 to 1839 worked in Austria and Italy, partly on statistical investigations and partly on commercial negotiations, which are the subject of later chapters. During this second period he was in the employ of the Foreign Office. In the earlier period his status is not clear, but it seems likely that he was in some way officially sponsored, for he stated in the Preface to his *Commercial Statistics . . . of all Nations* that it was originally intended to publish the results of these in-

[1] *Parliamentary Papers*, 1835, vi, questions 139, 899. It was stated that such journals already existed in France (*Archives de Commerce*), in Holland (*Handelsblad*), and in Denmark (*Handels und Industrie Tidende*).

[2] Ibid., questions 3, 538, 773, 904, 1147. Palmerston and Thomson were both members of this committee, but as the minutes of evidence do not state who asked which question, the matter cannot be settled conclusively.

vestigations as a Command Paper. As publication did not begin until 1843, during Peel's administration, which was markedly unsympathetic to this group of officials, the work was published at McGregor's expense.[1]

The second investigator of this kind was Dr. Bowring, whose studies of economic conditions in France, Germany, and other parts of Europe will be discussed in subsequent chapters. He was from the beginning a paid employee of the Foreign Office.[2] Both men carried out work of much the same kind and quality; and to both the frontiers between research, propaganda, and commercial negotiation were shadowy. Neither can be said to have done original work abroad—in the sense in which Jacob's work on the corn laws was original. For the most part they collected tables of already published official statistics, and digested the works of continental statistical writers. On one occasion this was untrue; in Bowring's work in France he used local reports, and tables collected in his tours of the country. His later work was executed more hastily, and contained little of this kind.[3]

It remains to try and form some assessment of the value of these statistical inquiries in the eighteen-thirties and forties, particularly in the field of commercial policy.

The immediate task, that of codifying existing information, had been fully carried out by the publication of *Porter's Tables*. The existence of the department by itself ensured that, from 1832 onwards, government statistics would be presented on a comparable basis every year, and that opportunities for the enlargement of statistical knowledge provided by new administrative measures would be noticed and exploited.

It could hardly be expected that the far-reaching objectives of the department could be attained. Porter deserves admiration for attempting as much as he did, but he had no means of compelling the public to supply him with figures, and his field of inquiry was very wide—perhaps too wide for effective results. To W. Armstrong of Newcastle upon Tyne, for example, he wrote: 'It is not possible

[1] See *Commercial Statistics*, &c. (London, 1843), vol. i, p. ix; and p. 226 below.

[2] See Chaps. 6 and 7.

[3] See p. 108 below for a violent attack on Bowring's work by Disraeli. In addition, a number of investigators, including David Urquhart, were sent by Palmerston in these years to the Near East and the Black Sea on similar kinds of inquiry. [V. J. Puryear, *International Economics and Diplomacy in the Near East* (Stanford, California, 1935), pp. 23–26.]

for anyone to pronounce as to the importance which the registration of even simple facts may come to have upon the general condition of the country, at some future period.'[1] Such wide terms of reference may well have inhibited the department from formulating its inquiries in such a way that they stood a fair chance of being answered. In years of slump and social upheaval such as 1839 or 1842 there is no sign, either in the records of the Board of Trade, or in collections of political correspondence such as the Peel, Russell, or Melbourne papers, that the Government had a firmer knowledge of the economic situation in the provincial centres than it had had ten years previously. And on such problems as the effects of foreign tariffs on British export markets, or the effects of British tariff changes on domestic prices and consumption—the questions which were to be the subject of so many pamphlets once the anti-corn-law movement got under way—a great deal of varied information had been collected, but it was too little to contribute decisively to the formation of policy. A later chapter will show that in the years 1840 to 1842 Gladstone and Peel complained of the lack of official information to guide them in their tariff revision, and that there was still a need for special missions of inquiry.[2] Consular reports, in spite of the Select Committee of 1834, do not seem to have altered much in numbers or character during this period. In 1854 the Northcote–Trevelyan report on the Board of Trade recommended that the compilation of statistics should in future be divided up among the different government departments. The original idea of a central organization which could, on demand, offer a reasoned assessment of the economic state of the nation had proved to be over-ambitious.

It has been suggested that the department failed to produce more substantial results because its objectives were too general. But it could plausibly be argued that, in other ways, its work was limited by the intellectual attitude dominant in the Board of Trade. They showed a preoccupation with the effects of what they believed to be unwise forms of state intervention, which tended to obscure to them other matters of equal importance. McGregor and Bowring wrote at length on the character of continental tariffs, and on the economic effects of high protection where they found it abroad. Where they found other forms of mercantilist regulation of industry they discussed them also. McCulloch in his *Dictionary* pro-

[1] B.T. 24/1.

[2] See pp. 226, 230 below.

vides much the same kind of information; and in his evidence before the Select Committee on Public Documents his criticisms of existing statistical sources hinged on the question whether they adequately showed the effects of duties on prices or consumption.[1] In McCulloch's work, though not in the work of the other two, this preoccupation with foreign tariffs can partially be explained by the fact that the *Dictionary* was designed for the use of the export merchant. But neither he nor McGregor showed any interest in economic organization in the countries he was studying. In this respect Bowring, with his Radical political sympathies, his linguistic abilities, and his zest for travelling, showed a broader imagination. His reports on France gave a lively and intelligible picture of how silk and wine were made and marketed, and provided the English reader with an idea of the kind of power wielded by different economic interests in France. His much slighter report on Germany was distinguished by being the first in England to foretell the importance of the German chemical industry.[2]

The same narrow vision can be seen in places in the *Progress of the Nation*. The book sets out to describe the progress 'not of this or that section of its inhabitants, but the progress of the whole social system in all its various departments, and as affecting all its various interests'.[3] No one, reading the *Progress of the Nation* at the present day, would find as clear or illuminating a picture of the whole social system as he would from the evidence collected by the major parliamentary committees of this period. On one hand, there is the same indifference to questions of economic organization, or to industrial processes or to their social environment, which suggests that the author was unaware of the complex amalgam of discontents which found expression in Chartism. Questions of taxation are considered in relation to two criteria, that of maximizing the yield to the Exchequer, and that of minimizing the interference with industry and commerce. The effects of different taxes on different classes of consumer were not considered.[4]

On the other hand, Porter's intellectual standpoint at times distracted him from questions which were relevant to his general theme, or blinded him to them. He was concerned above all to

[1] *Select Committee on Public Documents, Parliamentary Papers*, 1833, xii, questions 48 ff., 84 ff.

[2] See pp. 107 ff. below.

[3] *Progress of the Nation* (1847 ed.), p. 2.

[4] See Part III, pp. 145 ff. below.

measure progress, whether the progress of manners or the progress of industrial production. In spite of the letters, cited earlier in this chapter, which asked for evidence of the causes and development of commercial fluctuations, Porter showed little interest in this subject. He used the tables he possessed to demonstrate expansion, and not to show fluctuations, though they might have been thought to be of importance in the development of the 'whole social system', and certainly of great importance to the politicians charged with the framing of economic policy.

The attitude, not only of Porter, but of the Board as a whole, is perhaps most clearly seen in their handling of a subject of much interest now, namely the question of the value of imports and the terms of trade in this period. The Board did not undertake the working out of import values until 1854, two years after the death of Porter.[1] While there is no definite explanation, among the documents, of why the question was not tackled earlier, it is possible to suggest reasons.

There can be no doubt that many people, both in England and abroad, were strongly critical of the existing system for the valuation of imports. The French consul-general in London hardly ever sent home a return of British exports and imports without a lengthy explanation of their inadequacy. César Moreau, the French vice-consul, prepared a system of his own for the valuation of British imports, for the use of his own Government.[2]

The problem was canvassed by the Select Committee on Public Documents: both Marshall and McCulloch were extensively examined on the practicability of working out values for imports. Both believed that it could be done. It would not be difficult to produce a return showing the quantities of imports of particular commodities, the rates of duty, and the freights usually paid. The difficulty arose in establishing the prices at which they had been sold in this country. Where a commodity varied greatly in quality and price, the price-quotations would be of little help. Marshall's solution, if he were given control of the Statistical Department, would be to employ 'intelligent boys' who would attend the public sales and make notes of the proportions of goods sold at different

[1] It is not known whether there is any connexion between these dates.

[2] Ministère des Affaires étrangères, correspondance commerciale, London, e.g. consular reports dated 29 May 1835 and 29 Mar. 1836: Archives nationales, F[12] 6216.

prices. McCulloch suggested that they should get trade reports from the ports of shipment overseas.[1] Porter's solution given, not before the committee, but in the *Progress of the Nation*, was similar to Marshall's; it would be 'not only possible, but easy of accomplishment to arrive at a satisfactory approximation to the truth, if some competent persons in various lines of business were employed every year to affix an average value to the different descriptions of goods that had been imported in the course of the preceding year'.[2] Finally, as early as January 1830, before the question had been publicly raised, William Irving, Inspector-general of Imports and Exports, had written: 'I may be permitted to recur to the plan for ascertaining the real value of Imports and of Foreign goods exported which I submitted to their Lordships some time ago. The adoption of that plan would, I venture to believe, add most materially to the interest and the practical utility of the commercial records.'[3]

It is quite clear that they were not frightened away from the problem by its technical complexities. It appears likely that the problem was shelved for other reasons. To inquire closely into the balance of payments was, in McCulloch's opinion, to ask the wrong questions first. It is noticeable that while Marshall was eager to work in this field, McCulloch only conceded to the committee after questioning that the problem was a 'rather important' one: import values were chiefly needed to study the effects of import duties on consumption. He was anxious to know the quantities of goods imported in order to show the growth of British trade. He said nothing about the relationship of export prices and import prices.[4]

The problem of import valuations was bound up with current economic controversy in a way which was perhaps unexpected. At intervals between 1829 and 1832 the unreal and misleading character of British trade statistics was raised in the Commons by Alderman Waithman, a follower of Attwood. British export statistics provided an opportunity of showing the evil results of the resumption of cash payments in 1821. In 1798 the real value of exports had been above the official values; now, he said, the reverse was true. As the system of valuation had not changed, it

[1] *Select Committee on Public Documents, Parliamentary Papers*, 1833, xii, questions 142–4, 56–85.

[2] *Progress of the Nation* (1847 ed.), p. 359.

[3] B.T. 1/268.

[4] *Select Committee on Public Documents, Parliamentary Papers*, 1833, xii, questions 142–4, 60–65.

followed that export prices had declined. The inferences which he drew from this were muddled, and provided an easy target for Poulett Thomson, but Waithman came very near to describing what in modern terms would be an unfavourable movement in the terms of trade: 'By a return he held in his hand he found that within the last thirty years the price of weaving a piece of cloth had fallen from 10*s*. 6*d*. to 1*s*. 9*d*.: and the price of a quarter of wheat had fallen from about 80*s*. to about 50*s*.'[1]

Waithman's demand for the revision of the system of valuation produced varied consequences. It is possible that Irving's scheme of valuation of January 1830 was a response to these complaints. There was at least one follower of Attwood, Colonel Davies, on the Select Committee on Public Documents, and he may have led the discussion on the subject there. Joseph Hume, glad of an opportunity of pushing forward his follower, Marshall, approved the revision of the system of valuation, but attacked Waithman's point of view whole-heartedly.[2] Thomson was violent and perhaps unreasoning in his opposition. As Waithman's object was 'the depreciation of the standard, the House now knew how to meet him'.[3] He defended the existing system with the same sort of vigour as that of Wellington in defending the 'matchless constitution' of the unreformed House of Commons. He reiterated two propositions, the first that British imports would be paid for by British exports, and the second, that import prices, particularly of raw cotton, had fallen at the same time as export prices. McCulloch produced an article in the *Edinburgh Review* on the 'Recent Commercial Policy of Britain' which coincided with the debate of 1832 on the subject, and which followed similar lines.[4] Both ignored the idea implicit in Waithman's remarks, that export and import prices might be falling at different rates. This persistent refusal to venture into this field illustrates the gulf which exists between the process of policy-formation in the early nineteenth century, and the arguments which are sometimes today produced in defence of it.[5]

[1] *Hansard*, 2nd ser., vol. 22, cols. 305–9 (9 Feb. 1830). The subject was raised again by Waithman in Feb. 1831 (ibid., 3rd ser., vol. 2, cols. 556–84), and in Jan. and July 1832 (ibid., vol. 9, col. 779; vol. 14, col. 6).

[2] Ibid., vol. 9, cols. 15–17.

[3] Ibid., 2nd ser., vol. 22, col. 323.

[4] Vol. 55, 1832.

[5] Cf. A. H. Imlah, 'The Fall of Protection' in *Essays in Honor of George Hubbard Blakeslee* (Clark University, 1949), pp. 306–20. Thomson's antipathy to Attwood was shown in a letter to Edward Ellice of 9 Sept. 1832, where he claimed that 'every intelligent mechanic' confessed his theory of depreciation

The Statistical Department of the Board of Trade was a pioneer, and explored its field of work with great energy and enterprise. If it failed to play a more directly important part in the framing of policy, and the solution of current problems, it was partly for reasons beyond its control—its inability to collect statistics on a sufficient scale for some important lines of inquiry, and perhaps also the fact that it was too closely associated with one political party; its influence dropped after 1841. But Porter and his colleagues also suffered from intellectual limitations which prevented their giving attention to questions in which they might have achieved useful results.

Against these points, however, must be set their undeniable influence over the public, and over statistical writers abroad. It has been said in a previous chapter that, so far as is known, no equally significant writers of protectionist tendencies were at work in England at that date.[1] Nor has the writer discovered any workers in this field, at this date, who were not to some extent dependent on these sources of information. Abroad, the frequency with which the names of Porter, McCulloch, McGregor, and Bowring appear in contemporary writings on economic policy is remarkable. A writer such as Dieterici in Prussia drew his account of the trade between England and Prussia in corn and timber from English sources; and it was partly the fault of the English if he used their attacks on the corn laws and timber duties to reassert the importance of protectionism to Germany. Nebenius, the finance minister of Baden in the eighteen-thirties, and an influential advocate of high protective tariffs in Germany, was also dependent on English sources for many of his arguments.[2] In France complaints can be read that all that was known of French foreign trade had been collected and published by partisan British agents.[3] In these ways the statisticians of the Board spoke to a wider audience than did politicians such as Thomson.

to be 'utterly exposed'. He believed he would be able to 'lick the Attwoodites and Ruin preachers to the Devil' (Russell Ellice MSS., National Library of Scotland).

[1] See p. 30 above.

[2] Dieterici, op. cit., pp. 260 ff., 351; C. F. Nebenius, *Der deutsche Zollverein, sein System und seine Zukunft*, Carlsruhe, 1835.

[3] See p. 126 below.

6

COMMERCIAL NEGOTIATIONS WITH THE ZOLLVEREIN

THE regulation of British commercial relations was the field which, more than any other, gave the officials of the Board of Trade scope for exercising initiative and determining the course of policy. It was a field which was affected comparatively little by the limitations which have been described in previous chapters. Parliament, it has been shown, was always alert to the threat of foreign competition against British industries: some protectionist interests—notably the landed and shipping interests—were well-organized and old-established. Commercial negotiations with foreign powers, however, do not appear to have made so obvious an impact on organized business interests: certainly there is little sign, until the end of this period, of parliamentary interest in the development and safeguarding of British export markets. During this period the political and the commercial map of Europe was radically changed; Belgium broke away from Holland in 1830; the Polish rising of 1830 was suppressed; and in Germany, the Zollverein was consolidated during these years. All these changes involved, or at least threatened, changes in British trading relations, or restrictions on British exports, yet none of them seems to have attracted the serious attention of Parliament. In contrast to this, the Foreign Office was successful in removing tariff barriers to British trade in two important treaties, the Anglo-Austrian Treaty of 1838, and the Anglo-Turkish Convention of the same year. These, which were of great potential importance, also attracted little notice. Provided always that it was possible to negotiate favourable treaties without making inroads into the existing British tariff, the Government could proceed with their plans without hindrance: if they were slack, it does not seem that there was any section in Parliament which was determined to drive them on. On the other hand, the Manchester Chamber of Commerce was fairly active in this period in bringing to the notice of the Board specific difficulties which its members were encountering in foreign markets, and Poulett Thomson, as member for Manchester, was under a particular obligation to attend to them.[1]

Another circumstance gave the Board of Trade greater opportunities than it might otherwise have had. Palmerston was always prepared to exert himself to push forward any plan which would promote British commercial expansion. But his approach to the subject was not primarily determined by economic considerations. He saw the protection of British interests abroad in political terms, being more willing to act firmly to defend the rights and liberties of British trading communities in foreign cities, than to take the initiative in fighting for easier tariff conditions. An example of the contrast in points of view was shown in the autumn of 1839. Discussions about commercial treaties with Naples and with Sardinia were going forward. The former was being conducted by McGregor, and the latter by the British Minister at Turin, Sir Augustus Foster. Palmerston strongly criticized the proposed treaty produced by McGregor, and one of his grounds was that it did not sufficiently safeguard the freedom of worship of Protestant merchants.[2] On the Sardinian negotiations, Le Marchant in the Board of Trade complained that Foster did not 'know much about his business' since he was proposing terms for a reciprocity treaty which did not give equality of status to British shipping in Sardinian ports.[3] At the same time the Board wrote to the Foreign Office saying that it did not think it necessary to hold out for religious toleration for British merchants.[4]

The responsibility for keeping open markets for British exports, and for opening new ones, rested with the Board of Trade. In negotiations with France, with the Zollverein, with the Italian states, Austria, or Sweden, the work was carried out by the Foreign Office, but a considerable initiative in opening new discussions, or in driving languishing ones to a conclusion, rested with the Board. One possible exception to this is the Anglo-Turkish Convention of 1838. Here, the absorption of British foreign policy in the Eastern question, and the problem of Mehemet Ali, produced an abnormal situation.

It is not surprising that the interest of the Board of Trade in commercial negotiations should have been greater than that of the

[1] A. Redford, *Manchester Merchants and Foreign Trade, 1794–1858* (Manchester, 1934), chaps. vii and viii.

[2] B.T. 1/359.

[3] B.T. 1/357.

[4] B.T. 3/29 (letter dated 14 Dec. 1839).

Foreign Office. The demands of strategy and diplomacy and the demands of commercial expansion are not necessarily coincident. The course of negotiation for commercial treaties tended to be influenced by general diplomatic considerations. Palmerston's foreign policy was built on the idea of an entente with France, and prolonged efforts for a commercial understanding with France were made in this period without success. Yet the prospects for extensive trading relations between the two countries were never very great: France was unable to supply the raw materials or the food which Great Britain required to import: discussions between Britain and France were carried out in terms of Britain's imports of silk and wine. France on her side had her own textile and mining industries, which were technically unable to compete with British industries, and claims for protection from which would probably dominate the policy of the Orleanist régime.

The commercial advantages which would result from similar negotiations with Russia and Prussia seemed greater. This region exported a big proportion of the corn imported by Britain in the early nineteenth century, and as far as the timber duties allowed it, some of the timber also. There was already, before the Zollverein established itself, an export trade in hardware and textiles through Leipzig to Poland and beyond. The obstacle to a commercial convention with these states was always stated to be the protectionist British corn laws and timber duties—this argument was rammed home again and again by Cobden, and by the officials of the Board also. But it is noticeable that during the eighteen-thirties the argument was not really put to the test. The records of the Board of Trade do not contain any discussions about the need for commercial negotiations with Russia—even discussions of the most tentative kind. As far as Prussia was concerned, the formation of the Zollverein took place without any effective intervention from Britain. Britain did not attempt to investigate the possible effects of the union on British trade, nor did she open discussions with Prussia directly until 1836, when the Zollverein had been successfully formed. During the years, that is, when Britain was anxiously watching every development of commercial policy in France and Belgium, and to a slightly lesser extent in Spain, she paid little attention to progress of events in Germany. This can perhaps be associated with Palmerston's hostility to the Eastern Powers, and with his attempts to build up a quadruple alliance of England,

France, Spain, and Portugal. On the other hand, Cobden, the free-trader, was also the person in the eighteen-thirties who spoke out most publicly against the prevailing Russophobia.

If we look back from the vantage-point of today, there can be little doubt that the formation of the Zollverein overshadows all other events, during this period, in the field of commercial policy: the emergence of Germany, economically unified and industrially developed, was the subject of a more serious preoccupation to the makers of British commercial policy in the late nineteenth and early twentieth centuries than almost anything else.

Two questions are important to the present study: first, what interpretation did the Board of Trade put on the formation of the Zollverein, and secondly how, and how successfully, did they respond to it? The history of the problem can be divided into two phases, the first from 1828 to 1834, the critical years during which most of the non-Prussian states of Germany were drawn into the Zollverein, and the second from 1834 to 1841, during which the issue was becoming no longer one between economic unity and disunity but one between high protection and moderate tariffs.

Before discussing the impact of the Zollverein on English commercial policy, it is desirable to say something about the structure of Anglo-German trade in this period. As was also true of Anglo-French trade, it was far easier to define the advantages which Britain would derive from reductions in the German tariff, than it was to show the advantages which Germany would derive from British reductions.

In the first place, the statistical outline of the situation was exceedingly obscure. Partly because of the political disunity of Germany, and partly because of her geographical situation, the British Custom-House records of exports gave no clear picture of their total value or volume. The main trade routes into Germany lay then, as now, along the river valleys, particularly the Rhine and the Elbe. Goods imported from Britain via the Elbe and Weser, goods, that is, passing through Hamburg and Bremen, were classified as exports to Germany; those going to Stettin and Danzig, the Prussian ports in the Baltic, as exports to Prussia. Over and above this, Britain exported goods to Rotterdam which were trans-shipped there and sent up the Rhine: these were classified as exports to Holland. But it was not known what proportion of British exports to Holland was re-exported in this way, though it was generally assumed that it would be a large one: Nebenius, the German writer on the Zollverein, and McGregor of the Board of Trade both assumed that the whole of British exports to Holland went on into Germany.[1] This was plainly too much, but there was no obvious more precise way of dealing with the situation.[2]

A further considerable statistical problem was presented by the trade of Hamburg. For example, Brazilian coffee and sugar were sent to Hamburg on British account, and sold there: they would not therefore appear in the British Custom-House returns. Goods imported by Hamburg did not necessarily proceed inland into Germany: they were exported to Russia or Sweden.

Finally, goods sent to Germany did not necessarily stop there: a great deal, mostly of cotton textiles, went on into eastern Europe, and to Asia and Asia Minor. Here any attempt to offer figures inevitably broke down. Both Austria and Russia had prohibitively high tariffs, poorly enforced, and the trade from Germany to the East was largely a smuggling one.[3] For this reason, little could be found out about the scale of the trade:[4] indications are, however, scattered through the consular reports from Leipzig: the success of the Easter and Michaelmas Leipzig fairs was often stated to be dependent on the presence of merchants from Brody in Poland, or Tiflis in Persia.[5]

It is, therefore, not possible to produce figures of the volume of British exports to Germany which would be of any value. Goods went farther afield than Germany, and Britain received goods in payment for them from farther afield also. Both Russia and Sweden claimed substantial favourable trade balances with Britain: Russia exported hemp, flax, timber, and tallow to Britain, and Sweden iron ore and timber.[6] The trade between

[1] *Select Committee on Import Duties, Parliamentary Papers*, 1840, v, question 30.

[2] McCulloch, *Dictionary of Commerce*, 1835 ed., gave some thought to the problem of calculating the proportion of British exports to northern Europe which found their way into the different states of Germany. His solution, to assume that consumption of British goods was proportional to population, was not very much better.

[3] W. Thieme, *Eintritt Sachsens in den Zollverein und seine wirtschaftlichen Folgen* (Leipzig, 1914), pp. 55, 83.

[4] B.T. 1/331, consular report (J. J. Hart), Leipzig, 7 Apr. 1837. He had been especially instructed to report on the trade from the East.

[5] B.T. 1/332, consular report, Leipzig, 10 June 1837. The scale of the trade to Asia is indicated by the fact that one party of 20–30 Persian merchants arrived and each member was reputed to be bringing about £15,000 in gold with him.

[6] See McCulloch, *Dictionary*, articles on St. Petersburg and Stockholm.

Britain and northern Europe should, in short, be considered as a whole.

In considering the analysis of the problems presented by the Zollverein, which was made by the Board of Trade's advisers, these considerations are not of the greatest importance. As a previous chapter has shown, the Board's officials had little interest in researches into the value of British trade: they watched the progress of British trade from the more general reports of manufacturers or of British consuls abroad. Outside England, in Germany, as in France, these statistical obscurities mattered considerably more. Officials and writers were accustomed to thinking in terms of the balance of trade: and even had they possessed a satisfactory method of assigning current values to British imports and exports, these would inevitably have tended to give an exaggerated picture of the value of British exports to Germany. As it was, there were no estimates available of the value of British imports from Germany, and German propagandists tended to use the British figures of official values: for example, Nebenius, the finance minister of Baden, wrote in 1835 that in 1832 British exports to Germany had been £12·5 million, while imports from Germany had been merely £1·25 million.[1] Such figures were fantastic, but as protectionist propaganda in Germany they were admirable: no reader could fail to see that Germany was being swamped by British manufactures. It is curious that the statistically inclined officials of the Board of Trade made no attempt, as far as the writer knows, to check or counteract such arguments.

The story of the formation of the Zollverein is well known. It was one which gave Britain little opportunity for effective intervention. After 1815 Germany was divided into about thirty sovereign states, all pursuing different tariff policies, and all possessing tariff frontiers.

Between 1818 and 1828 the idea of Customs union was in the air, and it took concrete shape in 1828 when two unions were formed by treaty, one in the south between Bavaria and Württemberg, and one in the north, when Hesse-Darmstadt joined the Prussian tariff system. This second Customs union, the nucleus of the future Zollverein, was based on the Prussian tariff of 1818. This tariff, which had abolished Customs frontiers and internal tolls within the Prussian dominions, was more scientifically designed

[1] C. F. Nebenius, *Der deutsche Zollverein, sein System und seine Zukunft* (Carlsruhe, 1835), p. 334.

than most of the tariffs in force at that date, for it admitted raw materials free of duty, placed high revenue duties on imported colonial produce, and charged on the whole moderate duties on imported manufactured goods. On the other hand it was potentially an instrument which could discriminate against British goods: duties on cotton and woollen goods, which were intended to be equivalent to 10 per cent. *ad valorem*, were specific, and with the fall of prices, particularly of cotton goods, during the thirties they became very much higher. As well as this they were levied according to the weight of the goods, and thus fell particularly heavily on the cheaper grades of Lancashire goods (as compared, for instance, with Swiss muslins). By 1839, when Bowring attended the Zollverein conference in Berlin, he reported that the duties payable on cotton goods might be equivalent to sums varying between 30 and 120 per cent. *ad valorem*. The Prussian tariff had from the beginning been higher than that of the southern German states: as time went on it became distinctly protectionist in character.[1]

Once Customs unions of this kind had been established, it was probably inevitable that the strongest should attract new members from among the others. Between 1828 and 1834 Britain was well aware that the Prussian system was establishing control over the country, yet was uncertain how to respond. Palmerston reacted more strongly to the political expansion of the Prussian influence than did the Board of Trade to the economic aspects of the situation. At first the Board believed that it might be an advantage, since reciprocal benefits for the contracting parties appeared to be the object: 'this is not inconsistent with principles recognised by all nations, and it must be admitted that it is one which Great Britain has in some instances adopted'.[2] Deacon Hume, surprisingly, spoke of retaliation: 'they will hardly be able to adopt discriminating duties to our disadvantage without subjecting themselves to very severe retaliation. Upon the grounds of such duties the King can, under the authority of the Corn Act . . . prohibit corn from the offending country: and a little alteration of the Wood Duties would exclude Prussian timber from our markets.'[3]

[1] Much the same thing happened to Huskisson's alteration of the silk duties. Cf. pp. 169–70 below. The formation of the Zollverein is described in W. O. Henderson, *The Zollverein* (Cambridge, 1939).

[2] B.T. 5/38, meeting of the Board held 20 Aug. 1829.

[3] B.T. 6/67, memorandum dated 20 Oct. 1829.

This hesitation may partly be traced to uncertainty of the effects of the Zollverein, but free-traders were also faced with a difficult problem, for they had to weigh the advantages of a large German market, free of internal tolls and restrictions, against the risk that it might become surrounded by a prohibitively high tariff wall. Apart from this, the English utilitarians tended to regard the Prussian administration with reverence; McGregor spoke of 'Prussia, where every man is intelligent, and every man thinks, and where as soon as he sees an effect he immediately enquires into the cause'.[1] McCulloch showed the same tendency; in criticizing the Zollverein tariff in 1835, he wrote: 'We are indeed astonished that so liberal and intelligent a government as that of Berlin should, at this late period, become the patron of the errors and absurdities of the mercantile system.'[2] Bowring later recommended that the British tariff should be remodelled on the same principles as the Prussian tariff.[3] In Parliament, and in the country at large, little notice was taken of the development. Twice the question was raised in the Commons, in August 1833 and in August 1835, on each occasion by G. R. Robinson, the inveterate enemy of the Board of Trade. Each time Palmerston replied saying frankly that nothing could, or even should, be done to check the progress of the Zollverein: it was impossible to intervene in reciprocal arrangements between other states, and it was bad policy to retaliate.[4] In the country there is no clear indication of public anxiety on the subject, but further research into local reactions, particularly in the industrial towns of the north, might reveal it. The most spectacular expansion of the Zollverein took place in 1834 and 1835, in a period of good harvests and expanding trade, when there was little in the immediate circumstances of those industries which exported to Germany to focus their attention on it. It was not until 1838, in drastically changed economic circumstances, that the Zollverein tariff became a subject of public anxiety, as is shown, for example, by the petition of the Manchester Chamber of Commerce to Parliament of 20 December which drew attention to the industrial progress of Germany.[5]

[1] *Select Committee on Import Duties, Parliamentary Papers*, 1840, v, question 312.
[2] *Dictionary of Commerce* (2nd ed., 1835) under 'Danzig'.
[3] See p. 155 below.
[4] *Hansard*, 3rd ser., vol. 20, cols. 695–703; vol. 30, cols. 610–13.
[5] A. Prentice, *History of the Anti-Corn Law League* (London, 1853), vol. i, p. 85. Cf. p. 65 above.

There was in any case little opportunity for effective intervention. Britain made two attempts to check the progress of the Zollverein. A general encouragement and support was given to the formation of a third Customs union, the so-called Mittelverein, which was set up in 1828. The states in this union, which together commanded the main trade routes along the Rhine, Main, and Elbe valleys, did not form a Customs union, but pledged themselves not to enter either of the remaining Customs unions till 1834, and not to raise transit duties on goods passing through their territories.[1] A more positive attempt by the British to reply to the Zollverein was the signing in 1832 of a reciprocity treaty with Frankfurt, to run for ten years. There is no sign that this treaty owed anything to representations from the Board of Trade, though in general they 'saw no objection' to it.[2]

In 1831, in spite of her treaty obligations to the Mittelverein, Hesse-Cassel was forced through financial pressure into the Prussian system. In 1834 Saxony and the two states of the southern union, Bavaria and Württemberg, joined the Prussian union, and the greater part of Germany was united into one system. Two groups of states remained outside, those along the coast of the North Sea, which had a fair chance of remaining independent, and the states along the Rhine, Baden, Nassau, and Frankfurt, which found themselves surrounded with hostile territory. Within a year or two the latter were forced into the Zollverein. Baden and Nassau joined in 1835: on neither occasion was there the opportunity for Britain to intervene, nor did she attempt to do so.[3] But when in 1835 Frankfurt opened negotiations with Prussia, the situation was different. The treaty with Britain ran till 1842, and Prussia insisted that Britain should release Frankfurt from it before discussions could be begun.[4] In view of the economic hardship suffered by Frankfurt, whose trade was being increasingly diverted through neighbouring towns, Palmerston agreed to end the treaty. The Board of Trade viewed this decision with regret, but asked that a proviso be made that the Frankfurt fair be given

[1] The chief members of the middle union were Hamburg and Bremen, Hanover, Oldenburg, and Brunswick, Nassau, Hesse-Cassel, and Frankfurt-am-Main, and in the east, Saxony.

[2] B.T. 5/40, minute dated 25 Oct. 1831; Henderson, op. cit., p. 83.

[3] B.T. 1/311, Cartwright (British Consul-General in Frankfurt) to Palmerston, 20 May 1835.

[4] Henderson, op. cit., pp. 116–17.

the same commercial privileges as Leipzig.[1] Frankfurt entered the Zollverein in January 1836.

After this date two courses of action were open to Britain: to try to circumvent the workings of the Zollverein by one means or another, or to try and come to a tariff agreement with it. Within the administration, opinions remained uncertain. Consular reports from Frankfurt in this period were painted in the gloomiest colours, emphasizing any divisions of interest in Germany, and criticizing the effects of the tariff on the cost of living. To some extent this found a response in the Board of Trade: Poulett Thomson commented on one such report: 'Inform Lord P[almerston] that we would desire Mr. Küper to encourage as much as possible the dissatisfaction felt by the states alluded to.'[2] Against this, Lord William Russell, British Minister at Berlin from 1835 to 1841, agreed with the United States' Minister there, Mr. Wheaton, 'that it is not in the interests of Great Britain or the United States to desire or seek to bring about a dissolution of the Commercial Union: on the contrary he thinks that since its creation a larger market has been opened to the introduction of our manufactures and an impetus given to German industry which can only be supplied by importation. This opinion of Mr. Wheaton was adopted by myself at the formation of the Union and I have not yet seen grounds to alter it.'[3] Dr. Bowring came to the same conclusion in 1839.

The first sign of response to the new situation came in March 1834 when, apparently on the initiative of Auckland,[4] a German agent, Solomon Keyser, was sent to inquire into the workings of the Customs union. Bowring had been sent publicly to France: Keyser was warned of 'the importance of the utmost secrecy being observed by you both with respect to the object of your

[1] B.T. 3/25, letters dated 2 May 1834 and 1 July 1835; *Hansard*, 3rd ser., vol. 32, col. 856. At Leipzig, importers were allowed to introduce goods free of duty, and when the fair was over paid duty on the amounts which had been sold. Frankfurt's economic difficulties are described in consular reports of 3 Mar. and 23 Apr. 1834 (B.T. 1/303). The Frankfurt Senate, an oligarchy, wished to continue the struggle, but the Chamber of Commerce and the mass of the population were against it (R. Schwemer, *Geschichte der freien Stadt Frankfurt-am-Main* (Frankfurt, 1912), vol. 2, chaps. 12–13).

[2] B.T. 1/347, note dated 26 Dec. 1838. See also consular reports dated 11 Nov. 1836 (B.T. 1/327) and 24 Oct. 1838 (B.T. 1/346).

[3] B.T. 1/346, Russell to Palmerston, 14 Nov. 1838.

[4] B.T. 1/303, Auckland to Palmerston, 14 Mar. 1834.

journey and to your employment by His Majesty's Government'. He was to travel with the usual passports, and in the guise of a commercial traveller. He was to report on the economic effects of the union, but he was also to comment on 'the checks which one State interested in preventing a Contraband Trade may endeavour to establish over any other State interested in conniving at a more free admission of Merchandise. You will notice what are the places on the frontiers of the League and on the course of the Rhine which are favourable to such contraband trade.'[1]

Such instructions show that the Board were thinking, however vaguely, in terms of direct attack, legally or illegally, on the Prussian tariff. No record has, however, been found of Keyser's reports.

In July 1836 was held the first Zollverein conference, and this provided the first occasion on which the idea of a tariff convention between Britain and Germany was raised. In April another of the Board's experts, McGregor, was in Germany: he toured industrial and commercial centres—Frankfurt, Leipzig, Chemnitz, and Mainz, and it seems that he was particularly charged with reporting on the effects which the Zollverein tariff had had on the business done by British merchants at the Leipzig Easter Fair. His reports, coming at a time which was in other respects an extremely prosperous one in England, presented a gloomy picture: at Frankfurt the sale of British cotton and woollen textiles was reduced, and at Leipzig their sale for German consumption was 'nearly prevented'. Textiles for consumption in eastern Europe and beyond were still sold in great quantity, for they could still, after paying the Zollverein transit duty, compete with German textiles. British cutlery, he said, found an undiminished market in Germany. So far, then, Britain was not yet suffering severely from the effects of the new tariff, but the situation might easily become worse.[2] In England, the Select Committee on the Timber Duties had reported in August 1835, recommending a reduction of 15*s*. a load in the duty on Baltic timber, and it was hoped to offer this as an inducement to Prussia to reduce the duties on textiles in return.[3]

[1] B.T. 1/303, Henry Canning (British Consul-General at Hamburg) to Solomon Keyser, 26 Apr. 1834.

[2] B.T. 1/322, McGregor to the Board of Trade, 29 Apr., 2 and 8 May 1836; B.T. 1/324, 9 and 14 July 1836.

[3] This offer was genuine, for as late as Feb. 1837 Thomson stated that the ministry had not yet made up its mind whether to alter the duties or not

McGregor was sent on to attend the conference at Munich, and to explore the possibilities of a tariff agreement. Once again, it was considered desirable to put the discussions in the hands of an expert, rather than to leave them to professional diplomats, for an expert 'will also be able to make himself master of the workings and real interests of the Commercial Union which at present are quite unknown to the governments composing the Union'.[1]

McGregor's presence at the conference admirably fulfilled these expectations. The discussions about a tariff agreement were a total failure, but he returned home with first-hand knowledge of the subject. All the states singly would, he was told, welcome a commercial treaty with England, particularly if it brought with it political support. The representatives of Bavaria and Württemberg were particularly friendly to such a proposition; those of Saxony, in deference to the interests of their textile industries, were not. Prussia, which McGregor regarded as 'wielding the whole power of the Union', was at first favourable: they were prepared to reduce duties so as to allow the entry of British textiles, in exchange for reductions on timber, linens, corn, and a guarantee not to raise the duty on raw wool. But the Prussian commissioner 'took his stand upon Corn, saying the other reductions were of little consequence'.[2] In 1836, when Select Committees of the Lords and Commons were occupied in investigating agricultural distress, this made agreement impossible. The Board of Trade was brought sharply up against the argument, which was to be heard so often in the years after 1838, that the corn laws were directly responsible for the exclusion of British textiles from the German market.[3] Whether, if it had been possible to shake the corn laws in 1836, it would have also been possible to negotiate a satisfactory tariff agreement with the Zollverein, is another matter.

Between 1836 and 1839 the British Government made no further direct approach to the Zollverein. Their energies were diverted to establishing new points of entry for British textiles in

(*Hansard*, 3rd ser., vol. 36, col. 137). In the end the duties remained unaltered because of the volume of complaint from the shipping and colonial timber interests; see pp. 189–90 below.

[1] B.T. 1/323, Lord William Russell to Palmerston, 26 May 1833.

[2] B.T. 1/324, McGregor to the Board of Trade, 9 and 14 July 1836.

[3] The most notable expression of this point of view was given in the speech of Bowring to the Manchester Chamber of Commerce in September, 1838 (A. Prentice, *History of the Anti-Corn Law League* (London, 1853), vol. i, p. 60).

eastern and southern Europe.[1] During these years, as the Zollverein began to be recognized as a permanent and important feature of the commercial landscape, other countries became interested in negotiating with it: Holland signed a navigation treaty in 1837, and the United States was anxious to make a commercial treaty. But it was not until the winter of 1838–9 that, with the revival of the anti-corn-law agitation, the British Government again took up the question. The increased scale of corn imports, and the decline in cotton exports in 1837 and 1838, made the whole subject relevant. Added to this, a second treaty between Holland and the Zollverein in 1839 allowed the import of semi-refined sugar from Holland at reduced rates, and in December 1839 this concession was extended to Hamburg. Britain, as the third major exporter of sugar to the Zollverein, was anxious to share in the concession also.[2]

Accordingly, a British representative, in this case Dr. Bowring, was again sent to the Zollverein conference, held in Berlin in July 1839, to observe the proceedings and to investigate the possibilities of an Anglo-Zollverein tariff agreement. Observers were also sent by the French and United States governments. After two or three weeks in Berlin he made a short tour of the manufacturing districts of Saxony, Silesia, and Westphalia, and returned to England. In Germany, unlike France, the British diplomatic representatives paid tribute to the 'discretion' and 'conciliatory language' that he had shown, and endorsed his views of the situation.[3]

Bowring, in a long report sent home from the conference, confirmed what McGregor had said two years before, that there was no hope of agreement with Britain, unless the corn laws were drastically changed. But he added, which had not been said before, that time was short. Parliamentary opinion in Britain had not yet come round to the need for repeal, but 'a change might be forced upon us and we obtain no benefit from the change'. The population of Prussia was rising, and the country would soon cease to be an exporter of grain. At the same time manufactures were developing under the shelter of the Zollverein tariff which could not withstand

[1] See pp. 127 ff. below. Henderson, op. cit., p. 129.

[2] Henderson, op. cit., pp. 127–38. There were fears that Hamburg was being drawn into the Zollverein (B.T. 1/353, Henry Canning to Foreign Office, 21 June 1839).

[3] B.T. 1/355, Sir George Hamilton to Palmerston, 7 Aug. 1839.

English competition; the number of member states which were fighting for higher protection was increasing every year.[1]

Bowring then returned to England with an urgent mission to preach against the corn laws, and, under the auspices of the Anti-Corn Law League, he made a lecture tour of northern industrial cities.[2] At the same time he prepared a full *Report on the Prussian Commercial Union* which was published in the spring of 1840. The lectures, the *Report*, and Bowring's evidence given to the Select Committee on Import Duties in July 1840 together ensured that his main thesis was widely and rapidly diffused. It is a good indication of the latitude given by the Whigs to their subordinates, that this report, written by someone who had caused political embarrassment before, was printed before Palmerston or anyone at the Board of Trade had had an opportunity of seeing it.[3]

'The importance and the interest of the topic', wrote Bowring, 'seem to grow with the work . . .'; as he wrote himself into the subject, so the discretion shown in his earliest letters from Berlin weakened. In his anxiety to press the case for a tariff agreement with Germany, he went out of his way to justify the existing organization of the Zollverein. He dwelt at length on its achievements in removing internal Customs barriers, and in reducing smuggling. He described it, in terms which should have gratified List, as the expression of the German desire for national unity, and held that it was Britain's fault (through the corn laws) if the movement was being misdirected to serve the 'smaller and sinister interests of the Verein'.[4] He put forward two main arguments, which were later reiterated by his colleagues before the Select Committee on Import Duties, and which, in the welter of argument on the corn laws in the eighteen-forties, were much quoted, on the authority of the Board's officials. In the first place, the Zollverein was a direct response to Britain's introduction of the corn law of 1815, and its subsequent modifications; if, said Deacon Hume,

[1] Bowring's correspondence on his mission to Germany in 1839 is in F.O. 97/326.

[2] There is a quantity of correspondence from Bowring, and relating to him, on this subject in the J. B. Smith MSS. in the Manchester Public Library (see MS. 923.2, S 333).

[3] *Parliamentary Papers*, 1840, xxi. The report was published in Berlin in 1840 (*Bericht über den deutschen Zollverband an Lord Palmerston*). On the printing of the report see F.O. 97/326, Bowring to Palmerston, 4 Nov. 1839.

[4] *Report on the Prussian Commercial Union*, p. 1.

after the French wars 'we had thrown open our ports for raw produce, and removed protections, we should have had our manufactures in a most secure position, for the other countries who are now attempting to rival us would not have attempted it'.[1] Secondly, the Zollverein tariff was doing harm to the export trade of Britain.

Bowring's report failed to prove either of these contentions, partly because it was hastily prepared: in July 1840 Disraeli declared that of Bowring's German report, 'more than one half consisted of a mere compilation of several celebrated German statists whose works no doubt had obtained a place in the libraries of many Members of that House'.[2] More specifically, it was pointed out that Bowring offered no figures of German trade after 1837, though these were available in Germany, and though the heavy British corn imports of 1838 and 1839 made them particularly relevant to his purpose.[3]

It is doubtful how far either of his arguments could have been driven with the evidence available at the time. It has been shown that in Germany the impulse towards Customs union was not immediately or solely connected with agricultural depression after 1815, but was provoked by the over-running of the German market with British goods after the ending of the continental blockade. This was something which should have been known to the officials of the Board of Trade: it was, for example, emphasized in the prize essay of J. H. Thieriot, *Welchen Einfluß auf dem Felde des sächsischen Gewerbfleisses und Handels hat der Anschluß des Königreichs Sachsen an den preussisch-deutschen Zollverein bis jetzt gehabt?*[4] This source had been used by Bowring. The exclusion of British manufactures had been from the beginning one of the objectives of those who supported the Prussian tariff of 1818, and this desire still existed, particularly among those 'statistical' writers whose works were known to Bowring.[5] List, whom Bowring had

[1] *Select Committee on Import Duties, Parliamentary Papers*, 1840, v, question 1204. There is much use of these opinions in propaganda put out by the League and its supporters: see, for example, Hamer Stansfeld, *Compensation not emigration the one thing needful*, &c. *Lectures . . . delivered to the Leeds Parliamentary Reform Association 10, 17 and 24 January, 1842* (Manchester, 1842).

[2] *Hansard*, 3rd ser., vol. 55, col. 706. In this debate the Conservatives made a general attack on the Whig policy of sending *ad hoc* missions abroad instead of using the existing consular officials. Cf. pp. 85–86 above, and 226 below.

[3] *British and Foreign Review*, vol. xi, no. 22.

[4] Leipzig, 1838.

[5] The same attitude can be seen in C. F. Nebenius, *Der deutsche Zollverein*,

met at some earlier period, was violent in his criticisms, and construed the report as an attack on Germany's industrial development:

Dr. Bowring deceived himself very much if it were his belief that the Germans desired no better fortune than to be allowed to export corn to England, receiving in return British manufactures. Some few landlords on the lower Elbe, and on the farthest borders of the Baltic, might cherish such hopes and wishes; but it could hardly have escaped so keen an observer as Dr. Bowring, that since the commercial League had been established, the national spirit in Germany had acquired a giant's strength. . . .[1]

This article was quoted to good effect by the protectionist, Ormsby Gore, in the debate on Villiers's anti-corn law motion of April 1840.

But, even if it were granted that the Prussian tariff of 1818 was a direct reply to the British corn law of 1815, it did not follow that repeal would reverse this trend. Protected industries, as Bowring himself argued, would not lightly abandon a system under which they had flourished, nor did they always get what they wanted.[2]

sein System und seine Zukunft (Carlsruhe, 1835), which was also known in the Board of Trade.

[1] *Hansard*, 3rd ser., vol. 53, col. 500, quoting the *Augsburger Allgemeine Zeitung* of 28 Dec. 1839. List published a second long attack on Bowring in 1841. Both are printed in Friedrich List, *Werke* (Berlin, 1928), vol. v. The personal relations of the two men are described in C. Brinkmann, *Friedrich List* (Berlin and Munich, 1949).

[2] The governments of the various states were not necessarily impelled into the Zollverein by public pressure. In two states where commercial interests were strong and strongly organized, that is in Frankfurt and Saxony, this was the case: the Handels-deputation of Saxony was consulted by the Government on policy, and their advice was taken. (See p. 103, n. 1, above, and W. Thieme, *Der Eintritt Sachsens in den Zollverein und seine wirtschaftlichen Folgen* (Leipzig, 1914), pp. 42–44.) In Hesse-Darmstadt the Government took the lead: Du Thil, who negotiated the treaty, wrote afterwards that he doubted whether they would have entered the Zollverein successfully if the Estates had been in session at the time. Similarly in Baden, a commission of industrial and commercial representatives was consulted early in 1834 on the question of entry, and on economic grounds they decided against it. Yet the Government went ahead with negotiations. The treaty with Prussia, once completed, was violently attacked in the Chamber of Baden. (See H. Ulmann, *Denkwürdigkeiten . . . des Staatsministers Freiherrn du Thil, 1802–48* (Berlin, 1921), p. 303; F. Wallschmidt, *Der Eintritt Badens in den deutschen Zollverein*, &c. (Heidelberg, 1904), pp. 1–10.) By contrast, in both Hanover and Brunswick, which remained outside the Zollverein in this period, there were substantial sections of opinion which favoured entry into it. (H. Arning, *Hannovers Stellung zum Zollverein* (Hanover, 1930), pp. 39–41; R. Wittenberg, *Braunschweigs Zollpolitik von 1828 bis zum Anschluß an den deutschen Zollverein* (Göttingen, 1930), pp. 18, 42.)

This was a fact which he tended to ignore. It would be incorrect to see the formation of the Zollverein as an expression of popular national sentiment, but Bowring's point of view did not sufficiently stress the share of the various governments in the formation of economic policy: as in contemporary France, the economic strength of an interest, and the validity of its case, were of less importance than its political strength. One factor of importance in the formation of the Zollverein might well encourage a resistance to lower duties—namely that many governments were short of money (particularly after the upheavals of 1830) and were glad to strengthen sources of revenue which were beyond the interference of possibly liberal assemblies of estates.

It would therefore have been very much more difficult to forecast the response which Germany might make to changes in British tariff policy than Bowring would have had his readers believe. In his favour is the clear impression which McGregor had received in 1836, and Bowring in 1839, that the wishes of Prussia were dominant in the Zollverein, and that Prussia was willing to barter lower duties on cotton and woollen cloth for repeal or drastic reduction of the corn laws and timber duties. But this impression did not mean that agreement would necessarily be reached: the history of Anglo-French relations in this period shows that many such promising beginnings could lead to little or no result.

The second way in which Bowring's report may have given a misleading impression was in his discussion of the existing character of Anglo-German trade. In the first place, whatever the immediate effect of the corn law of 1815 had been, in the long run British grain imports had not been diminished. With a rising population to feed, Britain was importing more in each decade, as Peel was to emphasize in his memoranda on the corn laws in 1845. He showed that British imports of wheat had risen in the following way:[1]

Annual average import,	1801–10	555	thousand quarters
	1811–20	429	,, ,,
	1821–30	534	,, ,,
	1831–40	908	,, ,,

Of these quantities roughly half came, during the eighteen-thirties, from Germany. It could reasonably be argued that with repeal or

[1] Peel, *Memoirs*, ed. Mahon and Cardwell (London, 1856–7), vol. ii, p. 333.

with a low fixed duty the quantities of grain imported from Germany might increase, and that the arbitrary and uncertain workings of the sliding scale made the export of grain to England more difficult and more speculative than it need have been. But over the period in question the trade had undeniably increased.[1]

In the second place, Bowring did not sift carefully the evidence of the effect which the Zollverein had had on British exports. In the middle of a trade depression it was natural that those exporters who were suffering should look for the nearest scapegoat.

DECLARED VALUE OF CERTAIN EXPORTS FROM THE UNITED KINGDOM TO GERMANY AND THE LOW COUNTRIES, 1828–38

(Columns marked *a* give Bowring's annual average for the six years immediately before the Zollverein, 1828–33; columns marked *b* for the years 1834–8. The source is Appendix VI of Bowring's *Report on the Prussian Commercial Union*.[2])

	£ Thousand							
	Prussia		*Mecklenburg, Oldenburg, Hanover*		*Hanse towns*		*Holland and Belgium*	
	a	*b*	*a*	*b*	*a*	*b*	*a*	*b*
COTTON								
Piece goods	..	..	1	..	1,119	1,071	489	713
Hosiery	..	..	..	..	275	192	244	176
Yarn	2	1	..	4	1,525	1,985	791	1,360
HARDWARE AND CUTLERY	3	4	..	..	71	76	38	58
IRON AND STEEL								
Unwrought	2	7	3	4	28	52	41	105
Wrought and cast	2	3	1	2	28	39	37	75
SUGAR								
Refined	101	44	18	7	354	41	10	1
WOOL								
Piece goods	..	..	10	6	583	637	285	390
Hosiery	..	..	?	?	10	11	19	17
Yarn	..	..	..	..	86	186	38	70

These figures do not justify the pessimism expressed in England and by Bowring about the future of exports to Germany. They confirm that exports of both cotton and woollen yarns had increased; but exports of woollen cloth had increased also.

[1] The corn laws are discussed further on pp. 171 ff. below.

[2] The figures marked ? are missing from the tables given by Bowring.

Exports of cotton cloth had remained unchanged in value. Exports of cutlery and hardware, which were menaced by the development of Solingen, had increased. Exports of all kinds of iron and steel had very markedly increased. Two things had suffered considerably, the export of refined sugar, about which little was said by Bowring, and that of cotton hosiery, which was threatened, and threatened successfully, by the hosiery industry of Saxony. (It was claimed by witnesses before the Select Committee on Import Duties of 1840 that Saxon hosiery was competing successfully with British hosiery in export markets in the United States.[1]) The conclusion to be drawn from these figures would seem to be that the dangers to British commerce from the Zollverein were not yet being felt.[2]

It is in fact curious that consular reports from Frankfurt and Leipzig should have continued to be so gloomy in the teeth of this evidence, and, even more so, that they should have been accepted in Britain as giving a correct picture of the situation as a whole. Several things combined to create this misleading impression. First Frankfurt, from the beginning, had been the place where, largely on political grounds, the strongest criticism of Prussia had been heard: the British consuls there were writing in sympathy with the prevailing atmosphere.[3] Secondly, there was evidence, some of which was available to the Board of Trade, and was in fact mentioned in Bowring's report, that the trade fairs were diminishing in importance in Germany, certainly in their importance for the distribution of goods for the home market. Industrialists, to an increasing extent, distributed their goods by commercial travellers direct to the places where they would be consumed, and sent to the fairs only those goods which had been previously rejected by the home market, and which they hoped to export.[4]

Thirdly, writers on commerce, and the officials of the Board of Trade, tended to see the situation in terms of textiles alone. It was true that exports to Germany of cotton manufactures, as opposed to cotton yarn, were not increasing, and it was held that this was an unsatisfactory development since it involved the substitution of an

[1] See pp. 203 ff. below.

[2] It could be argued (though Bowring did not say this) that the figures for the years 1834–8 gave an unduly favourable picture of the position, since they included the boom years 1835–6.

[3] The British consul at Frankfurt, Christian Koch, was himself German.

[4] *Report on the Prussian Commercial Union*, p. 37.

article in which the proportion of British labour costs to total costs was lower.[1] And it was suspected, correctly, that this switch from the import of cotton cloth to the import of cotton yarn was itself a step towards the ultimate exclusion of both. When the German spinning-industry could supply the total German demand, a tariff which excluded British yarns would probably be imposed. During the eighteen-forties the protection of the German spinning-industry became a subject of controversy in the Zollverein.[2]

Bowring and his colleagues in the Board of Trade did not examine whether new commodities were beginning to find a place in British exports to Germany. List is remembered for two ideas, protectionism and railway promotion. Already before the publication of his book in 1841, the Zollverein had given a stimulus to railway-building. In February 1837 the British consul in Leipzig reported on the railway 'mania' in Germany: at the time of his writing there were under discussion lines between Leipzig and Chemnitz; between Halle, Magdeburg, and Leipzig; between Leipzig and Nuremberg; between Nuremberg, Munich, and Salzburg; between Mainz and Frankfurt; and a Prussian line between the Rhine and the Weser. It was in the same dispatch that the consul sent the news of the new rate of duty on iron and the special concession for iron rails. (It was generally conceded that British rails were the best.[3]) Bowring, in his travels in 1839, noticed the prevailing interest in railways, but never pointed out that this would provide an expanding market for British exports. Lady Charlotte Guest, wife of Sir John Guest the iron-master, who was travelling with her husband in Germany in August 1838, saw things in a different light from Bowring, and commented on the increasing scale on which British rails were being used.[4]

The figures of German iron imports in the early years of the Zollverein show that her impression had been a correct one, though the really dramatic increase in iron imports came after the time at which she and Bowring were writing.

Bowring's report, and the first public discussion of the tariff question in England, came at a time when the general commercial

[1] *Select Committee on Import Duties*, question 2736 (evidence of G. R. Porter).

[2] Henderson, op. cit., pp. 183–4.

[3] B.T. 1/329, consular report dated 27 Feb. 1837.

[4] Bessborough, *Lady Charlotte Guest: Extracts from her Journal* (London, 1950), pp. 77–78.

ZOLLVEREIN IMPORTS OF IRON (MINUS RE-EXPORTS)

(*Thousand Zentner*)[1]

	Pig iron	*Bar iron*
1836	51	129
1837	110	103
1838	245	331
1839	249	299
1840	703	377
1841	920	505
1842	1,132	889
1843	2,621	933
1844	1,385	1,472
1845	400	933
1846	1,558	977
1847	2,284	1,002
1848	1,418	596

tendencies of the Zollverein could not yet be predicted with any confidence. The conflict between free-traders and protectionists, between landowning interests on one hand, and textile and iron interests on the other, or between the followers of Prince Smith and those of List, were to take place in the next decade.[2] Bowring drew attention to what was significant with considerable skill—he showed the demand for protection on the part of new industries which had been expanding since 1834, particularly textiles, and pointed out how a tariff which had originally been low had in fact been rising over the previous decades. He pointed out in his report fields in which Germany possessed techniques which were in advance of those in Britain—in metal-working and in chemical manufacture.[3] Against this, he accepted too freely the German tendency to place responsibility for these developments on Britain, and encouraged exaggerated hopes in Britain of what repeal of the corn laws might bring. It is certainly true that he was one of the most important proponents of a line of argument which was extremely common in England in the forties. Lord Melbourne, whose

[1] C. F. W. Dieterici, *Statistische Übersicht . . . des Verkehrs und Verbrauchs im preussischen Staate, und im deutschen Zollverbande* (Berlin, 1836–58). A zentner of the Zollverein is equal to 110 lb.

[2] See Henderson, op. cit., pp. 179 ff.; and his *Britain and Industrial Europe, 1750–1870*, chap. iv, sect. 7.

[3] *Select Committee on Import Duties*, questions 834–5; Clapham *Economic Development of France and Germany*, ed. of 1921, pp. 102–3, discusses the value of Bowring's report.

interest in economic policy was small, but who was deeply concerned with the conciliation of public opinion, wrote in November 1839 to his brother, Beauvale, the Ambassador at Vienna, that the argument for repeal of the corn laws based on the need to offer a reply to continental protectionism 'has been made over and over again, and is the main argument in every pamphlet and every debate upon that side of the question'.[1]

[1] L. C. Sanders, *The Melbourne Papers* (London, 1889), p. 408.

7

COMMERCIAL NEGOTIATIONS AND THE RECIPROCITY SYSTEM

OUTSIDE the Zollverein commercial negotiations were carried on by Britain during the eighteen-thirties on a fairly extensive scale, particularly after 1838. The experience of all these negotiations led to two general conclusions. Of these the first, which has already been suggested by the account of discussions with the Zollverein, was that the factor determining success or failure was the degree of political support which Britain could mobilize in the country with which the negotiations were being held. A second general conclusion, which was less apparent in the history of relations with the Zollverein, was that the reciprocity system was on some occasions of very limited advantage to Britain.

From 1823 onwards Britain had offered reciprocity treaties to any countries who were willing to enter into negotiation, and in the eighteen-thirties the Board of Trade showed little desire to depart from this tradition. By these treaties each country gave equality of treatment, particularly in respect of port dues, to its own shipping and to that of the other country, and each gave most-favoured-nation treatment to the imports from the other. The treaties did not enshrine tariff alterations, which probably simplified the task of negotiating them. But the Board of Trade was convinced of the theoretical objections to commercial treaties. In discussing a commercial treaty with Naples in June 1831, it wrote of

a convention securing some exclusive privileges to the commerce of each country, an arrangement which does not appear suited to the present times. To leave each country at liberty to alter or modify its table of duties according to its means seems to be the best principle of commercial legislation, especially as experience cannot fail to show that it is for the interest of each state to take from the other its productions as little burthened as possible by fiscal charges.[1]

This was a principle to which the Board of Trade adhered

[1] B.T. 3/22, letter dated 18 June 1831.

throughout this period: in 1840 Deacon Hume reasserted it before the Select Committee on Import Duties. It was a principle which might be sound in theory, but which failed to tackle many of the commercial restrictions which were most obstructive to British trade. Discussions for reciprocity treaties were therefore often accompanied or followed by discussions about tariff alterations. In these discussions the British negotiators exerted strong pressure, but they aimed at general relaxations of import conditions, rather than at exclusive trading privileges for Britain.

The general terms of the reciprocity treaties were in practice less liberal than at first sight appears. Most-favoured-nation privileges were compatible with colonial preferential duties: thus Brazil, which signed a treaty in 1827, still found that the British tariff excluded foreign coffee and sugar. The equality of shipping dues should not disguise the fact that much was still reserved to Britain. The Act of 1825 still laid down a substantial list of enumerated goods which might only be imported into Britain in British ships, or in ships of the country of which they were the produce, or in ships of the country from which the goods were being imported.[1] This list was extended in 1833, when Customs legislation was consolidated,[2] and was still maintained in 1845. And there were stricter rules governing the import of non-European produce, which might not be re-exported from European ports, and which could only be imported in British ships or in ships of the country of which they were the produce *and* from which they were being imported. These rules, as they were applied to the shipping of a port like Trieste, which was rarely dealing with goods which were of Austrian origin, made nugatory the benefits of reciprocity.[3] Even the attempt to equalize port dues, which would appear to have been a straightforward undertaking, led in practice to endless discussion and difficulty: in Britain dues varied from port to port, and in negotiations with France, or with Sardinia, much time and energy was spent in arguing about suitable equivalent rates in these countries.[4]

From the point of view of the British exporter many of the treaties were of doubtful benefit. Huskisson had succeeded in

[1] 6 Geo. IV, cap. cxiv. [2] See p. 51 above.

[3] Adolf Beer, *Die österreichische Handelspolitik im neunzehnten Jahrhundert* (Vienna, 1891).

[4] The discussions with France are summarized in F.O. 97/207, and with Sardinia in F.O. 67/112.

obtaining reciprocity treaties with Austria, Prussia, Denmark, the Hanse towns, Sweden, Mecklenburg, Hanover, the United States, France, and with most of the South American republics. These treaties might be useful in the protection they gave to the status and rights of British merchants living abroad,[1] but in nearly all these countries tariff regulations were unsatisfactory to Britain. Prussia, Sweden, Hanover, France, and Austria all either prohibited, or burdened with heavy duties, the import of those goods in which Britain was most interested. The same could be said of many countries, such as Spain, Portugal, and Naples, which had not been willing to sign reciprocity treaties with Britain.

During this period the activities of the Board were directed towards two objectives, the extension of the reciprocity system to those countries which still remained outside it, and the persuasion of those countries with prohibitive tariffs—whether they were inside or outside the reciprocity system—to give an easier admission to British goods.

With this end in view prolonged discussions with France were undertaken, which illustrate better than anything else the kind of obstacles which such a policy encountered. Discussions were in progress from 1831 to 1834, from 1838 to 1840, and from 1842 to 1843.[2] The subject was raised again at intervals after that time, but it was not till 1860 that a commercial treaty was finally signed. In spite of a reciprocity treaty signed in 1826 there remained on both sides fairly substantial grievances. On the British side, in addition to the question of port dues, there were grounds of complaint in the French tariff. While Britain, under Huskisson and Wallace, had been moving towards greater commercial freedom, France had

[1] See p. 95 above, and pp. 129–30 below.

[2] There are three collections of private papers of importance for this subject. The most important are the Clarendon papers in the Bodleian Library. These appear to contain two separate collections: (1) three boxes of letters (mostly from John Bowring) and papers addressed to George Villiers, and (2) four volumes of letters and papers from Villiers and Bowring addressed to Poulett Thomson in London. It seems possible that these letters were removed from the Board of Trade in 1846–7 when Clarendon (as Villiers had then become) was President. There are also letters, mostly from Bowring, in the Auckland papers in the British Museum, and in the Granville papers in the Public Record Office. (Granville was Ambassador at Paris from 1824 to 1841.) There is also much correspondence in the Archives nationales and in the Ministère des Affaires étrangères (correspondance commerciale, relating to London) showing the impact on the French of these negotiations.

been reinforcing the system of protection which had survived from the Empire: the tariff alterations which had been made in the eighteen-twenties had been designed to protect French industries from British competition. After 1815 imports of cotton and woollen cloth and yarn were prohibited. Both the coal and iron duties were so arranged that, in spite of Britain's most-favoured-nation status, there was an effective discrimination against British imports. Lower duties were charged on coal imported over the land frontiers of France, than on coal imported from Britain by sea. Lower duties were also charged on charcoal-smelted iron than on coke-smelted iron.[1] From the French point of view it would seem that there was less ground for complaint: the most conspicuous British protective duties, those on timber and corn, sugar and coffee, hardly affected them. By contrast, imports of silk and gloves had been legalized in 1824–5, and in the Budget of 1831 Althorp spontaneously proposed to equalize the duties on Cape, Portuguese, and French wines.[2] On the other hand, there was still much complaint in France that the British silk duties were too high.[3] There was a further grievance that duties on British and colonial spirits, whisky and rum, had been reduced in 1824–5, while those on French brandy had not been touched. This, the French believed, meant that British tastes were switching from brandy to their own inferior products.[4]

The tariff questions dividing the two countries were therefore such as would emphasize divisions of economic interest in each. The demand for a more liberal admission of French silks came at a time when English silk manufacturers were mobilized against the relaxations which had already been made, though coal, iron, or textile exporters might welcome tariff discussions with the French. In France the July revolution had left protectionist views dominant in the Chamber of Deputies, as was shown in 1831 when a proposal to modify the corn law of 1821 was thrown out.[5] The three

[1] The operation of the coal duties was examined in the *Enquête sur les houilles* (Paris, 1833), and of the iron duties by the *Enquête sur les fers* (Paris, 1829).

[2] See pp. 46–49 above. The duties on French and Portuguese wines were equalized in Sept. 1831, but the preference given to the Cape wines survived.

[3] Archives nationales, F[12] 6207 and 6216 (especially the complaints of the Chamber of Commerce at Lyons). They complained that the nominal rate of duty in Britain, 30 per cent. *ad valorem*, was, in practice, often exceeded. Cf. pp. 169–70 below.

[4] See Archives nationales, F[12] 6207, 6216, and 6219, for these complaints.

[5] E. Levasseur, *Histoire du commerce de la France* (Paris, 1911–12), vol. ii, pp. 160–1.

conseils-généraux, of commerce, of arts and manufactures, and of agriculture, which had an important voice in the framing of economic policy, were also predominantly protectionist in feeling.[1] On the other hand, the manufacturers of Lyons were in favour of a more liberal tariff, and the wine-growers of the Gironde occupy the same sort of position in the history of French tariff policy as do the cotton merchants of Manchester in English history. Elsewhere opinion was divided and it is important to emphasize this division: it is impossible to make a clear antithesis between the interests of industry and agriculture or between those of particular regions and particular industries. Such antitheses are often stated in deceptively simple terms, and in the history of Restoration France this is particularly true. The coal and iron duties affected different regions very unequally in a country where transport costs might be very high. The industrialists of Rouen or Lille were liberal when they thought about coal or iron, but prohibitionists when they thought about textiles; a fact which helps to explain some of the complexities of negotiations in this period.[2]

[1] There is repeated complaint of this in Bowring's letters home. In France, unlike England, there was an organized hierarchy of consultative bodies who gave their views on economic policy. At the bottom the chambers of commerce were controlled by the central administration; the permission, first of the prefect, and then of the Ministry of the Interior was needed before one could be set up. The membership of the chambers was also controlled until a system of election was introduced by *ordonnance* in June 1832. There were also in many towns *chambres consultatives* which dealt with industrial questions. Above these there were three central *conseils-généraux*, of commerce, of agriculture, and of arts and manufactures, which in this period met annually in Paris at the invitation of the central government. Until 1831 the membership of these *conseils* was also controlled by the Government, but after that date some representatives of the chambers and councils in the larger towns were included. Above all these was the *conseil supérieur de commerce*, which included important permanent officials, and representatives of the two Houses of Parliament. It follows from this structure that it was far easier in France than in England to make estimates of public opinion on economic questions, and also far easier for the Ministry of Commerce to control the kind of opinions which were expressed. There is a manuscript note in the Archives nationales, written by the official who had been secretary at the meetings of the *conseils-généraux* of 1832 and 1833. It argues that the sessions of the *conseils* were of little value for the advice received by the ministry, but of great value in giving the ministry an opportunity for enlisting support for its own policy. (F^{12} 2493A.) On the chambers of commerce and higher bodies at this time see E. Levasseur, *Histoire du commerce de la France* (Paris, 1912), vol. ii, pp. 158–9.

[2] Opinions of chambers of commerce on free trade and protection were collected in the *Enquête relative à diverses prohibitions* (Paris, 1834). A similar division existed between the wine and textile interests of Rheims.

The political situation was on the whole favourable to negotiations. The British showed their good intentions by their proposal in the Budget of 1831 to equalize the wine duties. On the French side, the Government of Louis Philippe was anxious for British support and, like some of the German states, was interested in improving the Customs revenue.[1] But these favourable conditions were offset by personal antipathies. The English negotiators, who were in France from 1831 to 1834, were George Villiers and John Bowring, and Bowring, the more active of the two, rapidly antagonized the officials and politicians with whom he was dealing. He on his side suspected the personal motives of the French: Talleyrand, he believed, 'has much capital invested in iron mines, *so he is not to be trusted*'. So had the Duc Decazes, an important member of the *conseils-généraux* of agriculture and commerce: 'he has large stocks of rascally bad quality which he cannot sell and is terribly pushed for money'. The king himself was a considerable owner of forest land, from which the charcoal used in the French iron industry was drawn, and his lukewarmness to the treaty was ascribed to this.[2]

Thus, in the absence of powerful motives, either political or economic, the long-drawn-out negotiations of 1831–4 between the two countries achieved very little. Each summer tariff proposals were brought forward by the French, but they were rejected by the Chamber of Deputies. Finally, after attempts at direct negotiation had been abandoned, a series of tariff alterations was introduced by *ordonnance*, by which opposition in the chamber could be avoided. These included alterations of interest to Britain, in that they reduced the duties on raw wool, on coke-smelted iron, and on coal.[3] In addition to these, the prohibition on the export of raw silk had been abolished in the spring of 1833, which removed a frequently expressed grievance in England.[4]

A second attempt to negotiate in 1838–40 showed more clearly the kind of difficulty which was involved in tariff discussions with any country which feared Britain's industrial superiority. The French prohibition on the entry of cotton and woollen yarns and

[1] M. Marion, *Histoire financière de la France* (Paris, 1914–28), vol. v, chap. 3.

[2] Clarendon papers, French correspondence, 1834, Bowring to Thomson, 16 May; Granville papers, P.R.O. 30/29/16, Bowring to Villiers, 9 May 1833; J. Bowring, *Autobiographical Recollections* (London, 1877), p. 260.

[3] *Ordonnances* of 10 Oct. and 28 Dec. 1835.

[4] *Hansard*, 3rd ser., vol. 20, cols. 695–703.

cloth had never extended to linen. Through this loophole came very rapidly increasing imports of linen yarn, which rose from a declared value of about £7,000 in 1828 to nearly £900,000 in 1838.[1] This increase, which revived memories of the Eden–Vergennes treaty of 1786, provoked a strong demand for protection in France, which in turn roused anxiety in the British linen-producing districts, and led to further negotiations in which Porter and McGregor took part.[2] By the spring of 1840 a tariff agreement between the two countries had been drawn up, by which the British agreed to reduce the duty on brandy and to rearrange the wine duties. They also agreed to lower duties on a miscellaneous collection of goods—wall-paper, plaster of paris, confectionery, and so on. They were not willing to touch the silk duties, as this would be politically dangerous. In return the French offered substantial concessions, and agreed to substitute duties for prohibitions on most woollens,[3] on cotton yarns, cutlery, hardware, and earthenware. The proposals of 1840 came nearer to success than any, until the Cobden treaty of 1860, but in the end, as a result of the rift between England and France on the eastern question in the summer of 1840, they were abandoned. In 1842 the increase in the linen duties which had been threatened in 1838 was finally made.

Where the officials of the Board were perhaps weakest was in their underlying hopes and assumptions about Anglo-French trade. The case for a commercial treaty was formulated in general and rather unrealistic terms; they held that, 'There can hardly be a greater proof of the bad effect of that system than is exhibited by the small amount of trade that is carried on between two nations whose wants are so great, and each of which has it in its power to supply so materially the wants of the other.'[4]

France, they said, needed iron, coal, cotton, and woollen textiles; England needed wines and silks. It was a situation which provided a textbook illustration of the fact that different places were naturally suited to the production of different commodities

[1] *Select Committee on Import Duties, Parliamentary Papers*, 1840, v, question 2525.

[2] Archives nationales, F[12] 2490; *Réclamations de l'industrie française des fils et des toiles de lin et de chanvre* (Paris, 1842). The British protests are in B.T. 1/359 and 363; see also F.O. 97/207.

[3] The terms of the proposed convention are in F.O. 97/195.

[4] *Select Committee on Import Duties, Parliamentary Papers*, 1840, v, question 2517 (evidence of G. R. Porter).

(Ricardo had formulated the theory of comparative costs in terms of two countries exchanging cloth and wine). But they did not know how to deal with the pragmatic argument of French industrialists or officials who emphasized the difference in character between the demand for British goods in France and that for French goods in England. The French were certain that their iron, coal, cotton, or wool could hardly compete against imports from England: the effects of the treaty of 1786, and their current experience of British linen yarns, seemed to prove the point. Against this, the market for French products in England seemed problematical: imports of silk goods after 1825 had increased, but not in a spectacular fashion, and nobody could predict the effect of a reduction in the duties on French wine in England. Porter was encouraging: he told the French Commissioners that in England claret was the drink of the aristocracy and port and sherry of the middle classes; as the middle classes aped aristocratic habits as far as their means would allow, a reduction of duty would greatly stimulate consumption. But this argument was not wholly compelling to the French.[1]

Bowring and Porter recognized that the liberalizing of the French tariff could only take place slowly, but they hardly gave enough attention to the strength of economic isolationism in France, which was not entirely confined to the circles which gained most from the existing tariff. France, unlike England, was not dependent on imported food, and most of her smaller-scale industries could find a market for their products at home. England suffered from violent trade fluctuations, against which they thought it desirable to be insulated. Of the provincial chambers consulted in 1834, several, which had no economic interest on either side of the issue between high and low tariffs, argued in this way.[2]

These discussions also provide the best-documented example of an important feature of the commercial negotiations of this period, namely the extent to which the initiative was left to subordinate officials. This was by no means peculiar to the discussions with France: on two occasions, in 1839 and 1840, McGregor negotiated

[1] F[12] 6219. See also F[12] 6210, 6216. McCulloch, in his article in the *Dictionary* on Wine, argued that in 1669, when the duties on French and Portuguese wines in England were the same, very large quantities of French wine were drunk in England—again an argument which was not very persuasive.

[2] *Enquête relative à diverses prohibitions*, see opinions from le Puy, Nevers, Nancy, Rennes, Alençon.

draft treaties with Naples and Prussia respectively without instructions from above. The same freedom from control was shown in Bowring's relations with the French public. In a situation where opinion was broadly divided on tariff policy, Bowring attempted to act directly on public opinion, in much the same way as did the Anti-Corn Law League ten years later. In three successive summers of 1832–4 he made provincial tours, which are minutely documented in his letters home, and in which he had initially the blessing of the French Minister of Commerce, who provided him with letters of introduction.[1] On all these tours, his 'resurrectionizing', as he called it, followed the same pattern. On arrival he would, like the lecturers of the Anti-Corn Law League, address the local chamber of commerce, arguing that free trade would redound to their own advantage, and urging them to petition the Ministry of Commerce. At Lyons the chamber came to 'some very spirited resolutions . . . and indited an admirable letter to the Ministry of Commerce. . . . They also determined to address the other Chambers of Commerce in France urging their co-operation.'[2] On occasion more precise instruction was given: Villiers, who fully supported these activities, wrote that he had furnished a Bordeaux wine merchant with

> the Merchants' Petition to the House of Commons in 1820 as a model of sound uncompromising principle for the wine growers to follow, and I have written him my views of the way in which they should get up their memorials and organize a permanent though not factious agitation upon the subject. . . . I have been abstracting one or two debates and Althorp's and your speeches for translation and publication.[3]

As well as this Bowring operated extensively through the press, or through those sections of it which were unfriendly to the régime. When the Customs Bill of 1833 was under discussion, for example, he wrote to Villiers:

> I am come to a solemn league and covenant with Flachat of the Constitutionnel. The day after tomorrow they are to break out. I have settled with Perreira an article for the National, with Rodet for the Temps, with Guillemot for the Messager, with Parth for the Moniteur du Commerce,

[1] Archives nationales, F^{12} 2647.

[2] French correspondence, 1831–2, Bowring to Thomson, 24, 28, and 29 Apr. 1832.

[3] Ibid., Villiers to Thomson, 23 Dec. 1831.

with — (illegible) for the Journal du Commerce and Comte for the Courier. Every day you will have an article somewhere.[1]

Like the organizers of the Anti-Corn Law League, Bowring hoped to influence the Government by the united force of public opinion, as his letters from Lyons show. How far was his agitation successful? Bowring pitched his claims high, particularly in his tour of 1833. He claimed that 'the fire is strangely spreading' and that 'the provincial press which has hitherto shown indifference for the most part, hostility sometimes, has, as if by a spontaneous explosion, become the advocate of free trade'. Or again:

For what is our present position compared with that of last year? Lyons alone had spoken out energetically—now we have Bordeaux—la Charente—la Rochelle—Nantes—l'Orient—Morlaix—St. Brieuc—Caen and Havre. We had only one or two country newspapers pleading our cause. We have now every Journal without exception of the Gironde.

Even at Rouen I have the leading Journal thundering against the prohibitory system.[2]

The anxiety of the British authorities, as time wore on, is some confirmation of his story. Granville admitted that he had had 'an extraordinary success', yet in 1834 was compelled to ask the Board of Trade in London to persuade Bowring 'not to allow his zeal . . . to lead him into a course of general Hostility against the French government'.[3]

But the evidence of his impact must also be looked for in the provincial centres in which he was campaigning. A solitary example has been found of a petition drawn up under his guidance. It comes from the chamber of commerce at Lorient: 'C'est donc avec la conviction la plus intime, avec l'espoir d'un avenir fructueux pour les deux pays, que la chambre de commerce de Lorient adopte les

[1] Clarendon papers, box marked 'Anglo-French Commercial Treaty', Bowring to Villiers, 3 June 1833. One of these articles, from the *Journal du Commerce* of 22 Aug. 1833, has survived among the papers of the Ministry of Commerce (Archives nationales, F^{12} 6210). It is annotated by somebody in the ministry who, after criticizing its judgements and its statistics, correctly concluded that it was 'evidemment rédigé sous l'influence d'un système hostile au système de l'administration française'.

[2] Granville papers, P.R.O. 30/29/16, Bowring to the Lords Commissioners of Trade, 1 July 1833; Clarendon papers, French correspondence, 1833, Bowring to Thomson, 25 May 1833.

[3] Auckland papers, B.M. Add. MS. 34460, Granville to Auckland, 24 Feb. 1834.

hautes vues énoncées par le docteur Bowring et forme le vœu que le gouvernement entre dans cette voie de prosperité. . . .'[1] Elsewhere he commanded attention and drew support, but much of it seems not to have grown deep roots. Shortly after the last of his tours, Duchâtel, the liberal minister of commerce, sent round a questionnaire to chambers of commerce and *chambres consultatives*. The answers to this inquiry provide a corrective to Bowring's claims. The wine and silk districts, and some big seaports (such as Nantes), were still liberal. But the big manufacturing towns, Amiens, Rheims, Lille, Roubaix, Turcoing, were all predominantly opposed to any change of system. These were places which Bowring had tended to avoid, or if he had visited them, he had restricted himself to contact with those interests which were favourable to change. Thus at Rheims he reported that he got on well, but this was because he was studying wines and not textiles. The same thing happened at Rouen where the chamber of commerce 'determined to demand a diminution of the duties on coal, iron, machinery, and all the other elements of manufacturing labour'. But in reply to Duchâtel's inquiry, the chamber complained of English emissaries 'dont le talent ne peut être révoqué en doute' who were succeeding in persuading even manufacturers that there was a market for French textiles in England. And Dunkirk, where Bowring had been favourably received, warned the ministry of the imprudence of listening to the 'adroit' suggestions of the English.[2]

From this agitation Bowring emerged with the status of an expert. The results of his investigations in France were published in two reports, of which the first, signed by both Bowring and Villiers, contained a general attack on French tariff policy, and the second, signed by Bowring alone, contained an enormous amount of detailed information which he had collected at first hand on the organization of the French wine and silk trades. In the absence of anything equally effective to contradict them, these became a standard statement of the questions at issue. They were criticized in France for their failure to select facts fairly, and for their failure to mention British restrictions on imports from France, but no reply was produced.[3]

[1] Archives nationales, F[12] 2647.

[2] *Enquête relative à diverses prohibitions*, especially vol. i, pp. 84 (Rouen) and 70 (Dunkirk); Granville papers, P.R.O. 30/29/16, Bowring to Lords Commissioners of Trade, 1 July 1833, to Granville, 15 Aug. 1833.

[3] *Enquête relative à diverses prohibitions*, vol. i, pp. 102–3. The chamber of

Bowring operated against the French with an astonishing freedom and effrontery. He described his doings in daily letters to Villiers, Thomson, Auckland, and Granville—all people in responsible positions—and though towards the end they found him an embarrassment, they made no determined attempt to stop him, perhaps from a belief that his good effect on opinion would outweigh the resentment he provoked. In 1839, when there was again talk of sending him to France, Palmerston summarized the episode in the following way:

> The French government hate Bowring, but for no fault of his; they professed a wish to liberalise their Tariff, but said popular opinion prevented them—we said will you allow us then to help you by trying to enlighten public opinion in France. They could not say no though they well knew the Difficulty was as much with themselves as with public opinion, and they did not wish to lose their Excuse. Accordingly Bowring was sent upon an authorised Tour of agitation in the Provinces and produced much more effect than the French government wished but not quite enough to make them yield.[1]

Bowring also went on tours of investigation elsewhere: to Belgium in 1833, where he claimed that he was 'setting up the agricultural against the manufacturing interests', and had 'got most of the papers to take a right view of the question'.[2] He went to Switzerland in 1835, to the states of northern Italy in the same year, to Syria, Crete, and Egypt in 1838, and to the Zollverein in 1839. He made an attempt to go to Spain. McGregor went to Austria in 1838 and to Naples in 1839.[3] There is no record, however, of their dealings with the public on these other occasions. But it was from the knowledge acquired in this way that their standing in the debates on commercial policy of the eighteen-forties was derived.

Elsewhere in southern Europe tariff negotiations took a course closely similar to that in France. In Spain the import of cotton

commerce at Amiens was concerned that the only statement of the tariff question available in France was one which had been produced by servants of the British Government. The French Consul-General in London, Durand St. André, argued in the same way.

[1] Lord Melbourne's letters, Hertford County Record Office, Palmerston to Melbourne, 21 July 1839.

[2] Auckland papers, B.M. Add. MSS. 34459, Bowring to Auckland, 27 Sept. 1833.

[3] Reports on these tours are printed in *Parliamentary Papers*, 1836, xlv; 1839, xvi; and 1840, xxi.

goods was prohibited; in Sardinia, as in the Zollverein, duty was levied by weight, which penalized the cheaper British goods; in Naples it was levied according to the length of cloth, which made it desirable to manufacture and export especially wide pieces to that market.[1] With Sardinia a reciprocity treaty, unaccompanied by Sardinian tariff alterations, was signed in September 1841, though the British Minister at Turin, Sir Augustus Foster, complained of the 'excessive susceptibility of the king and his ministers who are apt to see a disposition to over-awe them'.[2] With Naples there were discussions which lasted, on and off, from 1834 until a treaty, satisfactory to Britain, and accompanied by tariff alterations, was finally signed in June 1845.

In Spain and Portugal, where the two queens, Maria II of Portugal and Isabella of Spain, owed their position to a considerable extent to the diplomatic support of Palmerston, the obstacles to British commercial negotiations were made yet more apparent. In Spain, George Villiers, who was a dogmatic free-trader, was British Ambassador from 1833 to 1839. He made repeated attempts to extract a liberal commercial treaty from the Spanish Government, offering in exchange, in 1835 to declare war on Don Carlos, and in 1836 and 1838 a British loan.[3] In the spring of 1839 a tariff commission was appointed which quickly revealed the political dangers of these suggestions: in February Clarendon wrote of a 'representation signed by all the senators of Catalonia . . . in which the Independence of that Province is insolently threatened if any change in the prohibitive system is made by the Government'.[4] In these circumstances a new tariff, which was introduced in November 1841, reaffirmed the existing prohibitions, and preserved the discriminating duties against British shipping. In Portugal, discussions took place intermittently from 1836 until a new commercial treaty was signed in 1842. But during these years, in which decisive steps to modify the British tariff were taken, the Portuguese tariff was raised twice, in 1837 and again in 1841, higher duties being imposed on textiles, earthenware, and

[1] A. Redford, *Manchester Merchants and Foreign Trade, 1794–1858* (Manchester, 1834), p. 91.

[2] B.T. 1/358. The negotiations are described in F.O. 67/112, and the text of the treaty is given in McGregor, *Commercial Statistics*, vol. i, pp. 1051–2.

[3] C. K. Webster, *The Foreign Policy of Palmerston* (London, 1951), vol. i, pp. 432, 446, 460.

[4] B.T. 1/349. Villiers succeeded his uncle as Earl of Clarendon in Dec. 1838.

hardware, all of which were items of interest to British exporters.[1]

In contrast to these failures there were two successes, the Anglo-Austrian treaty of 1838 and the Anglo-Turkish Convention of the same year. On both occasions commercial and general diplomatic considerations were in harmony. The fear of Russian expansion in the Middle East after the treaty of Unkiar Skelessi in 1833 prompted closer relations with Austria, and in Turkey, until the crisis of 1840, Palmerston was occupied in checking the claims of Mehemet Ali, and in countering Russian influence within Turkey. He was therefore prepared to show a more determined interest in commercial negotiations with both countries. Commercially, the emergence of the Zollverein had stimulated interest in this area: any action which would open fresh markets, or more particularly open fresh doors to existing markets, was very desirable. In Austria the negotiations, which were largely carried out on the British side by McGregor, led to the signing of a navigation treaty, which was accompanied by effective tariff reductions. Import prohibitions, except that on salt, were abolished. On cotton and woollen goods, iron, and fish, the duties remained high, but they could nevertheless now legally be admitted.[2] On the Austrian side, a desire to increase the Customs revenue and a desire for closer relations with Britain were both effective motives. When the treaty was signed, Lamb wrote home to Palmerston:

> The conduct of England in the negotiation of the treaty is considered as a return to the interest formerly felt by her for this country which she was supposed to have abandoned. However erroneous this latter supposition may be, it has been adopted here to an extent of which I was hardly aware, and it is only by Prince Metternich's congratulations upon its removal that I learn in what strength it has existed.[3]

In Turkey also political motives were of great importance. Negotiations, however, involved a range of grievances quite alien

[1] The text of the treaty and details of the Portuguese tariff of 1841 are given in McGregor, op. cit., pp. 1123–9, 1146. According to McGregor's calculations the rate of duty on cheap cotton cloth was raised from 15 per cent. *ad valorem* before 1837 to 45 per cent. after 1841.

[2] The correspondence dealing with this treaty is contained in F.O. 7/266–72. The navigation provisions of the treaty are discussed in J. H. Clapham, 'The Last Years of the Navigation Acts', in *E.H.R.*, vol. xxxv, July and Oct. 1910.

[3] F.O. 7/272, Lamb to Palmerston, 3 July 1838.

to the better-regulated administrations of western Europe. British merchants did not complain of a high import tariff, still less of an official policy of industrial protection. The import and export duties fixed by the Turkish empire were in theory no more than 3 per cent. *ad valorem*, so that 'Turkey is entitled to read a lesson to the most civilised European powers'.[1] The inconveniences and burdens suffered by British merchants sprang from the disintegration of the Sultan's authority: trade, particularly the export of olive oil and raw silk, commodities of much interest to Britain, was impeded by high local duties or by local monopolies. As in China at that time, the problem lay not in the tariff but in the internal economic organization of the country.[2] By the convention, signed in August 1838, Britain was granted most-favoured-nation status, and Turkey agreed to abolish monopolies, extra local duties, and restrictions on the activities of foreign merchants on Turkish soil. Against this a general increase of the export duty from 3 to 12 per cent. *ad valorem* was introduced. The real difficulty lay in the enforcement of these provisions, particularly in the districts which were subject to Mehemet Ali.

These were some important fields of commercial negotiation in this period, but they do not provide an exhaustive list. A treaty was signed with Peru in 1837, and there were discussions with Chile in 1833, with Greece in 1834, and with Haiti in 1838–9.[3] With Holland, a navigation treaty was successfully concluded in September 1837, which ended the situation, described in Canning's rhyme, whereby each country placed a surcharge on the goods of the other. When, after 1834, the German states of the Rhine entered the Zollverein, a serious threat to Dutch commerce was foreshadowed, and it was Holland which took the initiative in opening discussions with England. These were carried out by the British Minister at The Hague, and the Board had no direct hand in them, beyond giving a general approval.[4] Belgium, where industrial development was very rapid,

[1] McCulloch, *Dictionary*, article, Constantinople. He also produces information, drawn at first hand from merchants trading in this region, in his articles on Smyrna and Alexandria.

[2] The convention is described in V. J. Puryear, *International Economics and Diplomacy in the Near East, 1834–1853* (Stanford, California, 1935). Cf. M. Greenberg, *British Trade and the Opening of China, 1800–42* (Cambridge, 1951).

[3] B.T. 3/24–28.

[4] The negotiations are described in F.O. 37/204–6. See also B.T. 3/26, letters dated 24 May and 20 Aug. 1836.

was also dominated by protectionist sentiment, or by a desire for closer relations with France. Bowring paid a short visit there in 1833, and recommended that negotiations should be opened on navigation and on the transit dues on goods passing through Belgium. These were begun in 1834, and continued until 1839 without result.[1] On the contrary, the Belgian tariff was raised in June 1838, and again in 1842.[2]

In northern Europe there was a tentative approach to Sweden in 1835. Sweden had a considerable number of tariff prohibitions, and Norway—which was united with Sweden in 1815—had prohibitively high duties. When there was a renewed attempt in 1835 to alter the British timber duties, the Board of Trade persuaded the Foreign Office to approach Sweden to find out whether she would make tariff concessions in return.[3] Poulett Thomson believed that it was only by producing some concrete evidence of the probable response abroad that the Commons could be persuaded to accept a reduction in the duties. In Scandinavia, if anywhere, the general commercial advantages which should follow from a freer admission of foreign goods should have been capable of demonstration. Sweden, it is true, exported iron as well as timber to Britain, but was nevertheless keenly interested in the future of the timber duties: Norway's trade with Britain was wholly dependent on timber, and the country had suffered severely since the introduction of colonial preference in Britain.[4] The discussions had hardly begun when the very hostile reaction to the recommendations of the timber committee of 1835 killed the whole project at birth.

The omissions from this list of countries deserve comment. One, Russia, has been already mentioned: Britain had had no reciprocity treaty with Russia; no attempt was made to negotiate one in this period, and no attempt was made to whittle away the prohibitive Russian tariff. And, as will be shown below, little was done about commercial relations with the states of North and South America. In America, Britain had had her greatest success in spreading the system of reciprocity in the time of Huskisson, and

[1] Bowring's report on Belgium is in F.O. 10/28. (It is a much shorter document than his later reports.)

[2] The tariff of 1838 was chiefly a threat to the export of British earthenware (B.T. 3/26–27).

[3] B.T. 3/25–26.

[4] See evidence given before the committees of 1820 and 1821 on the timber duties (*Parliamentary Papers*, 1820, ii and iii, and 1821, vi).

to that extent there was little left to do in the eighteen-thirties. But, particularly at the end of the period under review, the general development of commercial relations with American states was unsatisfactory, and gave rise to considerable misgivings in the Board of Trade. These will be discussed below.

The drive to open markets in the countries of western Europe for British industry, and particularly in the years 1838–40 the British cotton industry, was uniformly unsuccessful. This was equally true of negotiations with countries such as Prussia or Sweden where it was plausible to argue that the British tariff was a real obstacle to such agreements, and of negotiations with France or Belgium, which countries had little cause for complaint. Bowring's attempt to set light to agitation in foreign countries was not successful. The silk and wine producers of France, or the merchants of Belgium, who might be interested in the development of a transit trade, were not strong enough—or convinced enough—to fight against the deeply rooted fears and suspicions of the protectionists. The same was true of negotiations with the reactionary Mediterranean states. In these—in Spain and Portugal, in Piedmont and Naples—governments were not prepared to take the risk of antagonizing powerful interests on which they depended for support. Where the Board succeeded in its commercial objectives, in Austria and Turkey, it seems to have been largely for diplomatic reasons. In dealing with autocratic states it was sometimes more useful to be able to suggest that tariff conventions might bring the political support of Britain than to suggest that they would bring economic advantages. Yet in Spain this recipe did not work.

This interpretation of the course of events suggests why the officials of the Board said with increasing conviction that the British tariff should be revised and reduced without reference to the state of commercial negotiations. In 1830 they had put this forward as good policy: it was as wrong to give exclusive privileges to the commerce of one country over its rivals as it was to exclude foreign goods by prohibitive duties. By 1840 it could be shown by experience that there was little to be gained by commercial negotiations, other than reciprocity in navigation. Protectionists in the eighteen-forties, and again in the eighteen-seventies and eighties, argued that to reduce a tariff unilaterally was to throw away a valuable bargaining counter: in 1840 there was little evidence to suggest that the counter was of much use. Suspicion of Great

Britain seems to have been too deeply rooted to encourage countries to open the door wider than was absolutely necessary to British goods. In relations with Germany it would be very hard to prove that the repeal of the British corn laws would have weakened the Zollverein's system of industrial protection. And in France, where Britain had in fact substantially eased the export of wines and silks, British commercial negotiation met with no response. The ill repute of the Vergennes treaty summarized a general attitude that Britain would be the only gainer by any tariff alterations, or by reciprocity. The principle of Huskisson's reciprocity treaties was that they should not confer exclusive benefits on the contracting parties, but should extend their benefits to any countries willing to trade on the same terms. Nevertheless, in spite of this, it was assumed that Britain would not be campaigning for reciprocity if she did not believe that she would be the chief gainer by it.

This atmosphere of suspicion was perhaps partly engendered by the system of approach to countries one by one. These discussions, particularly when they were in the hands of Bowring or McGregor, tended to concentrate on the specific advantages which the trade of each country would gain by freer admission of the goods of the other. The discussions ran into difficulties by not giving enough attention to the multilateral character of trade: it was impossible to suggest tariff alterations which would not appear to benefit the trade of one contracting party more than that of the other. But international conferences on such subjects were never suggested in this period by anybody. The most effective line of free-trade argument, and one which was often used in the House of Commons, namely, that increased imports are in the end bound to be paid for by increased exports of some kind, could not be used effectively in the missions of Bowring and McGregor.

From this point of view, the different attitude adopted by Britain in the eighteen-forties—the attitude which the officials of the Board were doing so much to develop—produced better results abroad. When free trade was no longer a gospel suitable for preaching abroad, but was also unconditionally accepted by the wily British for themselves, foreign suspicions began to be slightly allayed.

There remain three questions to be suggested. In the first place, how far did British trade suffer from the determination of many European powers to exclude British goods? In the second place, what sort of backing did the Board have from British industrial interests? And in the third place, how did British commercial relations develop with countries outside Europe, where political and economic traditions were different?

The first of these questions is far beyond the scope of this study, and was not a question to which the Board gave much thought. Porter, who in general showed comparatively little interest in commercial negotiation in the *Progress of the Nation*, gave no answer to it.[1] It may be noticed, however, that the actual effects of continental tariff changes on the value of British exports to those countries were far less conspicuous than the tone of contemporary writing would suggest. During the years 1830 to 1846, which cover the establishment of the Zollverein, the declared value of British exports to Germany and the Low Countries was tending steadily to increase, and in spite of the various tariff histories of these countries, it continued to increase in the same way after 1846, the proportion of exports to these countries to total British exports being about the same in the years 1835–9 as in the years 1855–9. In France, in spite of the repeated failure of tariff negotiations, the declared value of exports rose sharply, from an average of £754,000 in the years 1830 to 1834 to an average of £2,733,000 in the years 1840 to 1844.[2] In Italy and Spain and Portugal, in spite of attempts to keep British goods out, the total declared value of British exports remained fairly constant. The proportion of exports to Europe had declined, but very little, since the end of the war. From 1835 to 1839 the declared value of British exports to Europe averaged annually nearly £20 million out of a total export trade of £49 million, while the average figures for the years 1815 to 1819 had been £19 million and £43 million respectively. The officials of the Board tended to exaggerate the importance of existing tariffs. Given the ease of large-scale smuggling in some countries, and the great advantages in price of British cottons, exports could be maintained in the face of apparently prohibitive barriers. Also, they were not quick to foresee or to notice changes in the character of British exports. In Germany, the Zollverein were attempting to exclude British cotton cloth, but exports of cotton yarn, which were the more valuable of the two, increased. Exports of iron to Germany increased very

[1] He has a small amount to say on the development of trade with Germany (*Progress of the Nation*, p. 424).

[2] Ibid., pp. 364–7; *Parliamentary Papers*, 1897, Cmd. 8706.

rapidly; in general, the good export prospects of iron and steel were something which might have been foreseeable in 1840.

On the second question, that of the reactions and attitudes of British merchants, the evidence, such as it is, once again suggests that they played a very minor part in determining the policies of the Board of Trade. In correspondence with the Foreign Office, the officials of the Board laid emphasis, when they could, on the pressure which was being put upon them by trade organizations, yet this is mentioned comparatively rarely as the underlying reason for a course of diplomatic action. Pressure from commercial interests lay behind the protests made from time to time about the high rates of duty charged in Spain and Portugal on salt fish from Newfoundland. There was violent agitation, expressing itself in a flood of memorials to the Board, on the Sicilian sulphur monopoly. In Constantinople the local British merchant community had been pressing for government action to relieve them of the vexatious hindrances to trade from which they were suffering—the same thing may be true of the negotiations with other countries, for all reciprocity treaties included articles which safeguarded the rights of British merchants in foreign cities. But on the major trends of foreign tariff policy—the formation of the Zollverein, the long struggle to make a tariff agreement with France, or the American tariff of 1832, which is discussed below—the Board did not, to judge by the evidence which survives, receive communications of any kind from commercial organizations in this country. Nor were these subjects raised in Parliament more than occasionally.

The final question concerns the attitude of the Board's officials to the development of British trade in countries outside Europe. In dealing with the American states (and with the British colonies), both economic and political circumstances were different. In the first place, outside the United States, the continent was industrially undeveloped—British diplomacy would not have to contend with the same fears of Britain's industrial supremacy. In the second place, in the United States as well as elsewhere, the export of food or raw materials which Britain was capable of using was a major economic interest. It could be argued, by Jacob and others, that free trade in corn might not make much difference to the scale of exports from Prussia and Poland, but it could not possibly be argued that Brazil and the West Indies were not dependent on the export of sugar and coffee to Europe, or that it was not vital to the southern states of the United States to find markets abroad for their cotton and tobacco. Finally, all these states were 'constitutional states' in Palmerston's sense of the word—in them public opinion could find constitutional expression, and economic privilege was not dependent, as it might be in southern Europe, on court favours. If, in these circumstances, commercial relations with England did not develop satisfactorily—from an English point of view—then there was serious cause for anxiety. This began to become clear at the end of this period.

Until about the year 1838 the correspondence of the Board showed remarkably little interest in the course of trade with America. Reciprocity treaties had already been made with the United States and with most of the states of South America. British diplomacy was not much concerned with American affairs in this period, and it has already been shown that interest in commercial relations seems often to have been stimulated by general political considerations. In the United States a definitely protectionist tariff was introduced in 1832: it is perhaps remarkable that there is no mention of this, either in the correspondence of the Board with the Foreign Office, or in the letters received by the Board from the general public. (In 1833 a revised measure was introduced in the United States, which provided for the gradual reduction of tariff rates extending from 1833 to 1842, so that the problem passed away again.) After about 1837–8, British commercial relations both with the South American states and with the British colonies began to deteriorate. Partly this can be traced to the effects of the abolition of slavery, partly also perhaps to the depression of the later eighteen-thirties. The British colonies of Jamaica and Guiana attempted to make good their losses in revenue by introducing import duties on imported manufactures.[1] In the Latin American countries the combination of a somewhat reduced demand for their sugar and coffee in Europe, with the simultaneous shortage of these commodities in Britain, made them sharply conscious of the unreality of the most-favoured-nation status they had obtained by their treaties with Britain. The provisions of Huskisson's reciprocity treaties had never touched the structure of Britain's colonial preference: countries such as Brazil still found their sugar and coffee excluded from Britain. This was a real grievance, not only in Brazil, and at the end of this period the consular reports

[1] B.T. 3/30.

coming home from America told a general tale of rising anti-British sentiment, expressing itself in attempts to raise tariffs against British manufactures.

Thus, at the end of 1838, Britain opened negotiations with Haiti for a reciprocity treaty on the usual model.[1] At first, these went forward satisfactorily, but soon reports began to arrive of delays and difficulties which the British negotiator was experiencing.[2] Then in May 1839 he reported that the project had broken down: partly because the Government of Haiti did not wish for trade to be opened between the British colonies of the West Indies and themselves, partly because they possessed no merchant navy and would not benefit from the usual reciprocity provisions, but fundamentally because 'they betray a childish dread of binding themselves to place foreigners on the footing of citizens, or of giving them any influence in the country'.[3]

Similar events were reported from other states. It was reported from Lima in January 1839, that preliminary talks were being held there about a Spanish-American congress which should by commercial treaties introduce differential duties in favour of the Spanish American states.[4] A scheme of this kind had been under discussion since 1834, but was now increasing in favour. In spite of protest from Britain, these duties were introduced in April 1839.[5] There were consular reports of increased Customs duties from Uruguay and San Salvador.[6] In New Grenada the reviving support which was being given to the introduction of differential duties, in favour of their own shipping, was interpreted by the British consul as a move hostile to Britain. (Britain could claim equality of shipping dues under the terms of the existing treaty.) When a further claim against the Government of New Grenada arose, the British Chargé d'Affaires there wrote: 'To put forward such a claim would no doubt greatly exasperate the present bitter feeling against the provisions of the treaty between the two countries.'[7] In Mexico a new tariff designed to exclude all but the finest imported cottons, and therefore British cottons, was opposed by violent threats from the British Chargé d'Affaires. In Mexico, as in European states, people influential with the Government had established cotton manufactures, and the Government was acting on their behalf.[8]

[1] B.T. 1/345. [2] B.T. 1/351. [3] B.T. 1/353.
[4] B.T. 1/351. [5] B.T. 1/351; B.T. 1/354.
[6] B.T. 1/364; B.T. 1/360. [7] B.T. 1/355.
[8] B.T. 1/353; B.T. 1/359–60. Pakenham, the British Chargé d'Affaires,

But the most important development of anti-British commercial policy was probably that in Brazil. In December 1838 Ouseley, British Chargé d'Affaires at Rio de Janeiro, wrote home giving a depressing picture of the prospects of British commerce if there were no change in the British sugar and coffee duties. The treaty signed between Britain and Brazil in 1827 had, in addition to the terms usually made, included exceptional concessions to Britain: Brazil, a former Portuguese colony, inherited the terms of the commercial treaty signed with Portugal in 1810: they were limited by the treaty to a duty of 15 per cent. *ad valorem* on imports from Britain.[1] The treaty was to run for fifteen years, but its terms could be reconsidered at the end of this time. Two years' notice was to be given if either party wished to alter or denounce the treaty. (This question therefore came to a head in 1840.) Ouseley wrote:

I have every reason to believe that the Brazilian government will give notice . . . of their wish to put an end to the treaty. The present temper of this government, and particularly of the Chamber and of such people as think of these matters is decidedly hostile to any treaty being made or renewed with any country, especially with England, France, or the Great Powers. Late articles in all the leading papers and the speeches in the Legislative body sufficiently testify to this feeling. Yet if new treaties were to be made there is little doubt but that French and other commerce would be more favoured than our own, nor can we justly complain that it should be so. It must be admitted that France admits Brazilian produce although much of it enters into competition with her own Colonial Markets at a duty about one-third more than that paid by her own Colonies whereas our present duties are in fact prohibitory upon Brazilian produce.

That the attention of Commercial people here is fully awakened on

threatened that the independence of Texas would be recognized in London if such a scheme went through, and went on: 'But this is not all: Mexico stands indebted to England in a frightful amount for the interest on the loan advanced for the service of this Country. With a degree of moderation and forbearance of which there will not be found many examples, England has hitherto foreborne to exact from Mexico the strict fulfilment of her obligations . . . but from the moment that the government of Mexico shall shew itself so weak and so inconsiderate as to proclaim for the benefit of a few interested individuals a system of commercial hostility towards England, from that moment she must no longer count upon the generous forbearance of the British government.'

Pakenham wrote this note without previous reference to Palmerston; on receipt of it the Mexican Government abandoned their proposal (B.T. 1/353).

[1] A. K. Manchester, *British Preeminence in Brazil* (Chapel Hill, 1933), chaps. iv and viii, discusses the treaty of 1825, and describes it as 'the price of recognition'.

this subject may be seen by the fact of their having sent Coffee to the Cape of Good Hope to be there reshipped to England, and then admitted on payment of the same duties as those paid by East India Coffee. In a late Journal here an article on Commerce appeared, mentioning that no real reciprocity existed in the Trade between England and Brazil, as the latter paid 300% on her produce when by treaty Great Britain was only to pay 15% and strongly recommending to the particular attention of the Government 'now that the treaty with England was drawing to a close the necessity of adopting a *real* Reciprocity in their future dealings with us'. . . .

Perhaps the attention of people in England is not sufficiently called to the relative importance of Brazilian commerce. The Brazils have taken from four to five millions sterling[1] and sometimes more annually of British manufactures and its comparative importance to our country is enhanced by the circumstance that it is almost exclusively in English bottoms whereas the commerce of the United States is principally carried on in American Ships. The trade with the United States had, it is true, reached double the amount of that with this country but it must be recollected that it is a precarious and fluctuating trade, that in years of panic and distress it often causes, like all credit trade, a great loss to English capitalists; in 1837 for instance it fell to about three millions, if I recollect right, whereas the trade to this country is almost confined to English Houses established here, is regular and steady, subject to little risk and with ordinary prudence brings a certain Return, few or no failures to any extent occurring in the very extensive business carried on here and at Bahia, Pernambuco etc.[2]

Poulett Thomson's comment on this was, 'Very good paper'; it gives perhaps the clearest and most convincing account of the reasons why Britain was incurring hostility in the Americas, and why it was an urgent matter to do something to allay the causes of discontent. There might be grounds for questioning some of the arguments put forward by the Brazilians,[3] but there could be no doubt that, politically, a grievance existed.

The history of Britain's commercial relations in this period was predominantly an unsuccessful one. The successes—notably in Austria and Turkey—were few, and the failures were too many. In Europe the raising of tariffs against Britain could be explained away on political grounds, and this kind of explanation was often advanced by Bowring or McGregor. The British tariff could not be

[1] Official value. The declared value in the eighteen-thirties was between 2½ and 3 millions.

[2] B.T. 1/349.

[3] See p. 198 below.

said to be the only reason or even a very important reason for continental protectionism. But the situation seemed much more serious when the reports began to come in of increasing hostility to Britain from a region which a few years previously had been glad to make the commercial treaties which called its independence into existence.

PART III

THE BOARD OF TRADE AND THE ATTACK ON THE BRITISH TARIFF

8

INTRODUCTION

THE Select Committee on Import Duties was appointed in May 1840 to 'enquire into the several duties levied on imports into the United Kingdom; and how far those duties are for protection to similar articles, the produce of this country or of the British possessions abroad, or whether the duties are for the purposes of revenue alone'.[1]

An inquiry on these lines would be taking place in a favourable environment in the summer of 1840. Politically the Whigs were weak after 1839, and were conscious of dependence on Radical support in the House: and further than this, they were beginning to be embarrassed by the series of annual deficits which had persisted since 1837–8. In the country at large the agitation of the Anti-Corn Law League was increasing, and was directing public attention to the growth of hostile tariffs on the Continent.[2] In these circumstances, while the committee's terms of reference were not very wide, they took the occasion to make a general attack on the tariff on all its fronts. They not only criticized its administrative weaknesses, and its failure as an instrument for the collection of revenue, but they went on, outside their terms of reference altogether, to attack the principle of protection on theoretical grounds.

In this attack the organizers of the committee and the officials of the Board were working in close association, as a previous chapter has shown. McGregor, Deacon Hume, Bowring, and Porter were

[1] *Select Committee on Import Duties, Parliamentary Papers,* 1840, v, p. iii.

[2] See pp. 64–65 above.

all heard in evidence, the first two at considerable length; and a careful reading of the minutes of evidence suggests that the form and character of their statements, which moved systematically over the whole field of commercial policy, had been previously concerted between them and the chairman, Joseph Hume.[1] This committee provides, for this reason, a good starting-point for the study of the Board's opinions. But, on the other hand, it did not carry out its work on the extensive scale of the major parliamentary investigations of the eighteen-thirties: a report was drafted after fourteen meetings only of the committee, and no more than a handful of trade witnesses were examined. The evidence collected on this occasion must therefore be supplemented by that given before similar committees at this time, and by the opinions expressed in the writings and departmental memoranda of the Board's officials.

Their assessment of the situation will be summarized under the following headings:

1. The tariff as a revenue instrument.
2. The demand for protection in England.
3. The demand for protection in the British colonies.
4. The effects of the tariff on the British export trade.

[1] Cf. pp. 71 ff. above. For the chairman's handling of McGregor's evidence, see *Select Committee on Import Duties*, questions 282, 314, 360, 611, 646, 1055.

9

THE TARIFF AS A REVENUE INSTRUMENT

THERE could be no doubt, whatever people's views on free trade and protection might be, that in 1840 the efficiency of the tariff as an instrument for the collection of revenue was a matter of the greatest public importance: of a total tax revenue of £47 million in 1840, over £35 million was raised by Customs and Excise. The experience of the years since 1836 had shown the difficulties of estimating the yield of the Customs and Excise with any reliability, and in a period when it was assumed by all that it was necessary to balance the Budget from year to year, any discussion which would clarify these difficulties would be of political value.[1]

The opening sessions of the committee, at which McGregor was examined, were occupied with the attempt to establish which particular duties had originally been imposed for protective and which for revenue reasons. Much of the discussion was concerned with items of little importance to British industry, and of negligible interest to the revenue, but there were also items of much greater significance, where a duty originally imposed for protection had become of importance to the revenue, or where new interests had established themselves under the shelter of what had originally been intended as revenue duties. Such a situation was to be expected in a time of rapid economic change, and even more after the financial strains of the Napoleonic wars; as Deacon Hume put it:

> There are a great many articles which originally were at a low duty, and where no protection was contemplated; but during the war, year by year, and budget by budget, the duties being yearly increased, many articles at last had duties imposed upon them, which set people on the alert to make them at home, which was never thought of before, and thus incidentally those became protected. First, revenue alone was the object, but parties made the goods here, and in fact intercepted the revenue.

[1] See pp. 59–60 above.

Such protective duties, accidentally introduced, could themselves become the grounds for claims to protection by other interests.[1]

In 1839 the principal revenue duties were the following:[2]

Commodity	*Imports from colonies*		*Imports from foreign countries*	
	Rate of duty	*Yield to revenue (thousand £)*	*Rate of duty*	*Yield to revenue (thousand £)*
Sugar . . .	24*s.* cwt.	4,655	63*s.* cwt.	..
Molasses . .	9*s.* cwt.	238	23*s.* 9*d.* cwt.	..
Tea	..	..	2*s.* 1*d.* lb.	3,362
Tobacco . .	2*s.* 9*d.* lb.	..	3*s.* lb.	3,476
Spirits . . .	9*s.* gallon	1,413	22*s.* 6*d.* gallon	1,375
Wine . . .	2*s.* 9*d.* gallon (Cape of Good Hope)	342	5*s.* 6*d.* gallon	1,772
Timber:				
Square timber .	10*s.* load	244	55*s.* load	328
Deals,* battens, staves . .	..	114	..	886
Coffee† . .	6*d.* lb. 9*d.* lb.	564 121	1*s.* 3*d.* lb.	..

* Deals, battens, &c., were imported under a large number of different rates of duty, according to their different sizes, but all the rates gave a substantial preference to the colonies.

† The 9*d.* rate applied to coffee imported from British possessions within the limits of the East India Company's charter, 'not being the produce thereof'.

As well as these, smaller but still substantial sums were obtained from the duties on provisions (butter, cheese, &c.), on fruit, and in years of high domestic wheat prices, from the corn laws.

In these duties protective and revenue purposes were closely interrelated. The duties on sugar and coffee had been originally designed as measures of protection to the British colonies, and still were so, but together they accounted for about £5½ million of revenue. In spite of colonial preferences a large revenue was drawn from the wines and spirits of France, Spain, and Portugal. The duties on corn and provisions were designed to protect British agriculture. The only duties in this list which were solely for purposes of revenue were those on tea and tobacco.

[1] *Select Committee on Import Duties*, questions 1119, 1149.

[2] Ibid., Appendix I.

The criticisms made by the Board's officials of the tariff as a revenue instrument must be related to their general views on public finance. Their attitude was determined predominantly by the problems with which they were professionally engaged: their first concern was with the economic effects of protection in distorting the allocation of productive resources between one industry and another. Outside this question their interest in questions of taxation was more perfunctory. Porter devoted a section of the *Progress of the Nation* to a consideration of the sources of public revenue, and Deacon Hume, in the H. B. T. *Letters*, discussed extensively the claims of the landed interest that they were bearing an undue share of the country's taxation. Parnell's *Financial Reform* was explicit on this subject. In a general way they held that taxation should be proportional to income: Parnell held that 'security and good order are productive of universal advantage, and that without them there would not be any considerable accumulation of wealth', therefore 'no individual can justly complain that he is made to contribute, in the same proportion to his means as others, for their attainment'.[1] Poulett Thomson, in the debate on Injudicious Taxation of March 1830, quoted Adam Smith's canon that taxation should be designed to take as little as possible from the pockets of the people beyond what was received by the public treasury.[2] But they never got beyond these general statements: there is no consideration of the difficulties entailed in applying the proportional principle, whether to indirect taxation or to a property tax, the character of which was always left vague. They show none of the interest, whether in tax administration or in the social effects of taxation, shown a generation later by Mill among economists or by Gladstone among politicians.

In considering the tariff as a means of collecting revenue, then, the officials of the Board were not concerned to find out whether duties fell more heavily on the rich or the poor. If they stated that a duty—the sugar duties or the corn laws, for example—bore oppressively on the poor, this was because they had already condemned the duty on other grounds. Like Parnell, they had a sole criterion—the minimizing of the burden to the commerce and industry of the country. While, as will be shown later, some of the objections which they levelled against protective duties were applicable to import duties of all kinds, they did not object to revenue

[1] 2nd ed., p. 3.

[2] *Hansard*, 2nd ser., vol. 23, col. 857.

duties in themselves. Thus, the first objection which can be made to a system of taxation which leans heavily on indirect taxation, namely that it is almost bound to be regressive in character, was one which in practice they ignored. It was left to working-class Radicalism, both in the early thirties and in the Chartist movement, to place emphasis on this objection: the first reaction of the *Northern Star* to Peel's reintroduction of the income tax was one of warm approval.[1] The officials of the Board, like the school of thought to which they belonged, were much more concerned with attacking the monopolists—whether landowners, West India proprietors, or silk manufacturers—than they were with questions of incidence. In politics they were quick to discern and to attack statutory privilege, and they were keen in their investigations of administrative clumsiness, or of traditional practices which had lost their meaning with the passage of time. But they had less to say in fields which did not offer scope for these kinds of activity. In international trade policy their opportunities were good; but in talking of public finance their remarks were confined to criticisms of administrative method, as is illustrated by their almost total silence on the question of a revived income tax.

Assuming that it is necessary to raise a large revenue from import duties, what sort of criteria for distinguishing between good and bad import duties were put forward by the Board of Trade? The clearest statement of principle was given by Bowring:

> *Question 778.* (*Chairman*) What would be the fit limits, in your opinion, to duties on imports, if the interests of the public revenue were alone looked to?—It appears to me that the principle should be to raise the highest amount of revenue compatible with the non-encouragement of smuggling, and with the greatest extent of demand.

This can perhaps be translated into three criteria of wideness of consumption, inelasticity of demand, and ease of collection of revenue. The first of these tests was passed without difficulty by all those commodities which were the largest yielders of revenue (with the possible exception of wines). On sugar Porter wrote that 'it would be difficult to point out any article better fitted for the purpose [of indirect taxation] than sugar. Without being one of the absolute necessaries of life, long habit has in this country led almost every class to the daily use of it, so that there is no people in

[1] See p. 231 below.

Europe by whom it is consumed to anything like the same extent.' He added: 'It is besides, from its bulk, in proportion to its value, not likely to be clandestinely imported.'[1]

Revenue duties were, however, also levied on a very large number of articles (not discussed in any detail by the committee) which were not in general consumption and which yielded negligible amounts to the revenue: McGregor listed nearly four hundred articles, the total yield of which in 1838 had been about £6,500.[2] To a large extent these consisted of tropical produce which did not enter into competition with British colonial produce, or of raw materials and foodstuffs which were not produced in England.

On the criterion of elasticity, the Board had much that was important and new to the public to say, for it was in this respect that most of the biggest yielders of revenue (other than timber) were least satisfactory. As Porter put it:

> If by reason of the cheapness of provisions the wages of the labourer afford means for indulgence, sugar, tea, and coffee are the articles to which he earliest has recourse, and his family partake in the sober gratification. On the other hand it will often happen that where the power of buying these things is not enjoyed, the small sum that can still be spared after the purchase of his loaf is bestowed in procuring that stimulating draught which is then more than ever desired, and the man is driven from his cottage to the public-house. We may thus reconcile the apparent anomaly which has been so often remarked, that the Excise revenue maintains its level during even lengthened periods of distress.[3]

The consumption of tea, sugar, and coffee was therefore considered to be sensitive both to alterations in incomes and to alterations in price: in practice Porter was much more concerned with the latter question. One place where the Statistical Department had probably broken new ground was in its careful investigation of changes in prices on the consumption of these commodities.[4]

With sugar, he found that 'with one exception only, that of the year 1835, every rise in price has been accompanied by diminished

[1] *Progress of the Nation*, p. 551.

[2] *Select Committee on Import Duties*, Appendix I.

[3] Porter, op. cit., pp. 562–3.

[4] Parnell suggested this line of inquiry in *Financial Reform* (2nd ed.), pp. 31, 44–49.

consumption, while every fall in the market has produced an increased demand'.[1]

The trade in coffee he considered also to be

> pregnant with lessons of great value as regards taxation. There are but few articles fitted for general use which have been subjected in an equal degree to alternations of high and low duties and with respect to which we are consequently enabled with equal certainty to trace the effects of taxation in contracting or enlarging the enjoyments of the people, or to mark the comparative advantage to the Exchequer.[2]

The increase in demand which accompanied reductions in price was something of the greatest value to the propaganda of the free-traders, as it was to the postal reformers. But it presented difficulties when particular tariff proposals were under discussion, for it offered no clear rule of thumb which would tell the administrators at which point the greatest revenue yield would be obtained. The temptation, to which the postal reformers fell easy victims, was to hold that the greater the reduction in duty, the greater the gain to the revenue. This weakness had been the chief argument urged against the introduction of the Penny Post in 1839.[3]

To observe that consumption rose when prices fell was only the first stage in a complicated piece of forecasting: a change in the rate of duty was only one of many factors governing a change of price. It was also necessary to know the conditions governing the supply of commodities in foreign countries—the Board had, for example, no knowledge of the tea trade in China at first hand. In that country, it was the difficulty of finding goods which the Chinese were willing to import, rather than the British tariff, which prevented a greater expansion of trade. (Porter discussed the tea duties in much the same terms as the coffee or sugar duties.[4]) Again it was necessary to know something of the demand in other countries which imported the same commodity. In short, it was impossible, without prolonged and detailed investigation, to give expert advice on the effect on the yield of particular duties if the rates were reduced.

[1] *Progress of the Nation* (1847 ed.), p. 552. He produced a table showing average prices and consumption per head of the population since 1830 which bore out this statement (loc. cit.).

[2] Ibid., p. 558.

[3] See pp. 60–62 above.

[4] M. Greenberg, *British Trade and the Opening of China* (Cambridge, 1951), chap. 1; Porter, op. cit., pp. 561–3.

It was fortunate for the free-traders' thesis that many of the duties which were the biggest yielders of revenue also protected colonial interests. With these duties, the problem of forecasting was much simplified; and as they were in any case considered to be so much more damaging in their economic effects, to concentrate on the sugar, timber, and coffee duties was to kill two birds with one stone.

In these three examples, it was self-evident that alterations in the rate of duty would, in the circumstances of 1840, lead to an increased yield. In 1840 the rate on foreign-grown sugar (muscovado and clayed) was 63*s*. a hundredweight. The duty on sugar grown in British possessions, both in the East and West Indies, was 24*s*. a hundredweight.[1] Baring's Budget of 1840 added a further 5 per cent. on the existing rates of duty. Until 1840 these duties had excluded foreign sugar from the English market. (In the early thirties the prices of British colonial sugars had been no higher than those of foreign-grown sugars and the activities of Joseph Hume and his allies had been directed towards the reduction of the duty on colonial sugar.[2])

But since 1838 the supply of West Indian sugar had declined very seriously: the amount of sugar and molasses retained for home consumption in the United Kingdom had fallen from 4·4 million hundredweight in 1838 to 3·8 million in 1840. The price in bond of colonial sugars had risen far above the price of the foreign-grown article. Two witnesses before the Select Committee on Import Duties, J. B. Moore and C. Saunders, stated that for similar qualities of brown muscovado sugar the colonial price was 54*s*. to 56*s*. a hundredweight, and for foreign sugar was 20*s*. to 22*s*.[3] Where refined sugars were concerned, the disparity in prices was even greater—Brazilian sugars cost 24*s*. to 26*s*. in bond, and similar colonial sugars 62*s*. to 66*s*.[4]

There was, therefore, a wide gap between foreign and colonial prices: in the examples mentioned here it was one of between 34*s*. and 40*s*. The protection given by the existing scale of duties was 39*s*. a hundredweight. At the time the committee was sitting, the first rumours were in circulation that foreign sugar was being

[1] *Select Committee on Import Duties*, schedule 1.

[2] *Hansard*, 3rd ser., vol. 10, col. 1242. They had been particularly concerned to equalize the duties on East and West India sugar.

[3] *Select Committee on Import Duties*, questions 1793–4.

[4] Ibid., questions 1795, 1893.

bought in England for home consumption, paying the full 63*s*. duty.[1]

In these circumstances, a comparatively small reduction in the duty would clearly increase the consumption of foreign sugar: and any increase of this was bound to benefit the revenue considerably. McGregor proposed to reduce the duty on foreign sugar to 32*s*.[2] and he was justified in claiming that this would benefit the revenue to a considerable extent.

The coffee duties were in the same position, and for similar reasons. Another witness, R. Sheil, gave evidence on the prices of Ceylon and St. Domingo coffee. Before the equalization of the duties on East and West India coffees in 1835, the price of these two kinds of coffee had been about the same. Ceylon coffee had ranged from 48*s*. to 51*s*. a hundredweight in 1834, and St. Domingo coffee from 51*s*. to 53*s*. Since 1838, in particular, the supply of colonial coffee had declined. After the admission of Ceylon coffee to the British home market its price had risen rapidly, 'showing', continued the witness, 'that our favoured countries cannot supply the market'.[3]

By July 1840 Ceylon coffee was costing from 80*s*. to 85*s*. The existing rates of duty were 56*s*. on coffee in British possessions and 140*s*. on foreign coffee. This protection was still sufficient to exclude coffee legally imported from foreign countries, but it made it advantageous to import it via the Cape of Good Hope. Coffee grown in Brazil or St. Domingo was taken to the Cape of Good Hope, landed, and shipped again to England, thereby qualifying for the 56*s*. rate of duty.[4] A reduction in the duty on foreign coffee which would be sufficient to make possible its import into England direct would clearly benefit the revenue.

The timber duties in 1840 gave a large preference to colonial timber, the duty on square timber being 55*s*. a load for Baltic timber and 10*s*. a load for colonial.[5] It was clear that a rearrangement of the duties would increase the revenue, Deacon Hume suggesting that the increase might be as much as £1 million

[1] *Select Committee on Import Duties*, questions 582, 1947.

[2] Ibid., question 666. He went further, however, and offered an estimate of £3 million a year as the probable gain to the revenue (question 630).

[3] Ibid., questions 1266–8.

[4] Ibid., questions 887–97, 1250–4, 1745–6, 2361–4.

[5] The duties on deals varied according to the size of the deals concerned, but in general gave a similar preference.

annually.[1] But the reasons were different. The estimates of the increased yield of the sugar and coffee duties, which would follow reduction in imperial preference, were based on the current shortages of colonial produce. With timber the danger, if it existed, was of a shortage of Baltic timber. But the committee of 1835 had suggested that the danger was being exaggerated by colonial interests: one witness, John White, held that there was no shortage of any of the many kinds, shapes, and sizes of timber in general use. A second witness was the Radical politician, Henry Warburton, who was a London timber merchant. From the records kept by his firm he argued that the prices of various kinds of timber in the ports of the Baltic had hardly varied since 1800, the fluctuations in price being entirely explained by those in freight rates.[2]

There was a general preference among British users in the early nineteenth century for Baltic timber, both among builders and among ship-builders. Much of the Canadian timber used in shipbuilding during the Napoleonic Wars had proved unusually susceptible to dry rot: Sir Robert Seppings, the chief naval architect to the Admiralty, had taken a prominent part in the attack on the timber duties of 1820–1, and had given detailed evidence of the unreliability of Canadian timber. The same prejudice against colonial timber existed in the building trade, and had been strongly expressed in 1820–1. The American yellow pine, which accounted for more than three-quarters of the total imports of square timber from the colonies, was held to be wasteful, for it was badly squared, liable to dry rot, and also so soft as to be unusable for structural purposes.[3] But it appears from scattered indications that these opinions were less strongly held in 1835: more than one witness explained that the preparation and seasoning of timber were now better understood in Canada, and that English builders and shipbuilders now had more experience of the uses for which it was suitable. Two witnesses, David Bellhouse and John White, had both told the committee of 1821 at length of the faults of Canadian timber: in 1835 they were speaking in its favour. Nevertheless, the

[1] Ibid., question 1449.

[2] *Select Committee on the Timber Duties, Parliamentary Papers*, 1835, xix. But J. Potter, 'The British Timber Duties', *Economica*, vol. xxii, no. 86, argues that the threat of shortage of Baltic timber was a real one.

[3] *First Report from the Select Committee on Foreign Trade, Parliamentary Papers*, 1821, vi. The Select Committee on Manufactures, Shipping, and Commerce of 1833 also discussed this question.

prejudice had not altogether disappeared: buildings of the best quality, the National Gallery or the British Museum, were built of Baltic timber.

But the decisive reason why it could be expected that reduction of the preference would increase the demand for Baltic timber lay in the difference in the freight charges from the two areas: as Deacon Hume said, 'no power of man, no lapse of time, can equalise, for our use, the position of a forest on the Ottawa with that of a forest in Norway or Sweden'.[1]

On the third criterion by which indirect taxes for revenue may be judged, that is, ease of collection, evidence was presented of two kinds: that the tariff encouraged smuggling, and that it levied duties on large numbers of small items which it was a waste of administrative energy to collect.

The existing tariff was held to give a premium to the smuggler in a number of instances—instances that is, where the articles were small in relation to their value, and were charged a high duty. This was not a new complaint. When the revision of the silk duties had been under discussion in 1823, Joseph Hume had asked members of the House how many of them could not produce a smuggled silk handkerchief from his pocket. A reduction in the duties on colonial spirits in 1824 had brought a very large increase in the legal importation.[2] In the Select Committee on Import Duties evidence was produced about silver plate, about hats and gloves, and, above all, about silk.[3] On gloves there was an import duty of 20–40 per cent., yet 'French gloves can be purchased in London at about the retail price of Paris, and they must of course be introduced by contraband'.[4]

Where hats were concerned, McGregor had a similar tale to tell:

I believe there is scarcely a boat comes over from Calais, or a vessel which arrives, in which smuggling in various articles to some extent does not take place. I had a German servant the year before last, and I discovered afterwards that inside his hat he smuggled several of these bonnets. He bought a large hat with a broad crown, and he contrived

[1] Badham, op. cit., p. 201.

[2] W. Smart, *Economic Annals of the Nineteenth Century, 1821–30*, p. 198.

[3] *Select Committee on Import Duties*, questions 110, 127, 261. Similar administrative problems were raised by the export of machinery. See pp. 164–5 below.

[4] *Select Committee on Import Duties*, question 127.

to smuggle several Tuscan hats rolled round within the lining of that, and he boasted of it afterwards, and stated the profit he had made.[1]

This argument, that a high rate of duty encouraged smuggling, had been used repeatedly by Huskisson, and had been given great prominence by him in his speeches on the silk duties in the House of Commons.[2] Deacon Hume, in evidence before the Select Committee on the Silk Duties in 1832, dealt with the same problem.[3] He suggested that when the import prohibition on silk manufactures had been abolished in 1825, the rates of duty had been fixed with the smuggler principally in mind.

Upon being asked if in the table of 1829 the duty was fixed at the minimum cost of smuggling? Mr. Hume replied that such was the intention of the Government of the day: it was believed that the articles on which they left the higher duties unreduced were less likely to be exposed to smuggling than those on which they had reduced the duties.... In 1826 he had entertained a hope upon the subject as to the 30%, that it could be collected; but smuggling, like everything else, had been lowered in price.[4]

The long investigations into Anglo-French trade which had occupied the Board during the thirties had produced much information on the extent of smuggling between the two countries. Bowring's Reports had investigated the way in which the fine cotton yarns used in the manufacture of tulles and muslins were smuggled into France over the Belgian frontier.[5] He also gave the Select Committee on Import Duties evidence about the scale on which French goods were smuggled into England.[6] Porter, before the same committee, produced damning statistics of the illicit imports of brandy and silks into England. He compared the French official returns of exports to England with the English returns of imports from France: these showed that the quantity of silks exported from France exceeded that legally imported into England, by amounts

[1] Ibid., question 110.

[2] *Speeches of the Rt. Hon. William Huskisson* (London, 1831), vol. ii, e.g. speeches of 8 Mar. 1824 and 25 Mar. 1825.

[3] *Parliamentary Papers*, 1831–2, xix (evidence of J. D. Hume).

[4] Badham, op. cit., pp. 141–2.

[5] *First and Second Reports of Bowring and Villiers on the Commercial Relations between France and Great Britain, Parliamentary Papers*, 1834, xix, and 1835, xxxvi.

[6] *Select Committee on Import Duties*, questions 837–42.

varying in different years from 35 to 45 per cent.[1] He produced similar evidence relating to the import of brandy.[2]

Of this general course of argument two points can be made. In the first place there can be no denying that an administrative rule which is widely evaded is a bad rule: the need to offer no incentives to the smuggler was one which was agreed by all parties. The officials of the Board of Trade, as professional administrators, and as the people who had knowledge of Customs administration and access to the official records of seizures of contraband, were the people best in a position to emphasize this point.

But it was not a point which was wholly apposite to an attack on protective duties alone. It was one which could be applied to an unduly high revenue tariff equally well. It was in fact applied by Parnell and McCulloch to the revenue duties on tea and tobacco, which between them yielded in 1839 nearly a third of the total Customs revenue.[3]

And it was legitimate to reply that more efficient enforcement would solve the smuggling problem equally well. The extension of the Zollverein over Germany had been accompanied by a notable improvement in the efficiency of Customs collection,[4] but this had not been achieved by a general lowering of tariff rates.

The lowering of tariffs is undeniably an effective answer to the smuggler. But in general this aspect of the case for freer trade was much less emphasized in the eighteen-forties than it had been in the time of Huskisson: Peel, for instance, in his Budget speech of 11 March 1842 did not offer it as a reason for his tariff proposals.[5]

The tariff could also be criticized on another administrative ground, namely that of a total Customs revenue of nearly £23 million in 1839 £21 million were raised on ten commodities, and the

[1] *Select Committee on Import Duties*, questions 2528–37.

[2] It appeared that the officially recorded exports of brandy from France had been greater than the officially recorded British imports down to the year 1833, but that since then French exports had been considerably less than British imports. Porter concluded that the French Government were conniving at the smuggling trade. The French explanation, which does not seem very convincing, was that they measured exports of brandy by their alcoholic content, and not, as the British did, by their total bulk (Archives nationales, F^{12} 6208).

[3] See p. 144 above.

[4] W. O. Henderson, *The Zollverein* (Cambridge, 1939), pp. 41, 50, 110.

[5] *Hansard*, 3rd ser., vol. 61, col. 422.

remaining £2 million on 1,142 minor articles.[1] This argument was not a new one: it could be found in Sir Henry Parnell's *Financial Reform*, and before that in the work of the Finance Committee of 1828 of which Parnell had been chairman.[2]

In 1840 the subject was discussed in some detail by Deacon Hume, who, since he had worked under Huskisson on the codification of the laws of the Customs, was the person with the longest experience of the question. In addition to the articles named in the tariff, there were two unenumerated classes—those which had undergone any degree of manufacture, and those which had not. The former paid a duty of 20 per cent. *ad valorem*; the latter of 5 per cent. These, together with a great range of the articles which produced a negligible revenue, he proposed to group together into a single class, paying extremely low duties. 'Mr. Huskisson's . . . object', he explained, 'was . . . to open our ports for new commodities by lowering the duties, with the intention of placing rated duties upon any which might be brought in in large quantities.'[3] Huskisson, and Deacon Hume after him, regarded this low rate of duty as something which provided the means of recording the imports of particular commodities.[4] This provided a certain ground of disagreement between McGregor and Deacon Hume: in 1840 the tariff enumerated 1,150 articles at different rates of duty, and to McGregor, and to the committee, this had in itself been a ground of reproach—the Zollverein tariff enumerated few articles and contained 43 rates only.[5] Deacon Hume, with a much longer administrative experience, defended this long enumeration of articles:

Question 1474. Are you aware under how many heads the commerce of that country (Germany) is collected?—Yes: at the same time the trade of this country are very desirous of having specifications of goods that they may know what the importations are. The general account of the importations governs many mercantile houses in their proceedings. . . .

Deacon Hume suggested that, while retaining the full list of articles, the tariff could be simplified by the substitution of *ad*

[1] *Select Committee on Import Duties*, question 45.
[2] *Financial Reform* (2nd ed., London, 1830), p. 120.
[3] *Select Committee on Import Duties*, question 1100.
[4] See Part I, Chap. 5 above. The removal of trade restrictions between England and Ireland in 1825 had created great difficulties for the statistical department: see *Progress of the Nation* (1847 ed.), p. 344.
[5] *Select Committee on Import Duties*, question 285.

valorem duties, at a uniform and very low rate, for the existing duties, which were predominantly specific. This reduction of duties would simplify work at the Custom-House in another way: merchants importing a consignment of goods would have less incentive to warehouse the whole, and withdraw it bit by bit, each transaction requiring a separate entry in the Custom-House records.[1]

Over all these proposals there can be little argument: no issue of protection versus free trade was involved. These were the sort of questions on which Deacon Hume's authority was unrivalled.

This kind of criticism was later to become widespread, yet in retrospect it would appear the least serious of their lines of attack. The fact that the rates of duty are many and varied is not of very great importance to the merchant who habitually trades in a particular range of goods, provided, that is, that the rates of duty are not constantly changing, as in this period they were not. A great variety of rates is a piece of administrative untidiness, and it is perhaps an indication of the Benthamite influence on the Board of Trade that they should have placed so much emphasis on it. Its success as a line of propaganda lay perhaps in the fact that, once exposed, it was an obvious absurdity the reorganization of which would do little harm to anyone.

It could, however, be argued that the great variety of rates discouraged new enterprises. According to Bowring, 'people in all parts of the world are in a state of great perplexity what they are to do; they do not know what articles you will receive, and what articles you will not receive; and all commercial transactions of a novel character, out of which many important operations might grow, are involved in obscurity'.[2]

In conclusion, the case against the tariff of 1840 as an instrument for the collection of revenue, as it was developed by the officials of the Board, contained several lines of criticism. There was still, in spite of the liberalizing activities of Huskisson, evidence that silk and gloves and other minor articles were smuggled into England, although, in the nature of the case, there could be little satisfactory evidence of the extent to which this took place. There was at least a chance that the revenue would gain if the duties were lowered to a point at which there ceased to be any incentive to smuggle. Where this point would be could only be established by trial and error.

[1] *Select Committee on Import Duties*, question 1482.
[2] Ibid., question 777.

With many of the most important revenue-producing items in the tariff there was a reasonable probability that the revenue would gain from the reduction of the rates of duty. With some, such as tea and tobacco, it was difficult to say anything definite, and neither was discussed before the committee of 1840. With the others, on sugar, coffee, and timber, it could be clearly shown that lowering of the imperial preference would increase the yield of the duties.

It should be emphasized again that Radical free-traders of this kind expressed no objections to the general principle of deriving a large proportion of the public revenue from import duties. To the regressive character of taxation which leant heavily on duties on tea, coffee, and sugar they were, as has been shown, largely indifferent, perhaps on the grounds that they were not necessities.[1] There is also a final point. None of these duties, except those on timber, which were strongly attacked, and the duty on Swedish iron, were levied on raw materials used in industry, so that they could not be said directly to raise the price of exports.[2] But in criticizing the corn laws a great deal of emphasis was placed on the argument, which was itself based on a subsistence theory of wages, that the corn laws raised wages and therefore indirectly the price of exports.[3] This line of argument could equally well be applied to duties on tea, coffee, and sugar, but it was not used. The reason for this distinction was probably the commonsense one that there is a large difference of degree between the effects on the cost of living of the price of bread and the effects of the price of tea. Altogether then, there was nothing in the Board of Trade in 1840 comparable to the late Victorian propaganda for the 'free breakfast table'.

[1] See pp. 145–6 above.
[2] See p. 159 below.
[3] See pp. 200 ff.

10

PROTECTIONISM IN ENGLAND

THE case put forward by the Board of Trade against the protective element in the tariff followed along lines which were for the most part traditional, but, as in their discussion of the Customs revenue, the officials of the Board added the weight of their official knowledge, and a considerable quantity of significant detailed argument, to the existing body of opinion.

First, they held on substantial statistical evidence that certain major industries needed no protection: a comparison of the value of the exports with the value of the British imports of the commodities in question showed that they could withstand foreign competition without difficulty. This argument was used frequently before the Select Committee on Import Duties, by McGregor, Deacon Hume, Bowring, and by Sir John Guest.[1] It could be applied to coal and iron, to cotton and woollen manufactures, and a similar case could be made against the retention of protecting duties on brass, china and glass, and copper manufactures.[2]

There is no novelty in this argument; Huskisson had defended his alteration of the Navigation Laws and his reduction of the silk duties on these grounds in the eighteen-twenties. In the absence of statistics of the value of imports, it is impossible to give a simple picture of the situation: in 1839 it can best be summarized as shown in the table opposite.[3]

These figures by themselves could hardly support general conclusions: in McGregor's evidence they were backed up by some examination of the competitive position of the industries concerned. But on a question of such importance, which was the key to the whole case for revision of the tariff, the discussion was surprisingly desultory, perhaps because the answers were taken for granted by all concerned. Over cotton there could be no argument: previous

[1] *Select Committee on Import Duties*, questions 20–26, 419, 421, 720, 1152–4.

[2] Ibid., questions 50–64, 75–83.

[3] Export values are taken from the *Progress of the Nation* (1847 ed.), p. 372: those of the revenue and rates of duty are from the *Select Committee on Import Duties*, Appendix I. In some cases they refer to 1838 (see p. 257).

	Declared value of exports from U.K. 1839	*Revenue from import duty*	*Rate of duty*
	thousand £		
Brass and copper manufactures	1,281	4	30% *ad val.*
China and porcelain	771	5	,,
Coal	543	..	£2 a ton
Cotton manufactures	16,378	3	20% *ad val.*
Cotton manufactures imported from East Indies	..	3	10% ,,
Glass*	371	4	..
Iron	2,720	29	30*s.* a ton
Woollen manufactures	6,272	32	15% *ad val.*

* Different types of glass were imported at different rates of duty.

chapters have shown that it was very extensively exported even to countries, such as those of the Mediterranean, where it had to surmount a very high tariff.[1] The agitation against the coal duties in northern France had shown that British coal could compete successfully against Belgian if it were given equality in the French tariff.[2] But the remaining items in this list required further examination.

The duties on iron were an example of duties which had originally been imposed for revenue during the French wars, and which had survived the peace. They could not be considered to be protective, for British iron was the cheapest in the world. Sir John Guest gave evidence that in the United States discriminating duties in favour of Swedish iron were in force: nevertheless, British iron was exported there on a considerable scale. The comparatively large amount of revenue collected by the iron duties had a particular explanation: it was paid on imports of Swedish iron which was necessary to the cutlery trade of Sheffield: 'There is something peculiar in the Swedish and Russian iron, with regard to the peculiar fitness for making steel, which we cannot understand.'[3]

Similar arguments could be applied to china, brass, and glass. In each case there were particular categories of goods which were imported in spite of British manufacturing superiority, and in spite of fairly high import duties. Mostly these were luxury goods, confined to a small section of the population—French porcelain

[1] See p. 134 above.
[2] See pp. 120, 125 above.
[3] *Select Committee on Import Duties*, question 403.

and looking-glasses, 'improved' German brass coffee-pots, and so on. They could not compete in cheapness with the bulk of British manufactures. In the same way the comparatively large amount of revenue collected on imported woollen goods was probably derived from luxuries, such, for example, as cashmere shawls. In talking of wool, however, McGregor hesitated to say that the woollen industry stood in no danger from foreign competition: he echoed the currently expressed fears of Saxon competition, and suggested that the 15 per cent. *ad valorem* duty might soon become an effective protection against imports from Saxony.[1]

In addition to these, the major export industries, it was also important, particularly in view of the political aspects of the problem, to consider those industries in which the statistics of imports and exports did not give convincing answers.

Embroidery, for example, had yielded £8,875 by an import duty of 30 per cent. *ad valorem* in the year 1839.[2] The term 'embroidery', however, covered a variety of products, and McGregor claimed that the types imported could not come into competition with the English types: they were of a different kind, of finer workmanship and greater cost. But at the same time he spoke of Swiss embroidery, which could compete with English, both in price and in the uses to which it could be put, but which was at present excluded by the rate of duty. In this example the effect of reductions of duty could not be reliably forecast.

The same was true of the hat industry. Imported hats were charged a duty of 20*s*. a dozen, in order to protect the Dunstable manufacture. McGregor claimed that here, again, there was no real competition between the imported and the native product. The imported Leghorn hat was something of finer quality: 'My own opinion is that two different classes of person would wear them; I am not aware that persons who wear the Dunstable would wear the Leghorn; but it is impossible to judge as to fancy or fashion.'[3] Here again the future was unpredictable, and the fact

[1] *Select Committee on Import Duties*, question 26. Cf. pp. 200 ff. below. The threat of Saxon competition, where wages and the cost of living were much lower than in England, was an important line of anti-corn-law propaganda.

[2] Ibid., questions 113-26.

[3] Ibid., question 101. J. G. Dony, *History of the Straw Hat Industry* (Luton, 1942), shows that the Luton and Dunstable industry complained of competition from Leghorn hats after 1815. The duty on imported straw plait was reduced in 1842. (In the fifties and sixties the English hat industry was very prosperous.)

that some Leghorn hats could be sold as cheaply as *2s. 6d.* each emphasized the fact.

In the same way, it could be shown that wall-paper, clocks, and looking-glasses were imported from France, though they were no cheaper than the most expensive English products. All these had one thing in common: they were all things which would only be bought by the comparatively rich. For one reason or another—fashion, traditional preferences, the difficulty of substitution of, for example, one kind of embroidery for another—consumers were unlikely to change their style of living. In all these examples the question of price and therefore of the rate of duty, was a secondary consideration. Reductions of duty would merely have the good effect of reducing the incentive to smuggle. But in discussing this, McGregor paid little attention to the possibility that such reductions might let in new types of goods altogether, such as the Swiss embroidery of which he spoke. Even then, according to his evidence, Swiss clocks were made more cheaply than English ones.[1]

In an assessment of the competitive position of British industry and the case for its protection, a discussion of import duties by themselves was not enough. In the eighteenth and early nineteenth centuries there had existed alternative measures for the protection of British manufactures, in the prohibition of the emigration of skilled artisans and of the export of machinery. The former of these had been abolished in 1824[2] but the latter still survived to a limited extent. Joseph Hume's Committee on the Combination Laws of 1824 had also had within its terms of reference the emigration of artisans and the export of machinery: they had recommended the removal of the prohibition from most kinds of machinery, but in view of public opposition this had never been carried into law. The system had, however, been much relaxed by administrative action. Since 1825 it had been possible, by licence given by the Board of Trade, to export nearly every kind of machinery, the only important class excepted being spinning-machinery; for it was from hosiery, textile, and lace manufacturers that most opposition had been received. Machines which carried out any preparatory processes could be exported, but nothing which actually twisted the fibre.

[1] *Select Committee on Import Duties*, question 70.

[2] Smart, op. cit., p. 231.

The export of machinery was not within the terms of reference of the Select Committee on Import Duties, but it was investigated in the spring of 1841 by a further committee, which, unlike so many committees of this period, appears to have been a genuinely impartial one. On the Tory side were Lord Sandon, Lord Francis Egerton, and Peel himself, all of whom attended faithfully and cross-examined the witnesses: among the Whig free-traders were Emerson Tennant and Mark Philips. They investigated the question with great thoroughness: their findings are important both as a complement to the evidence presented on import duties, and as a commentary on opinion at the time among the manufacturers concerned. McGregor had claimed that cotton and woollen textile manufacturers had disclaimed any wish for protection: he stated that the demand for protection had been confined to glass manufacturers, to manufacturers in some of the minor industries mentioned above, and to the three recognized protectionist interests—the shipowners, landowners, and silk manufacturers.[1] The discussion on the export of machinery suggested that his claim was exaggerated.

Although the surviving prohibition was restricted to the export of spinning-machinery, the question involved a complex interplay of economic interests. It was discovered that the hosiery and lace industries of Nottingham were vertically organized, the manufacture and export of knitting- and lace-frames being controlled by the hosiery and lace manufacturers themselves: no conflict between the makers and users of the machines could therefore arise here. But it was also clear that it was the hosiery trade which, in its fear of Saxon competition, and possibly in an unwillingness itself to introduce technical innovations, was the most strongly hostile to a repeal of the prohibition. The representative of the Nottingham hosiery industry pleaded that, if the prohibition were to be generally repealed, there should still be an exception made for stocking-frames and bobbinet machines.[2]

In the textile industries there was potentially a conflict of interest between the manufacturers of machinery and the spinners. The former were strong in their demands for repeal. They claimed

[1] See p. 181 below.

[2] *Select Committee on the Export of Machinery, Parliamentary Papers*, 1841, vii (evidence of William Felkin), questions 2116–26, 2176. See also evidence of Richard Birkin, Thomas Herbert, and — Sewell.

that in the slump since 1837 they had suffered severely: they could have been kept busy with orders from abroad, had they been allowed to export spinning-machinery, but the demand for it at home had almost disappeared.[1] It was as a result of these representations that the committee of 1841 was appointed; unlike the Import Duties Committee, it was the direct result of pressure from an industrial interest.

Among textile manufacturers opinions were significantly divided. Two witnesses, Thomas Ashton of Hyde, the cotton-spinner, and James Marshall, the flax-spinner of Leeds, both very large and efficient manufacturers, argued on general grounds in favour of repeal. They held, as did Deacon Hume, that anything which encouraged the consistent application of liberal commercial principles should be supported. It was better to allow the export of machines than to encourage the emigration of skilled labour to make them abroad. Prohibition could only stimulate the development of machine-making abroad; already the quality of some Belgian machinery was not much inferior to that made in England. On the essential question, whether the British spinners could afford to let the latest kinds of machinery fall into the hands of their rivals, both Ashton and Marshall replied that they could; superiority in mechanical equipment was but one of many elements which accounted for English manufacturing prosperity.[2]

But there were also plenty of witnesses who held to the opposite point of view, perhaps because they were less confident of their ability to meet all rivals. One such witness was Holland Hoole, Vice-President of the Manchester Chamber of Commerce. The chamber itself was divided on the question and had not been able to make representations to the Government about it.[3] Hoole held that to allow the export of spinning-machinery was to begin the work of free trade at the wrong end: it was necessary to repeal the corn laws before removing the 'restrictions from that which forms the very foundation of our manufactures'. Another witness who argued in favour of maintaining the prohibition, unlike Ashton, Marshall, and Hoole, who spoke as private individuals, was the representative of a trade organization. This was John Herdman, of the flax-spinners of Northern Ireland, who stated that his

[1] Ibid., evidence of William Jenkinson and Peter Fairburn.
[2] Ibid., questions 235–9, 252–6, 2710–11.
[3] Ibid., 2nd report, questions 3990–4007.

associates were opposed to repeal as they feared the progress which had already been made by Belgian and French spinners.[1]

It was therefore clear from this division of opinion that it was not true that textile manufacturers invariably disclaimed any desire for protection, if protection were construed, as it should have been, to include protection to their manufacturing processes.[2] They might be willing to forgo an import duty, but where, as with the export of machinery, the consequences could not be clearly foreseen, they were unwilling to take risks. It was only those few who believed that they would be able to maintain an unchallengeable position who were prepared to treat free trade as a dogma to be applied systematically.

Of the officials of the Board, Deacon Hume alone gave evidence before the Select Committee on the Export of Machinery, and followed the same line of argument as Ashton and Marshall. But as well as this, he produced important administrative arguments to show that the prohibition was ineffective:

> the export trade, not being a source of revenue, as the import is, very little general attention is paid to the shipping of goods . . . and consequently in the immense mass of exports that go from this country, it does appear to me that nothing could be more easy than to insert among those various goods, almost to any extent, those small parts of machinery which are the important things, and which it is most important to retain, if you retain any at all.[3]

The information collected subsequently by the committee fully confirmed Deacon Hume's suspicions. He had made it clear that—whether from their disapproval of the system or not—the Board did very little to check the smugglers: only when they had definite knowledge that goods were about to be smuggled did they inform the Customs authorities.[4] Customs officials confirmed that it was impossible to search every package, or to check the movements of coasting vessels which might easily carry prohibited machinery out of the country.[5] With machinery, as with silk, it was generally

[1] *Select Committee on the Export of Machinery*, 2nd report, questions 3329, 3481–3552. Their fears seem surprising in view of the rapid increase in exports of linen yarn to France at this time. See pp. 122 ff. above.

[2] The same sort of situation can be seen in a memorial sent in to the Board by Staffordshire potters in the summer of 1839, against the continued export of china clay to France (B.T. 1/353).

[3] *Select Committee on the Export of Machinery*, question 5.

[4] Ibid., questions 83–84.

[5] Ibid., evidence of R. B. Dean, I. Haimes, W. Ride, and D. H. Watson.

known that there was a regular smuggling trade, with recognized scales of charges. A number of witnesses, both English industrialists who had visited continental establishments and Englishmen who had worked in them, described the frequency with which they had met the newest English machines in Belgium or Prussia.[1] Whatever the wishes of English textile manufacturers might be, the existing legislation was largely useless, as the committee's report emphasized.

There remain to be considered those major industries, or economic interests, which still in 1840 enjoyed substantial protection; that is, the silk industry, the landed interest, and the shipping interest. A few years previously all three had been expressing their fear of foreign competition.

In the years between 1826 and about 1833 the silk industry had been one of the loudest in its complaints of distress, and a great deal of information about its problems was collected by Lord Grosvenor's Silk Committee of 1832, and by the Select Committee on Manufactures, Commerce, and Shipping of 1833. The committee of 1832 was, until the arrival of Bowring from France, heavily biased in favour of protectionism; Grosvenor had said in the House without irony that it would be hostile to its purpose to select members who were free-traders.[2] The tone of the evidence which it heard was therefore noticeably different from that of the evidence heard in 1840.

Yet, in spite of the efforts of the protectionists, the evidence given before this committee was not very substantial. Witness after witness complained of distress and unemployment in his branch of the industry, but very few could support their contentions with adequate statistical evidence. The silk industry was highly localized: a picture emerges of a variety of local problems, but not necessarily of one of decline over the industry as a whole. And even with these qualifications, the evidence of different witnesses was conflicting.

Four manufacturing areas in particular were considered, and of these Spitalfields was loudest in its complaints of distress. A large number of witnesses appeared, all of whom blamed the tariff arrangements of 1824–5 for their distress. While they did not give

[1] Ibid., evidence of Thomas Ashton, Grenville Withers.

[2] *Hansard*, 3rd ser., vol. 10, col. 1040. See pp. 38–40 above.

figures of the amount of thrown silk used before and after 1825, nor of the number of looms at work, they complained that their trade had been reduced in volume, and that the weavers' wages had declined since 1825.[1] There was no reason to doubt that Spitalfields was in decline, but it would have been possible to advance alternative explanations. It would probably have been more correct to say that the Spitalfields industry had not been able to adjust itself to a change in the character of the demand for silk goods. In 1840 a witness, T. F. Gibson, held that it manufactured goods for the higher classes, and Manchester for the lower classes. The expensive and beautiful waistcoat silks, for which Spitalfields had been famous, were no longer worn. Nor was there any longer the same demand for silk furnishing brocades.[2] The demand was greater for plainer and cheaper materials, and in this branch of the trade Spitalfields was unable to compete with Manchester.[3]

The second district from which evidence was heard was Coventry, which specialized in the manufacture of ribbons. Here again there were complaints of distress, but here again the evidence was conflicting. One manufacturer of gauze ribbons, R. S. Cox, stated that he had had 300 looms engaged on this manufacture in 1826, and nineteen only in 1831. On the other hand his manufacture of other kinds of ribbon had increased over the same period.[4] Another witness, Richard Baggallay, held that the sales of Coventry ribbon had diminished between 1827 and 1829, but had recovered again in 1831, in spite of competition, chiefly from Switzerland.[5] Behind these complaints lay the evidence, which had also been noticed at Spitalfields, that prices were falling: those branches of the industry which could adjust themselves to this fact could survive, but the rest could not. R. S. Cox stated that, compared with 1824, satin ribbons had declined in price by 33 per cent., figured and fancy goods by 40–50 per cent., and gauzes by 50–65 per cent. No figures were produced which showed the activity of the ribbon trade as a whole.[6]

[1] *Select Committee on the Silk Duties, Parliamentary Papers*, 1831–2, xix (evidence of J. Ballance, W. Beckwith, R. Bennett, A. J. Doxat, R. Graham).

[2] *Select Committee on Import Duties* (evidence of T. F. Gibson).

[3] *Select Committee on the Silk Duties* (evidence of Richard Baggallay and Vernon Royle).

[4] Ibid., questions 2053–4.

[5] Cf. *Hansard*, 3rd ser., vol. 24, cols. 570 et seq. (Coventry ribbon trade).

[6] *Select Committee on the Silk Duties*, question 2058.

Macclesfield and Manchester specialized in the manufacture of plain silks, and particularly, in Macclesfield, of silk handkerchiefs. John Brocklehurst, a notable Macclesfield manufacturer, produced figures[1] showing a decline in Macclesfield of the following proportions:

	Number employed	*Number of spindles employed*	*Wages per hour*
1824	10,229	276,000	$1\frac{3}{4}$*d.*
1828	5,254	160,000	1*d.*
1831	3,762	122,000	$\frac{3}{4}$*d.*

A possible alternative explanation of this decline was given by a witness, William Haynes, a silk merchant, before the Select Committee on Manufactures, Commerce, and Shipping of 1833: he suggested that there had been a transfer of some of the silk industry from the old centres of Macclesfield and Norwich to Manchester, as a means of escape from strict trade union regulation of wages.[2]

Witnesses from Manchester who appeared before the committees of 1832 and 1833 did not share the general hostility to the tariff changes of 1824–5. Since that time, they said, the manufacture of silk in Manchester had increased 'prodigiously' and was now fully able to compete with the French. The price of such goods had fallen, and as a result, 'silk goods have got into a different class of consumers, and the manufacture rests upon a much wider base than it did before the alteration'.[3] In Manchester, as in Coventry and Spitalfields, there was a suggestion that the real enemy was not foreign competition but falling prices. The price of the finished goods had fallen, but the price of the raw material had not; as a result wages and profits had fallen.[4]

The case against the existing tariff was not proved by these witnesses, for in each centre alternative explanations could be

[1] Ibid., questions 11326–36.

[2] *Select Committee on Manufactures, Commerce, and Shipping*, *Parliamentary Papers*, 1833, vi, questions 4935–6. Cf. J. H. Clapham, *Economic History of Modern Britain* (Cambridge, ed. of 1939), vol. i, pp. 210–11, for a description of systems of wage-regulation in Macclesfield and Spitalfields.

[3] *Select Committee on Manufactures, Commerce, and Shipping*, question 1380 (evidence of Thomas James).

[4] Ibid., questions 4946–8 (evidence of William Haynes).

advanced. Raw material imports, on the other hand, before and after the alteration, were as follows:[1]

Annual average imports	*Raw silk*	*Waste silk*	*Thrown silk*
		(thousand lb.)	
1814–23	1,522	59	361
1824–33	3,291	29	388

It is clear that there had been a very great increase in the total imports of silk for manufacture, and that by far the biggest increase had been in the import of raw silk: there was no justification for the complaint, made by Brocklehurst in 1832, that the 'throwing interest was ruined'. Both Huskisson, and following him, the officials of the Board, countered complaints by arguing that the increased scale of raw material imports showed that foreign competition could not be blamed for the distress of the industry. The declared value of exports, after an initial setback, had increased substantially since 1824:[2]

Year	*Value*	*Year*	*Value*
	£ thousand		*£ thousand*
1820	372	1830	521
1821	374	1831	579
1822	382	1832	530
1823	351	1833	737
1824	443	1834	636
1825	297	1835	972
1826	169	1836	918
1827	236	1837	504
1828	256	1838	777
1829	268	1839	868

In face of these import and export figures, complaints of general distress, which had been produced by foreign competition, were clearly untenable.

In 1832 the Board was fighting a defensive battle, but in 1840 it was recommending a further reduction of duty from 30 to 20 per cent. *ad valorem*. It is arguable that the case for this was less easy to substantiate: if complaints in 1832 and 1833 were exag-

[1] *Progress of the Nation* (1847 ed.), p. 218.
[2] Ibid., p. 222.

gerated, it did not necessarily follow that less protection would bring greater prosperity. Almost all the witnesses, Bowring among them, believed that the French had considerable natural advantages in the manufacture of silk which, other things being equal, would always enable them to compete successfully with the British. Their chief and insurmountable advantage lay in their possession of the raw material: the silk-worm was extensively cultivated in the central and southern regions of France, and the advantage of a native source of supply was reinforced by a prohibition, until 1833, of the export of raw silk, which was a source of grievance to the English manufacturers.[1] In 1832 Bowring, as an expert newly arrived from France, gave the committee a long and very thorough description of the way in which silk was grown and marketed in France.

Beyond this the French had another more intangible advantage, that is, a reputation in England for superior taste. This was something on which all witnesses agreed, whether they appeared before the protectionist committee of 1832 or the free-trading committee of 1840. Other things being equal, British consumers would prefer French designs. Bowring expressed the situation of the French in the following way: 'Taste descends down to the lowest classes of the community, and there is a remarkable contrast between them and those of a similar rank in this country in this particular; taste is in fact cheap in France, and is dear in England.'[2]

In a luxury trade such as the silk trade a reputation of this kind was worth a great deal, and it was not easy to suggest ways in which the British manufacturer could compete against it. Bowring in 1832 took occasion to lecture the committee on the importance of securing public access to national collections of works of art. In 1840 discussions were taking place on the need to provide schools of design, which existed in France, and on the importance of a copyright of designs.[3]

As well as these arguments, there was also the fact that the actual rates of duty in 1840 were considerably above the nominal rate. Huskisson had imposed *ad valorem* duties, but very soon specific charges on the various kinds of silk goods imported had

[1] See p. 121 above.

[2] *Select Committee on Silk Duties*, question 8757.

[3] See p. 21 above; also *Select Committee on Import Duties*, questions 2274, 2413–20, 2862.

been substituted for them: the decision whether to charge the duty at the specific or at the *ad valorem* rate rested with the Customs authorities, and they had been in the habit of opting for the former. With the fall in prices since the eighteen-twenties, the rates of duty had therefore tended to become heavier: in 1840 it was estimated that the duty on velvets, which was nominally 35 per cent., in reality amounted to 45 per cent. It was considered that velvet manufacture was the most flourishing branch of the Spitalfields trade.[1]

There was then an essential difference between the positions taken by the Board's officials in 1832 and in 1840. On the first occasion they could draw on statistical evidence, the reliability of which all parties were compelled to accept, whatever individual experience might say to the contrary: on the second they were venturing on speculation. While they might feel confident of their advice, the manufacturers in 1840 still appeared to show considerable misgivings: in their negotiations with the French, Porter and McGregor had said that it would be politically impossible to allow the easier entry of French silks into England.[2]

It was probably for this reason that the Select Committee on Import Duties had much to say about the effect which they believed the corn laws had in raising the prices of manufactures, and in checking the demand for British goods abroad. Both the silk manufacturers interviewed by them said that they would be willing to forgo protection if the restrictions on the import of provisions were removed, but could not show conclusively that their opinions were generally shared in the trade.[3]

In view of the partisan character of the work of the Select Committee on Import Duties, little weight can be attached to the unsupported testimony of these witnesses: these extracts are important as showing that the committee used anti-corn-law propaganda as a means of overcoming any protectionist hesitations which they encountered among manufacturers. In this field, therefore, they were compelled to admit that there was, as yet, no public demand for the removal of protection, and they could not produce incontrovertible evidence that some sections of the industry would not suffer from its removal.

[1] *Select Committee on Import Duties*, questions 2232, 2237.

[2] See p. 122, above.

[3] *Select Committee on Import Duties*, questions 2345–6, 2439–41.

The Board of Trade cannot be shown to have exercised any decisive influence on the discussion on the claims of the landed interest. Of the officials whose work is under discussion, only one, Jacob, was professionally concerned with the question, as Comptroller of Corn Returns. He gave evidence before the Select Committees of the House of Commons of 1833 and 1836, and before the Lords' Committee of 1837. The subject was not specifically under discussion in 1840.

His evidence forms a consistent whole, and does not disagree in any essential point with his published reports of 1826 and 1828 on the corn trade in northern Europe.[1] He reiterated two arguments which were of some value, since they received little emphasis during these years from anyone else in a position of comparable authority.

In the first place, he took every opportunity of reminding these committees of the scantiness of official statistics on the subject. There was, he said, 'no accumulation of facts in the Board of Trade excepting what has been printed'[2]—except, that is, the statements of average prices in various English markets, the statements of the quantities of grain imported from various countries abroad, and the compilations of facts given in the appendixes of his own published reports. The quantities of grain imported from Ireland, for example, had only been 'recorded in a very irregular manner'.[3] His statements about stocks in England, and about sources of supply on the Continent were, he said, entirely based on his own private observations and unofficial contacts.[4]

The second point which he made, before all three committees, was a reassertion of the central thesis of his two published reports of the eighteen-twenties—that it was unlikely that the supply of wheat to this country from north-eastern Europe would be greatly increased by a change in the scale of duties in England. In the eighteen-twenties he had argued that the primitiveness and expensiveness of transport in Poland and northern Germany were such that supplies could only be drawn from the interior of the

[1] *Report on the Trade in Foreign Corn*, &c. (London, 1826); *Report respecting Agriculture and the Trade in Corn* (London, 1828).

[2] *Select Committee on Agriculture, 1833, Parliamentary Papers*, 1833, v, questions 3–5.

[3] *Select Committee to Enquire into the State of Agriculture, 1836, Parliamentary Papers*, 1836, viii, questions 17–20.

[4] Jacob seems to have solved the problem of establishing regular and unofficial contact with leaders in the trade better than his colleagues at the Board.

country at prohibitive cost. There was, he said, no risk that the English landowners would be overwhelmed with cheap foreign grain if the corn laws were repealed. In the eighteen-thirties he carried this argument a stage farther: he suggested that the real risk was not one of agricultural depression created by the competition of cheap foreign grain, but a risk of famine if there were a succession of harvest failures in Britain.

The yield of the English harvest could fluctuate within wide limits: Jacob asserted that in 1816 the deficiency supplied by imports was equivalent to four months' consumption. Since then the population had increased; should a harvest as bad as that of 1816 recur it would be very difficult to make good the deficiency: corn merchants now tended to hold smaller stocks than they had done previously. (He held that since the introduction of the sliding scale of 1828 it had become more attractive to speculate in foreign than in home-grown corn.) At the same time, he believed, though this was something which could only be a matter of opinion, that the production of wheat in Poland and northern Germany was declining. Nor did he believe that Britain could draw on an alternative source of supply in North America, whose exports of wheat were normally very small, and found a better market nearer at hand in Cuba:

> if the English markets were at all times open and the price very high, or rather if you could make corn as fixed in its price as cloth or iron, you might certainly obtain from the United States a large quantity of flour: but the Americans, knowing the uncertainty of seasons in this country, will not change their course of cultivation in the speculation of what may happen next year in a country so distant as England.[1]

It does not appear that Jacob's work exercised much influence in the Board of Trade: he was not regarded with respect by McCulloch or by Poulett Thomson, and neither Porter nor Deacon Hume shows the influence of Jacob in his writings on this subject. It is certainly true that events proved that his warnings of famine prices given to the committees of 1833 and 1836 were greatly exaggerated: in 1838 nearly 2 million quarters of wheat were imported for consumption, and in each of the following years, 1839 to 1842, about 2½ million, yet the annual average price of wheat (varying between 70·6*s*. in 1839 and 57·2*s*. in 1842) did not rise spectacularly high.[2]

[1] *Select Committee on Agriculture*, 1833, questions 15–53; 1836, questions 202–4.

[2] R. C. O. Matthews, *A Study in Trade-cycle History* (Cambridge, 1954), pp.

Porter, in a pamphlet of 1839, *The Effect of Restrictions on the Importation of Corn*, agreed with the thesis that British agriculture stood in no immediate danger from foreign competition. He quoted the experience of the years 1829 to 1831 when the price of wheat in England had been between 64*s*. and 66*s*., while at Danzig it had been about half that amount: in such conditions, the quantities imported into Britain had been very small—354 thousand quarters in 1829, 518 thousand in 1830, and 299 thousand in 1831. Since British farmers now considered that 55*s*. a quarter was a remunerating price, and since the prices of wheat and rye in Germany were tending upwards, the danger to British agriculture was plainly receding: he did not accept the claim of the landed interest that British agriculture was at a natural disadvantage compared with the agriculture of northern Europe. In any case, the general advantages to be gained from steadier supplies, from steadier prices, and above all from more regular trading relations with eastern Europe outweighed any risks to the farmer. The Select Committees of 1833 and 1836 had failed to discover all this: they 'would have achieved more, if members of the Committees and the individuals brought before them as witnesses had been less exposed to the blinding influence of personal interest'. He added that the forecasts of the committee of 1833 had all been proved wrong.[1]

The third published statement of opinion on the subject which came from the Board of Trade in this period consisted of the letters written by Deacon Hume in the winter of 1833–4 to the *Morning Chronicle*, which were afterwards reissued as the *H.B.T. Letters*.[2] The first of these letters was called forth as a reply to the doctrines of Robert Owen, but their polemical force was quickly turned against Hume's favourite enemy, the landed interest. The letters attacked the claims made by the landed interest that, because of the particular fiscal burdens they were carrying, they had a better claim to protection than any other economic group. These arguments, based on the burden of taxation, on the incidence of tithe on landed property exclusively, on the burden of highway rates and poor rates, were attacked violently, and often unfairly, by

35–37, discusses the value of Jacob's work. (Poulett Thomson, in a letter to Russell of July 1838 (P.R.O. 30/22/3), described a report prepared for him by Jacob on corn supplies as containing a 'vast deal of rubbish'.)

[1] G. R. Porter, *Effect of Restrictions on the Importation of Corn* (London, 1839), pp. 18, 21.

[2] London, 1834.

Deacon Hume.[1] He argued that British interests would acquire new or bigger export markets in foreign corn-producing regions, but did not discuss the corn market in any detail.

He gave evidence before the Select Committee on Import Duties on the probable effects of repeal on agriculture, and, unlike Porter and Jacob, he held that corn would be imported on a scale which would entail a considerable reduction of the area under wheat in this country:

I believe that much land would be thrown out of arable cultivation, and I believe that one of the great evils of our agriculture is the misappropriation of the soil; I believe there is a great deal too large a proportion of land under the plough, and too small a proportion under grass. The difficulty of raising lean stock in this country for the purpose of fattening is so great, that it is the chief cause of the high price of meat . . . there being a power of increased consumption . . . of meat that is almost immeasurable . . . there would be no want of good employment for any of the land that we possess within our boundaries.[2]

This argument, that repeal would entail a more efficient use of resources, was not taken further: McGregor's evidence was confined to criticism of the effects on trade to eastern Europe of the sliding scale, and he supported a fixed duty, if total repeal of the corn laws were not possible.[3] On this question there were important differences of emphasis between the officials. It does not appear that in this question their views were of much influence: they were little used by Cobden, or in the parliamentary debates on the subject.

The remaining protectionist interest, the shipping interest, seems to have been the peculiar bane of Deacon Hume. He described it contemptuously before the Select Committee on the Timber Duties of 1835 as: 'Those parties who think it is desirable to neutralize all facilities of trade and as nearly as they can, to turn commerce into a handy-cap race.'[4] In his article on the timber

[1] For example, in talking of the poor rates, he stated that they had been borne without complaint in the eighteenth century, and said nothing about the enormous increase in their amount since then.

[2] *Select Committee on Import Duties*, question 1378. Those agriculturists who were favourable to repeal presumably argued along similar lines.

[3] Ibid., questions 1035 ff.

[4] *Select Committee on the Timber Duties, Parliamentary Papers*, 1835, xix, question 29.

duties in the *British and Foreign Review* of 1836,[1] he delivered a further violent attack on them: 'The "timber bounty" has been to the alms-begging shipowners what the "allowance system" was to far more pardonable paupers, and the analogy is as strong in the remedy as in the evil.'[2] In dealing with the shipowners, more than anywhere else, hostile bias can perhaps be seen.

Both political and economic reasons can be given for this. Politically, the shipping interest was very strongly organized. They were a recognized parliamentary group,[3] voting together, and always alert to resist anything which might hurt their interests; they were always able to claim that the welfare of the merchant navy was a matter of particular national importance, since for generations it had been a nursery for the seamen of the Royal Navy. (In this period the chief spokesmen in the Commons of the shipping interest were G. F. Young, Alderman Thompson, and Aaron Chapman.)

At the same time, the General Shipowners' Society acted in the same way as a modern trade association. They took care to keep the Board of Trade regularly informed of their views, sending them each year their annual report.[4] (In this they seem to be unique among the commercial societies of this period, most of which seem to have sprung into activity only when a particular grievance was being felt.) And they put forward far-reaching claims to be consulted. For example, they wrote to the Board on the navigation provisions of the Anglo-Austrian Commercial Treaty on which, they said, they had not been consulted, expressing their

Deep regret ... at being compelled ... to complain of a departure ... from that course of frank and considerate communication in matters affecting the shipping interest which has usually been observed towards them by their Lordships.

Le Marchant's comment on this letter was as follows:

Mr. Oviatt [who signed the letter] assures me that the letter was written with the view of recording the opinion of the shipowners that

[1] *British and Foreign Review*, vol. ii, No. iv.

[2] C. Badham, *Life of James Deacon Hume* (London, 1859), chap. viii, reprints this article.

[3] In the general election of 1835, for example, the General Shipowners' Society distributed a handbill in Hull, saying that the shipping interest was inadequately represented in Parliament, and asking for support for their candidate, Carruthers, who was duly elected. (He died in June 1835.) See also Porter, *Progress of the Nation* (1847 ed.), pp. 398–400.

[4] Copies were also circulated to the Foreign Office.

they ought to be consulted previous to the passing of any government measures affecting the shipping interest. . . . Mr. Hume, I believe has since informed Mr. Oviatt verbally that the letter was wholly uncalled for.[1]

Deacon Hume, therefore, approached their problems with something like exasperation. The shipping interest was affected at a number of points by the development of commercial policy after 1815. It had been as much owing to their efforts as to the complaints of the British North American colonists that the attempts to modify the timber duties had repeatedly failed. They claimed that the carriage of timber across the Atlantic provided their oldest ships with employment when they could not be used for any other purpose. In 1831 they had joined forces with the Tory opposition, and had secured the rejection of Althorp's Budget proposal to reduce the protection given to Canadian timber.[2] But while they had succeeded in blocking change in this field, they had failed to make any headway against Huskisson's relaxation of the Navigation Laws; they believed that the system of reciprocity in shipping dues was favouring foreign shipping, particularly Prussian shipping, at the expense of the British.

For political and economic reasons, the shipping interest (with the landed interest) provided the backbone of protectionism in this period. They conducted a parliamentary agitation for a Select Committee to consider their complaints, and they hoped to recommend the abandonment of the reciprocity system. In 1827 they introduced a motion to this effect, which was successfully resisted by Huskisson. (Poulett Thomson's maiden speech was made on this occasion in support of him.[3]) In 1833, with the appointment of the Select Committee on Manufactures, Commerce, and Shipping, they finally got their opportunity; a very large part of the proceedings of that committee was devoted to the examination of their witnesses. Two years later, when the attempt to alter the timber duties was renewed, they had a further opportunity of receiving a hearing. Thereafter, little more was heard from them until 1844, when, once again, the relaxations of the navigation system came under attack.[4]

The economic basis of their discontent had its parallels in the situation of the landed interest. As Huskisson and later Porter

[1] B.T. 1/346.

[2] See p. 48 above.

[3] Smart, op. cit., p. 425.

[4] *Parliamentary Papers*, 1844, viii.

pointed out, the demand for merchant shipping tonnage was bound to decline after the end of the war.[1] From 1816 to about 1829 the tonnage on the British register was declining, and freight rates were falling until the forties. With this, and with the post-war fall in prices, ship-building costs were falling: those who had bought ships during the war found that their ships had depreciated in value faster than they had expected—like the landowners, they stood to lose in post-war conditions. It became clear from witness after witness heard by the 1833 committee that when shipowners spoke of 'distress' they meant that trade had become less profitable: they could not say that there was any large tonnage of shipping unemployed.[2] This situation nevertheless explains why they held on so tenaciously to the colonial timber trade.

In searching for causes of their difficulties, some shipowners blamed foreign competition, brought about by the reciprocity treaties; others blamed the lower operating costs which foreigners enjoyed. Ship-building costs were lower in the Baltic, where good timber could be had cheaply, and the cost of provisions for a crew was much less in Prussia than it was in England.[3] Huskisson, and Deacon Hume after him, argued that the fall in profits was inevitable; even if it were desirable to do so, there was no way of insulating the shipowners against it. To abandon the reciprocity system would lead to retaliation from Prussia and the United States.[4] They had more sympathy with the complaint of high operating costs—to the Select Committee on Import Duties this could be quoted as an argument against the corn laws. The irrationality of the shipowners' position had been illustrated when the duty on ship-building timber had been discussed with them by Huskisson. He suggested that a rebate on the duty should be paid on Baltic timber used in ship-building: this would reduce the difference in costs between Britain and Prussia. The shipowners rejected this proposal, holding that to reduce the cost of new British

[1] Huskisson, *Speeches*, vol. iii, p. 77 (speech of 7 May 1827); Porter, op. cit., pp. 401–4.

[2] *Select Committee on Manufactures, Commerce, and Shipping* (evidence of R. A. Gray, J. Ewart, W. Woolcombe, J. Nickols, H. Tanner, J. Spence, W. Richmond, R. Anderson, R. B. Roxby).

[3] This was extensively quoted as a contributory cause of distress (see evidence of Forest, Gray, Richmond, G. F. Young, and Shelly).

[4] Huskisson, *Speeches*, loc. cit. There is a correspondence on this, and on the shipping problem generally, between Huskisson and John Gladstone in B.M. Add. MSS. 38,749.

ships would further reduce the value of those already in commission. They were complaining, not only of competition from abroad, but of competition from each other.[1]

Beyond this there was not much which could be done to alleviate the situation. Deacon Hume and Huskisson believed that it was aggravated by the system of classification for insurance at Lloyd's, where ships were classified according to their age alone, and irrespective of their condition. This system, which gave every encouragement to the construction of large numbers of ships of poor quality, and discouraged the repair of them, was altered in 1834.[2] Apart from this, Deacon Hume could only make the Utopian suggestion that, at the end of the Canada timber season, all those ships which were fit for nothing better should be valued, broken up, and compensation given to the owners by the State. He did not suggest that the owners had any moral claim to compensation, but he held that the damage done to the country's economy by the timber duties was so great that his scheme would be a sound business proposition.[3]

By 1840 the agitation of the shipping interest had largely died down, though argument on both sides continued in traditional terms. Throughout the thirties the tonnage on the British register was increasing fairly steadily, which suggests that the post-war problems of the industry had been left behind. During the thirties the additions to the reciprocity system were mostly insignificant, and were accepted without organized protest. It was later argued that the heavy corn imports of 1838 and subsequent years had brought prosperity to the shipping interest.[4] Little was said about them before the Select Committee on Import Duties, beyond a general assertion by Deacon Hume and McGregor that free trade, in making possible imports of sugar and coffee from outside the British colonies, in permitting the import of foreign meat, and in reducing the disparity between British and Prussian operating costs, would be to their advantage.[5]

It seems that the Board of Trade was right in saying that the shipping interest could make no justifiable claim for protection. In

[1] Porter, op. cit., p. 398.

[2] Ibid., pp. 467–8; Badham, op. cit., p. 229.

[3] *Select Committee on Import Duties*, question 1236. Cf. p. 207 below.

[4] *Select Committee on Extending the Employment of British Shipping, Parliamentary Papers*, 1844, viii (evidence of T. Thompson), question 1839.

[5] *Select Committee on Import Duties*, questions 359, 1450.

spite of the reciprocity treaties, the proportions of British and foreign shipping entering British ports were not significantly changed. (On the other hand, the total tonnage of British colonial shipping increased at a much faster rate between 1825 and 1840 than the tonnage of British shipping. This would seem to have been as serious a threat to the shipping interest as any increased foreign competition encouraged by the reciprocity treaties.[1]) But in theory a claim for protection was justifiable, according to Deacon Hume's general ideas, if it could be shown that an industry was burdened by restrictions imposed upon it by the State for non-economic reasons. (The West India planters, for example, had some claim to special treatment since they, unlike their rivals in Brazil or Cuba, were debarred from using slave labour.) In the same way, the merchant navy, because it was a nursery of British seamen, had had restrictions imposed by legislation on its organization. They could not find their masters and crews in the cheapest market: the master and three-quarters of the crew had to be British subjects.[2] In arguing thus, Deacon Hume again reflected the teaching of Ricardo.

The Select Committee on the Employment of British Shipping of 1844 provides an interesting postscript to this subject. Once again, the shipowners complained of distress; their trade had, they said, been worse in the preceding three years than for many years. Once again they produced a variety of reasons why this should be so, and of these the reciprocity treaties were most frequently quoted. As a group they still remained protectionists. Two years previously Peel had carried through the first major attack on the Canadian timber preference, and it is interesting to see that this, which had so long been the most valued asset of the shipping interest, was allowed to disappear unregretted. It was never mentioned as a cause of distress; on the contrary, more than one witness said that its abandonment had been of great benefit to them.[3] The discontent expressed in the demand for a committee in 1844 was less strong than that in the eighteen-twenties and thirties: when the session ended before the committee had completed its inquiries, the subject was dropped, and it was not reappointed in the following session. While it had been sitting, freight rates and the

[1] Porter, op. cit., pp. 402–6.

[2] *Select Committee on Import Duties*, question 1411; 3 & 4 Will. IV, cap. 54, sect. 12. Cf. p. 193 below.

[3] *Select Committee . . . on Employment of British Shipping* (evidence of H. C. Chapman, J. Somes, J. Straker).

employment of shipping had both improved. But the proposal to repeal the Navigation Acts in 1847 brought a powerful revival of the shipowners' opposition, and the repeal was only passed after a long and bitter struggle. The shipowners were in alliance with the agricultural protectionists led by Lord George Bentinck, and remained protectionists down to the outbreak of the Crimean war.[1]

If shipping and agriculture are left out of account, it seems that by 1840 there was no major industry in England which could make a reasoned case for protection from foreign competition. Sections of some industries, such as the Spitalfields velvet manufacturers, might be endangered by a change of system; so might various small and politically unimportant industries such as the wall-paper manufacturers. But with these qualifications, the officials of the Board of Trade succeeded in proving their point.

They were on much less secure ground when they tried to assess the state of opinion in the country. This was, in the nature of things, something on which it was impossible to give an unchallengeable answer. Had the Board of Trade wished to do so, they had no authoritative body representative of manufacturing opinion to which they could refer. They were compelled to judge from the petitions and memorials which came in to the Board of Trade, and from their unofficial contacts with industrial leaders. Since they belonged to a certain school of thought, they were most likely to discuss the question with people sympathetic to their views. Thus the only unofficial meeting of this kind which is recorded is one described by Badham, with a party of Manchester manufacturers: J. B. Smith described it in the following way:

> As President of the Manchester Chamber of Commerce, I went to town upon one occasion with a deputation, and we met Mr. Deacon Hume and Mr. Porter at Mr. MacGregor's. Many members of the House of Commons, and other advocates of free trade, came in during the evening, and there were animated discussions upon the question which had become one of great interest.[2]

It remains to ask how far the point of view of J. B. Smith and his associates had become generally accepted in the country. It was McGregor, among the witnesses from the Board of Trade, who

[1] W. S. Lindsay, *History of Merchant Shipping*, &c. (London, 1876), vol. iii, chaps. 3–10.

[2] Badham, op. cit., p. 335.

spoke on this side of the question. He suggested that leaders among the major exporting industries had disclaimed any desire for protection, but he could not produce any documentary evidence to prove it:

Question 21. . . . Are there any official documents which would show that the trade do not require any protection for cotton?—I am not aware that there are any official documents before the Board, but this has been frequently stated by deputations.

24. (*Chairman.*) Have you any means of knowing how far the manufacturers of woollen cloths and yarns consider that they require protection?—Since I have been at the Board of Trade we have had several woollen manufacturers, amongst various other manufacturers, at the Board, and they have invariably to me disclaimed requiring any protection whatever.

McGregor made no assertions of any kind about the coal, iron, or pottery industries: his statement that manufacturers disclaimed any protection was in practice confined to the cotton and woollen industries. In these latter industries, the evidence produced publicly before the Select Committee on the Export of Machinery does not seem to have proved his point. But even McGregor was constrained to say that in certain other industries opinion was predominantly hostile to a change of system:

Question 72. Are you able, from any information at the Board of Trade, to state what would be the effect of lowering this protective duty? (on watches)—No; the only information that I have publicly known is, that we have had frequent deputations from the silk and glass manufacturers, and from paper-hangers, and a few others, requiring protection; but from watch-makers never.

On this crucial question, then, the evidence was exceedingly insubstantial: McGregor and his colleagues rested their case on statistical and not on political foundations. It is noticeable that none of the witnesses before this committee appeared as delegates of regular commercial or industrial organizations, though it was the usual practice for such organizations to demand a hearing from select committees on matters which concerned them. The Board was not so much concerned to show that overwhelming public opinion demanded a change as to show the public the reasons why they believed a change to be necessary: but it could still be argued that they gave a misleading impression of the extent of the support which they actually enjoyed.

It is not easy, on this question, or indeed on any such question, to make confident assertions about the state of public opinion. Manufacturers may have tacitly agreed that the removal of protection would do them no harm, but unless they felt so strongly on the subject as to organize meetings and petitions, no record of their feelings is likely to survive. And such demonstrations, even if they were as imposing as those of the Anti-Corn Law League, still leave unanswered the question how far they were representative. In this period there did not exist, in sufficient numbers, the kind of institutions which would give a continuous and balanced account of the development of opinion on commercial subjects; there was virtually no trade press, and, on the whole, the chambers of commerce did not fulfil the kind of function which might be expected of them.

In 1840 the existence of sixteen chambers is recorded,[1] many of them in seaport towns. In the important manufacturing centres they were not so firmly rooted: the movement initiated by Wedgwood's General Chamber of Manufacturers had not led to lasting results. In Birmingham the chamber dated from 1813, but between 1832 and 1842 it was in a dormant condition.[2] In Manchester there is a gap between the collapse of the Manchester Commercial Society in 1801 and the founding of the Chamber of Commerce in 1820; and in Leeds there is a gap between 1800 and 1851, when the second Chamber of Commerce was founded.[3] The Chambers of Commerce of Glasgow and Edinburgh were continuously in existence from the seventeen-eighties, and the former was fairly active. The Manchester chamber was active in promoting the interests of the cotton industry, but it is clear that it was not until December 1838 that it was roused from its 'seven years' sleep' and under the leadership of Cobden put forward an uncompromising demand for the removal of protection. Even so, it does not appear that Manchester merchants were fully converted: in May 1840 Joseph Hume wrote to J. B. Smith, the chairman of the chamber, asking him to organize either a public meeting or a statement of the chamber disavowing publicly the need for protection to the cotton industry. He hoped that this would provide valuable evi-

[1] M. W. Beresford, *The Leeds Chambers of Commerce* (Leeds, 1951).

[2] G. H. Wright, *Chronicles of the Birmingham Chamber of Commerce, 1813–1913* (Birmingham, 1913).

[3] Redford, op. cit., see Preface; Beresford, op. cit. Between 1840 and 1850 three more chambers only were founded, at Leith, Swansea, and Liverpool.

dence for the Select Committee on Import Duties, but he did not receive it.[1] Even in 1841 there were important sections of opinion in the chamber who were not prepared to go as far as Cobden.[2] In Sheffield a similar request from Joseph Hume to the cutlers to provide evidence for his committee met with a similar refusal. (The election results of 1841, which provide further evidence of public apathy of this question, are discussed in a later chapter.[3])

It seems probable that the important trade associations of this period, the London West India Committee, the General Shipowners' Society, the East and West India Associations of Liverpool and Glasgow, the Brazilian Association of Liverpool, the Society of Merchants trading to the Continent, played a more important political role than chambers of commerce.[4] (The Manchester Chamber of Commerce is perhaps more properly regarded as a trade association of cotton exporters.) But trade associations, like the chambers of commerce when they were active, usually confined themselves to their own immediate practical problems, and did not formulate demands in general terms. The Merchants' Petition of 1820, which attracted so much attention both at the time and later, appears to have been an isolated phenomenon. In the eighteen-thirties only one chamber, that of Dundee, sent in memorials to the Board of Trade asking for the removal of protection in general terms.[5]

In formulating a general criticism of the tariff it would seem that the Board of Trade was leading a new movement of opinion, rather than expressing one which was already there. For where industrial or commercial interests were conscious of a grievance they were fully able to express themselves effectively. The sugar and coffee duties, like the corn laws, had long been the subject of complaints, which grew in volume with the shortages of 1840. These complaints were led by merchants of Liverpool and Glasgow, and there is evidence that they tried to organize opinion elsewhere on

[1] A. Prentice, *History of the Anti-Corn Law League* (London, 1853), vol. i, p. 88; J. B. Smith MSS. Manchester Public Library, Hume to Smith, 9 May 1840. In Feb. 1839 Cobden described the chamber as 'that hitherto worse than useless body' (ibid., letter of 8 Feb. 1839).

[2] See p. 163 above, and 215–16 below.

[3] See p. 224 below.

[4] Cf. J. H. Clapham, *Economic History of Modern Britain* (Cambridge, ed. of 1939), vol. i, pp. 198 ff. on these associations.

[5] B.T. 1/347, 353, and 363. Dundee, one of the members for which was Sir Henry Parnell, had a very strong interest in the linen duties abroad.

the subject.[1] On minor questions too, a very substantial volume of complaint could be quickly and effectively organized. In 1840 there were three of these campaigns; against the linen duties, against the Sicilian sulphur monopoly, and in favour of a reduction in the duties on Honduras mahogany, which was a valuable timber for shipbuilding, but less so for the making of furniture. On all these occasions between ten and twenty memorials, often couched in identical terms, arrived within a short space of time at the office of the Board. But all these campaigns were not presented in general terms, and they were supported only by those who were immediately affected.[2] The prominence which the history of the corn laws has given to Manchester, and the history of the East and West India questions has given to Liverpool, must not disguise the fact that nothing much was heard from the Black Country, from Leicestershire and Nottinghamshire, from the West Riding or from Tyneside.

[1] Redford, op. cit., p. 146. In 1829 Liverpool merchants organized joint action with Bristol, Birmingham, Manchester, and Glasgow against the East India Company's charter (Wright, op. cit.).

[2] On linen see B.T. 1/359 and 363; on Honduras mahogany B.T. 6/276 and B.T. 1/358; and on sulphur see B.T. 6/276.

11

PROTECTIONISM IN THE BRITISH COLONIES

IN discussing imperial preference, the Board of Trade was drawn into questions of urgent political importance. Colonial policy, unlike fiscal policy, was a subject on which Radicals held definite opinions. Some held that the colonial tie between the colonies and the mother country was one which was bound to weaken and disappear in time, and they tended, in dealing with questions of administration, to assume that anything which was working in the contrary direction was probably undesirable. Others, of whom Roebuck, Buller, and Molesworth were the best known, were concerned with state-assisted plans of colonial development. In the Board the opinions of Deacon Hume and Porter, as far as they can be discovered, inclined to the second point of view: Porter wrote eloquently of the mutual benefits which would be enjoyed by colonies and mother country under a system of free trade, and never suggested that colonies were undesirable in themselves.[1]

Two events of major political importance had taken place since 1830, the emancipation of the slaves in 1833, and the decision in 1839 to adopt the principles of the Durham report. These decisions gave questions of tariff and commercial policy a considerable topical importance. The Tory opposition were more likely to make a political issue out of a tariff change which threatened to damage the West India planters or the Canadian colonists than they were to make one out of the current commercial negotiations with foreign powers. As well as this the Canadian timber trade was capable of attracting the support of those who regarded schemes of assisted emigration as the best solution for pauperism in England and Ireland. Emigrants who were employed for wages in lumbering were being given an opportunity to save the money with which in the end they could acquire land.

It is difficult to define the precise status of the Board of Trade in the handling of colonial questions. Officially colonial policy was the

[1] *Progress of the Nation*, sect. viii, chap. 1.

province of the Colonial Office, under the guidance of Sir James Stephen. On questions of economic policy it was, like the Foreign Office, in the habit of consulting the Board of Trade. The records of the Board contain documents, not only on preferences enjoyed by colonies in the British market, but also on colonial tariffs and colonial currencies. (The Board of Trade seems to have retained a vestige of the functions it had originally had as the Council of Trade and Plantations.) On the other hand there seems little in the records to suggest that anything was done to ascertain the views of the Colonial Office when the revision of the timber duties was under discussion, whether in 1831, 1835, or in 1840–1.[1] Once again, as in the history of commercial relations with foreign powers, it seems that the Board had a free hand, within government departments, to make what suggestions it liked, limited only by what was politically possible.

The extensions of the system of commercial reciprocity which had been carried out in the eighteen-twenties and thirties, had not shaken the massive privileges which were enjoyed by colonial produce—coffee, sugar, and timber—in the British market.[2] But at the same time the colonies still suffered from restrictions imposed upon them by the mother country in imperial interests. These were a potential source of grievance. McGregor mentioned the system whereby goods, even if they came in British ships, must first be landed at certain free ports, and then reloaded to be taken to their ultimate destination; the regulation that some goods, such as tea and fish, might only be imported from Britain or from British possessions; and the imperial duties, levied by the imperial parliament on goods imported into the colonies.[3] Whereas in most questions of commercial policy Huskisson had made a decisive breach with the past, in this field the old system was still substantially alive. Huskisson, unlike the Whigs of a generation later, had never been anti-imperialist in his ideas.

Before the Select Committee on Import Duties discussion was concentrated on the British West Indies and the British North American colonies. In both cases the evidence of the Board of Trade was concerned to establish whether the colonists would

[1] Nor does the correspondence (in the Public Record Office) of Lord John Russell, who was Colonial Secretary from Sept. 1839 till 1841, concern itself with this problem.

[2] See p. 144 above.

[3] *Select Committee on Import Duties*, question 953.

accept willingly a reduction of their preferences in the British market if they were at the same time freed of imperial restrictions.

In discussing the North American colonies the essential question was the extent of their dependence on the timber trade. The preference given to Canadian timber dated merely from 1810, when it had been imposed as a temporary war measure, at a time when the Baltic was closed to British shipping. But the Canadian trade, once established, had brought into being vested interests in the colonies as well as among British shipowners, and had resisted attempts at alteration in the duties in 1820–1, 1831, and 1835.[1] It was necessary to find out how important the trade was to the colonies, and how strong resistance to change would now be.

It was clear from the figures of exports in 1839 given in the *Progress of the Nation* that timber was the most important item in the export trade of the colonies as a whole, but that its importance varied greatly from colony to colony.[2]

	Exports of timber	*Total exports*
	(Thousand £)	
Upper and Lower Canada	880	1,099
New Brunswick	610	690
Nova Scotia	143	643
Prince Edward Island	..	14
Newfoundland	..	818
Total	1,633	3,264

The timber trade represented nearly the whole of the external trade of New Brunswick, and was very important to that of Upper and Lower Canada also: at the other extreme it did not exist in Prince Edward Island or in Newfoundland. McGregor's evidence in 1840 was therefore concentrated on New Brunswick and the Canadas (which, together with Nova Scotia, were also the places from which protests had been received in 1831 and 1835). There were no figures available which would relate the value of total exports to total production in the various colonies, and the question was only incidentally referred to by McGregor. But he had lived in North America and had some first-hand knowledge of conditions in them. He stated that 'the province of New Brunswick alone, . . . from the labour and industry of the country having been directed so much more to saw mills and timber

[1] See pp. 48, 51 above.

[2] Sect. viii, chap. 6.

cutting, than to agriculture, would experience inconvenience and loss'.[1] The extent of its concentration on the timber trade was shown by the fact that it imported its supplies of food from the United States. He held that in Upper and Lower Canada the timber trade was of less importance, except to a few merchants at Quebec and Montreal, though he offered the committee little information about these colonies. Upper and Lower Canada together had a far larger population in relation to the size of their export trade in timber than had New Brunswick, and Porter records that in 1830 there existed there woollen and linen textile industries, and some iron foundries and paper-mills. In the eighteen-thirties the colony had usually a small exportable surplus of agricultural produce.[2] This suggests that timber exports were relatively unimportant, a view which was strengthened by the behaviour of the population in 1841 when the terms of the Whigs' Budget became known there. Then Sydenham reported that except at Quebec the proposal had been quietly accepted.[3]

The reduction in the preference to Canadian timber proposed by McGregor was drastic; instead of rates of 55*s.* and 10*s.* a load on foreign and colonial timber, he suggested rates of 22*s.* 6*d.* and 7*s.* 6*d.* Such a reduction would certainly much diminish the trade with Great Britain, and McGregor suggested, though not in any precise detail, that Canadian timber interests might be given compensation from the British Exchequer. Both he, and Deacon Hume (in an article in No. IV of the *British and Foreign Review* of 1836) believed that the timber trade as it existed was a doubtful benefit to the colonies; and the same point of view was put forward by writers outside the Board of Trade, such as Samuel Revans, who had given evidence before the committee of 1835.[4] Their objections were partly moral, partly economic: they were concerned to attack the belief held in England that timber cutting provided a valuable means of employing pauper emigrant labour from England. Particularly in New Brunswick, the timber trade deflected immigrants from the more important task of clearing the land for agriculture. Agriculture and lumbering were not, as might have been supposed, complementary occupations: the settlers and lum-

[1] *Select Committee on Import Duties*, question 932.

[2] Ibid., question 948; *Progress of the Nation*, loc. cit.: the population of New Brunswick in 1838 was 155,000, while that of Canada in 1844 was 1,177, 000.

[3] See p. 223 below.

[4] *Select Committee on Timber Duties, Parliamentary Papers*, 1835, xix.

berjacks were distinct classes of people, and the timber which found a market in Britain came from forests far inland and was floated down the rivers. The kinds of timber found on land suitable for agricultural settlement was not, generally speaking, used for export.[1] McGregor and Revans gave full descriptions of the disruptive effect which the lumberjacks were having on the colonies. They lived a wild life in the woods, and came down in the spring to the ports of shipment of timber to squander the high wages they had earned. In all this there was no support or confirmation from the other witnesses before the committee of 1835, and it does not seem that there was much justification for their sweeping charges.[2]

It was generally accepted that a reduction in duties such as that proposed by McGregor would bring loss to the colonies: in what circumstances would the colonists be willing to accept such a reduction? In 1840 both Deacon Hume and McGregor believed that they would not oppose a change if it were accompanied by the removal of imperial restrictions on colonial trade: 'As far back as 1834', said McGregor, 'the people of the Canadas expressed the opinion distinctly: "Remove these restrictions and prohibitions, and you may legislate as you think wise and fit in regard to the timber duties." ' (In 1835 he had been less explicit; he had merely stated that the Assembly of Upper Canada had said that the abolition of imperial restrictions would remove a great grievance.)

This presents the same questions as were presented by the duties, for example, on silk. First, would the loss of one kind of duty be an adequate compensation for the loss of the other? Secondly, did the people of the Canadas really see things in this light?

The 'restrictions and prohibitions' in question covered a wide variety of commodities. There was a protective duty of 5*s*. a barrel on wheat and flour, which was equivalent to a fixed duty of 9*s*. a quarter. On the other hand, during the thirties, the Canadians were exporting wheat periodically to the United States, and in the early thirties to Britain, where it enjoyed a preference, being admitted at a duty of 5*s*. a quarter when the price in Britain was below 67*s*., and 6*d*. a quarter when it was above.[3] Hence this restriction

[1] Badham, op. cit., pp. 211–13.

[2] A. R. M. Lower, 'Huskisson to Peel, a Study in Mercantilism,' in *Essays in Honor of W. C. Abbott* (Cambridge, Mass., 1941), p. 394.

[3] D. G. Creighton, *Commercial Empire of the St. Lawrence* (Toronto, 1937), pp. 244–52.

on imports of wheat into the North American colonies cannot have been a serious one. Similarly there were protective duties shutting out foreign-grown timber, but while Canada had in the past imported from the United States, she now exported timber there. There was a prohibition on tea imported from foreign countries, which was a genuine restriction, evaded by large-scale smuggling over the frontier from the United States.[1] There was a preferential tariff to protect British manufactured goods: but many of these goods—cotton, silk manufactures (of many kinds), paper, glass—had been shown by McGregor at an earlier hearing to be produced as cheaply in England as elsewhere. The prohibition on the import of foreign fish and fish products can hardly have operated very seriously against the North American colonies.[2]

Altogether, the prohibitions and restrictions cited by McGregor do not appear to amount to very much. It is difficult to see how the attack on the most important item of their export trade could have been exchanged gladly by the Canadians for the loss of any number of import restrictions. In point of fact it was quite untrue that they were indifferent to the fate of the timber duties. Henry Bliss, legislative agent in London for the colony of New Brunswick, and John Neilson, deputed by timber interests in Lower Canada to bring petitions to the king and the two Houses of Parliament, had given evidence before the committee of 1835, and had argued strongly for the continuance of the timber duties unchanged.[3] A reduction of the colonial preference in 1821 had provoked a strong outcry from Canada; so had the attempt to alter the duties further in 1831. In 1835 protests to the Board came from Nova Scotia, Upper and Lower Canada, and New Brunswick.[4] And, as in discussion of protective duties on English manufactures, the Board of Trade's witnesses could produce no documentary evidence to support their assertions.

In discussing the sugar and coffee duties, and the position of the British West Indies, the evidence of McGregor and Deacon Hume was very much more convincing. On one side, the imperial preferential duties which had been of so little importance in the North

[1] *Select Committee on Import Duties*, question 951; B.T. 6/276.

[2] Supplies for the Newfoundland fisheries entered duty-free. On British manufactures cf. pp. 158 ff. above.

[3] *Parliamentary Papers*, 1835, xix, question 1960.

[4] B.T. IND. 14106. Further protests were received by Parliament in 1836 (*Hansard*, 3rd ser., vol. 35, col. 227).

American colonies mattered far more to the West Indian colonies. In these islands, sugar-cane had been cultivated to the virtual exclusion of anything else, and they were dependent on imports of wheat, salted beef and pork, fish, timber, and staves for making casks, and equally dependent on their exports of sugar and coffee. If food supplies and staves were imported from the nearest source of supply—the United States—they were subject to import duties: corn from the United States was charged at the rate of 5*s.* a barrel. The committee spent some time in showing that these duties of foodstuffs were of little benefit to British agriculture, but had been imposed for the benefit of the northern colonies. Goods from these colonies, and goods from the United States exported by the St. Lawrence, entered duty-free.[1]

Thus the extent of the 'taxation', as they called it, on the West Indian colonies depended on the extent to which freights were greater over the longer distance, and the extent to which Canadian merchants could make undue profits through this system.

The fact that in the West Indies supplies were regularly drawn from Europe, from Hamburg,[2] suggests that there was a real grievance here. What would be needed to prove this would be some statement of comparative prices of provisions in the British colonies and in, for example, Cuba and St. Domingo, a statement which was not given.

It would, however, hardly be possible to argue that the restrictions on the import of provisions were an important reason for the great advance in the prices of sugar and coffee. In the early eighteen-thirties, British colonial sugar had been as cheap as any other, and had been re-exported by Britain on a considerable scale to the Continent. Deacon Hume himself made this point clear to the committee.[3] At that date the restrictions on imports in the West Indies had been the same as they were at the time the committee was sitting.

The main explanation of this development lay, as Deacon Hume and McGregor both stated, in the economic upheaval which had followed the abolition of slavery in 1833, and the premature ending of the apprenticeship system in 1838. Negroes on the sugar plantations had now to be employed for wages; hence the rise in

[1] Creighton, op. cit., pp. 247–8.

[2] *Select Committee on Import Duties,* question 620.

[3] Ibid., questions 1161–3.

the costs of production and hence the importance of getting rid of the prohibitions and restrictions on their supplies of food and timber.[1] As in discussion on the corn laws, it was assumed that wages were dependent on the cost of living. 'I believe', said Deacon Hume, 'that the working population in the islands could be supported with less wages, and that thus the planter would be enabled to raise his produce so much the cheaper.'[2] In conditions of slavery, where the slave-owner feeds and clothes his slaves, this is true.[3] It does not follow that it is true elsewhere, least of all in the labour market of the West Indies at this time. The committee, and the Board of Trade's witnesses, could not understand this environment. It is true that they had only a very short experience of free-labour conditions, but the two trade witnesses, Martineau, a sugar refiner, and Warner, a wholesale grocer, appear to have had a much more realistic understanding of the position. Prices had risen because the supply had fallen, and this was 'owing to the slaves not working'.[4] The correctness of this judgement can be proved by a comparison of sugar production in different colonies: in Jamaica, which had a bad traditional relationship between planters and slaves, and which had large areas of undeveloped land in the interior, the exports of sugar to the United Kingdom had fallen from an annual average of 1,384,000 cwt. in 1829–33 to 1,040,000 cwt. in 1835–8. (The trend became more pronounced after the time of this committee: in 1842–5 the exports fell to 678,000 cwt.) In Barbados and Antigua, where there was no undeveloped land, exports were better maintained: in Barbados they rose from an annual average of 333,000 cwt. in 1829–33 to 409,000 cwt. in 1835–8. In Antigua over the same periods they fell only from 160,000 to 144,000 cwt.[5] The complaints against the negroes were that they left the estates and lived in squatters' camps inland: or that, in other cases, they had obtained wages which allowed them to subsist on three days' work a week. In a situation of this kind, where the work had always been

[1] *Select Committee on Import Duties*, questions 668–70.

[2] Ibid., question 1415.

[3] Porter stated that, before the abolition of slavery, planters had said that they would be willing to exchange the protective duty on sugar for the introduction of free trade in provisions. But he maintained, in spite of persistent pressure from the committee, that they had made no suggestion of this sort more recently (ibid., question 2703).

[4] Ibid., question 1894.

[5] *Cambridge History of the British Empire* (Cambridge, 1940), vol. ii, chap. xiii, p. 511.

hated, discussion of the cost of provisions was of very secondary importance. (The committee tried to imply that lower costs of provisions would encourage emigrants: but Deacon Hume drily remarked: 'People seldom emigrate to the West Indies, nor go there without some positive object in view.'[1])

But, in spite of their tendency to exaggerate the effects of import restrictions on the production of sugar in the West Indies, Deacon Hume and Porter did not put forward any easy solution to the problem. Their evidence on sugar was less dogmatic than their evidence on timber. Deacon Hume emphasized that the fact that slavery was abolished in the British colonies, and not in Brazil or in Cuba, made the claims of the West India planters different in kind from the usual claims of protectionists. His view of the question is worth quoting, as it was later to be quoted by Peel as authoritative advice:[2]

Question 1411. (*Chairman*) Do you consider that the produce of our British colonies should be protected in our market, if the restrictions and impediments which now exist in the colonies are not removed?—I am strongly of opinion, that all our colonies would be able to compete with the world, and to become exceedingly prosperous, if they themselves had free trade offered to them; and having granted that boon to them, I think it would be wholly unnecessary to support them by any protection in their commodities in this country. At the same time I must be understood, that they must be colonies that are placed in all respects upon an equal footing with those countries which produce similar commodities. I cannot conceive, that having 30 years ago abolished the slave trade and now abolished slavery itself, that any question of free trade can arise between Jamaica and Cuba; Cuba with abundance of rich and fresh soil, not only having the advantage of employing slaves, whatever that may be, but notoriously importing the enormous amount of 40,000 or 50,000 slaves every year; they have, in fact, the slave trade and slavery; and as the laws of this country have deprived the planter in Jamaica of that means of raising his produce, I conceive that that is a question, like several others, that are taken entirely out of the category of free trade. . . . These are therefore the cases . . . involving matters of security and morality, which are taken out of the class of free trade, because they are by the law interfered with, for purposes independent of trade.

If, however, the slave trade and slavery were universally abolished,

[1] *Select Committee on Import Duties*, question 1425.

[2] Peel, *Speeches*, vol. iv, p. 393 (speech on sugar duties of 17 June 1844).

then, he believed, the British colonies would again be able to compete. This was as far as he would go.[1]

In the debate on the sugar duties of May 1841, and generally in the discussions on the question in the eighteen-forties, Parliament showed itself to be more deeply concerned with the future of imperial preference than with the need for protection to British industries. It was not easy to argue that the sugar interests of the West Indies or the timber interests of Canada could survive without protection: in dealing with this question, Deacon Hume himself showed hesitation in making recommendations about sugar. But, apart from these misgivings, the Board showed little appreciation of the strength of the arguments on the other side, and little understanding of the scrappy nature of the information they possessed.

[1] *Select Committee on Import Duties*, question 1411. McGregor had, on the contrary, held to the view that if both the protection to sugar were reduced, and the import restrictions in the West Indies were abolished, the West Indians would be as prosperous, or more prosperous, than they were in 1840 (ibid., question 668). Cf. p. 179 above.

12

THE TARIFF AND BRITISH EXPORTS

PREVIOUS chapters have shown that, in the view of the Board, there was little to be lost from a drastic reduction in protective duties. It remains to describe the reasons why they suggested that such an alteration was an urgent matter, and finally to offer some assessment of their work and of its political importance.

The thesis that British trade was being endangered proceeded on two levels: it was partly a diplomatic case, and partly an economic one. The diplomatic case, developed before the Select Committee on Import Duties, that the British tariff was provoking retaliation abroad, has already been described in the chapters on British commercial relations with foreign countries. It is certainly true that tariffs were rising abroad on all sides against British manufactures, and particularly against cotton manufactures. But it is not nearly so easy to show that they were rising in direct retaliation against the exclusion of foreign goods from England. It could hardly be said that the Italian states, Spain, Portugal, France, or the United States, had serious grievances against the British tariff, yet in all these countries measures hostile to the export of British manufactures had been in force during the period under consideration. In Europe it seems most probable that fear and jealousy of the scale or efficiency of British industry was the political motive behind this hostility. It is possible that the Prussian tariff of 1818 was influenced by the British corn law of 1815, but here again, so many other forces, political and economic, lay behind the formation of the Zollverein, that the motive of retaliation cannot be given much emphasis. In one country, Brazil—admittedly an important exception—and perhaps elsewhere in Central and South America, it is justifiable to argue that retaliation was the major reason for the general wish to abandon existing treaties with Britain as soon as possible.[1] And in the making of the reciprocity treaties in the eighteen-twenties, the threat of foreign retaliation, if Britain

[1] Cf. pp. 136 ff. above.

discriminated against foreign shipping, had been an influential motive.

It was also possible and plausible to argue that the motive behind rising tariffs abroad was one of imitation. Foreign countries, according to Deacon Hume, 'imagine that we have risen to our present state of prosperity through the system of protections, and that they have only to adopt the same system in order to succeed as we have done'.[1] A reversal of British policy might establish a fashion for more liberal commercial policies. In the event, the adoption of free trade by Britain was followed in the fifties and sixties by a trend abroad towards lower tariffs. But in 1840 the evidence, to which the officials of the Board gave due weight, was that the existing protectionist interests had strong political support in France, Germany, or the Mediterranean countries in question. A second relevant point was not made: it was also necessary to remember that the need for protection to infant industries was a doctrine which commanded reasoned and influential support abroad, notably in Germany.

The remaining arguments can be divided into two. In the first place it was held, not only in the Board, but also by the leaders of the Anti-Corn Law League,[2] that British merchants were losing markets abroad because Britain could not import in payment the goods of the country to which they were exporting.

This argument was chiefly applied to Germany. Against it, it might be urged that the scale of British wheat imports from Germany had in fact been steadily increasing since 1815, and had increased greatly in the eighteen-thirties, and that the rising population in Britain meant that the market there for German wheat would be an improving one. Until they appeared before this committee, the officials of the Board did not believe that the effects of repeal on British agriculture would be catastrophic, and placed the main burden of their criticism on the uncertainties accentuated by the sliding scale of 1828.[3] In this question, as elsewhere, they allowed the opportunity for propaganda presented by this committee to tempt them from the more judicious positions which they had adopted in private.

[1] *Select Committee on Import Duties*, question 1155.

[2] Prentice, op. cit., pp. 65, 138. On both occasions the thesis had been put forward to them by Bowring.

[3] See pp. 107 ff. and 171 ff. above.

A similar argument was applied to trade with the United States: in relation to a country which sold more of her tobacco and raw cotton to Britain than to any other country, it seems extravagant.[1] Three witnesses, however, J. B. Smith of Manchester, Joseph Walker, an ironmonger of Wolverhampton, and William Leaf, a London merchant (the last only after some prompting by the committee), all asserted that the United States would take more British goods if they could send flour and corn in exchange. Britain, they said, imported from the southern States, but took nothing from the northern ones: they, and the committee also, tended to look at international trade as a series of bilateral trade bargains, not only between sovereign states, but between sections of them.[2] (In a political sense there was something to be said for this, as protectionist and free-trading interests were often geographically separated from each other, and it was hard to persuade the protectionist that he had any common interest with the free-trader. This was true in Germany and France, as well as in the United States, where the tariff was an issue dividing northern and southern States.)

These witnesses were speaking specifically of the conditions of 1840, when British exports to the United States did in fact fall in value from £8·8 million in 1839 to £5·3 million in 1840, for which a shortage of foreign exchange was responsible. The consular reports from the United States gave favourable accounts of the harvests of 1838 and 1839, and these had been years in which the British crop had failed. Thus 1840 was a particularly good year in which to put forward this thesis. It was not confined to the committee. In December 1839 a memorial from a group of Sheffield cutlers was sent in to the Board of Trade, describing the unemployment which had been caused in Sheffield by the stopping of exports to the United States: £600,000 worth of bad debts were owing to Sheffield firms alone. They suggested that American flour should be imported duty-free for twelve months. They did not suggest that the problem was more than a temporary one.[3]

[1] Both raw cotton and tobacco were subject to duties in the British tariff. The height of the tobacco duty was criticized by Porter (op. cit., pp. 574 ff.) who stated that the consumption per head of tobacco in Ireland in 1839 had fallen to one-half of that in 1801. But the tobacco duties, not being protective, did not come within the Select Committee on Import Duties terms of reference.

[2] *Select Committee on Import Duties*, questions 1563, 2114, 3294.

[3] B.T. 1/357. The financial history of the United States, between 1837 and

Considered over a longer period, the Board's thesis was weakened by the fact that even more than in discussion of Germany, no one could make a reliable forecast of the effect of repeal on imports of American grain. As far as the immediate future was concerned, the fact that Canada was exporting wheat occasionally to the United States in this period suggests that the English corn laws were not of much significance in Anglo-American trade:[1] and this was confirmed by the course of events after 1846.

It was also claimed that the sugar and coffee duties were impeding Anglo-Brazilian trade in the same way. According to McGregor and three of the trade witnesses, Moore, Saunders, and Cockshott, all Liverpool merchants trading with South America, it was impossible to bring return cargoes from Brazil and sell them in Britain. Brazil was one of the most important foreign markets for British cottons: total British exports there were worth about £2½ million annually. Of the three main exports of Brazil, cotton, sugar, and coffee, cotton alone found a market in this country, and that to a comparatively small extent. Thus British merchants were compelled to take payment in sugar and coffee and to sell them on the Continent—principally in Hamburg. If they could sell sugar in England they would, they said, be able to turn their capital over more quickly, and increase their scale of operations.[2]

The force of this argument is plain; nevertheless, this triangular arrangement had always existed, and the British export trade with Brazil had grown and flourished on that basis, as Deacon Hume himself recognized:[3] 'The high duty upon foreign sugar was no doubt always intended as a protection; but it has never operated as such until lately; it was nominal and useless, because till lately we were the cheapest producers and chief sellers, not buyers; and yet Brazil always transmitted a large portion of her sugars through her commerce with this country, to the markets of the ultimate purchasers.'

In discussion of the effects of the coffee duties, the preferences of English coffee drinkers were also relevant. It was mentioned in passing by Moore and Saunders that Brazilian coffee was unpopular in Britain: 'There is not five per cent adapted to the consump-

1840, as it affected the British export merchant, is described in R. C. O. Matthews, *A Study in Trade-Cycle History* (Cambridge, 1954), pp. 55 ff.

[1] See p. 189 above.

[2] *Select Committee on Import Duties*, question 1760.

[3] Ibid., questions 1161–3.

tion of this country, unless the duty was so low as to enable the poor people to purchase it.'[1] In a minute written in the Board of Trade, Deacon Hume had said the same thing; a moderate reduction of the duty on foreign coffee would allow St. Domingo coffee to enter, while, he said, Brazilian coffee would remain excluded.[2] It was implied that in order to have noticeable effects on imports from Brazil it would be necessary to make more drastic reductions in duty than those which were contemplated; and in the event, the reduction in the duty on foreign coffee from 1*s.* 3*d.* per pound to 8*d.* and on colonial coffee from 6*d.* to 4*d.* in the Budget of 1842 did not immediately provoke a great increase in the quantity of coffee imported from Brazil. But it is also desirable to set against this the evidence of the London coffee-house keepers that coffee was in fact becoming a normal article of working-class consumption at this time.[3]

The claim that Anglo-Brazilian trade was being inhibited by the difficulty of making payments from Brazil needed more careful examination than it received. It might be true, as McGregor maintained, that under free trade the 'natural' increase of exports to Brazil might have been greater, and it was certainly true that all the reports reaching London suggested that the Brazilians were discontented with a very one-sided treaty. But too little could be predicted with certainty to justify dogmatic assertions.

None of these three examples which were discussed bore out very satisfactorily the general thesis. Given a system of multilateral trade, it would require a much more elaborate investigation to establish the ways in which British restriction of imports would restrict exports. It might have been easier to demonstrate a direct connexion between the value of imports and the value of exports in relation to trade with countries with which Britain's trading relations were bilateral,[4] but in these examples the effects of British import duties might not necessarily figure very largely in the picture. In any case it was not possible to say much on this subject when statistics of import values were unobtainable. It was safer to argue generally, in the words of Deacon Hume: 'I go upon the principle that it is impossible for us to import too much, and that

[1] Ibid., question 1779.
[2] B.T. 1/347 (Jan. 1839).
[3] See pp. 74–75 above.
[4] Such, for example, as the West African colonies. Cf. Matthews, op. cit., chap. vi.

we may be quite sure that the export will follow in some form or other.'[1] As Joseph Hume and Poulett Thomson had argued as far back as 1829, and as Gladstone was to emphasize in debates in the forties, if Britain were to increase her imports, some other countries would, in the long run, have to admit increased exports from Britain.[2]

The second main ground for arguing that the reduction of import duties was a matter of urgency lay in British costs of production of goods for export: Britain was losing trade to foreign competitors because their costs of production were less. Such differences in costs might be traceable to differences in raw material prices or to differences in wage rates. There was little to say on the former question, for in practice there were very few examples of raw materials on which in 1840 high import duties were still being levied, the most important exceptions being those on timber and Swedish iron. Elsewhere, on raw cotton, silk and wool, on hemp, tallow, and so on, duties had been reduced to a low level, mostly by Huskisson in 1825, and were in practice borne without public complaint.[3]

Discussion was concentrated on the difference between wage rates in England and abroad, particularly in Saxony. There it was stated that money wages of textile workers were about half of those of English workers, and that the cost of living was also much lower.[4] Thanks to lower wages the Saxons were able to compete effectively against British goods in North and South America. Reduction of the duties on foodstuffs in England would improve Britain's competitive position. Deacon Hume said:

> I cannot bring my mind to believe that we should not make stockings, or manufacture silk very largely in this country, if all protection were removed, provided that the system was general, so that the expense of living of the labourers . . . should be reduced to the natural amount. That must certainly be understood to mean that the corn trade should

[1] *Select Committee on Import Duties*, question 1172.

[2] Smart, op. cit., p. 491; F. E. Hyde, *Mr. Gladstone at the Board of Trade* (London, 1934), chap. v.

[3] See p. 159 above for iron and timber, and p. 3 on the Budget of 1825.

[4] This was one of the few subjects on which the protectionist members of the committee cross-examined the Board's witnesses with any vigour. But they were concerned to prove a thesis of their own, namely that high wages in England could be attributed to heavy taxation, which gave British goods a claim to protection in their home market.

be free, that meat, that every article of consumption should for the future be free.[1]

This implies a subsistence theory of wages, which was held in the Board of Trade: in the *Progress of the Nation* Porter had written: 'If the cost of living to a labourer's family were permanently increased, there can be no doubt that wages must rise proportionally.'[2] But it was politically dangerous to argue in reverse that repeal of the corn laws would make reduction of wages possible, and it was an argument which was going out of fashion at this time. In the eighteen-forties it was necessary for the Anti-Corn Law League to spend much effort in denying that this was their real aim. The relationship of wages and food prices was extensively discussed during the course of the anti-corn law agitation, and before 1846 Peel had come to the conclusion that wages did not vary with the price of provisions, and stated this as one of the grounds for his conversion to repeal.[3]

The theory, if it were accepted, was one which could be appropriately applied to Saxon competition in cotton hosiery. The hosiery industry in Britain was not known to enjoy advantages in techniques or organization over its Saxon rival: in both countries it was organized on a domestic basis, and used the same sort of machines, and in both countries hosiery workers had the reputation of being among the lowest paid.[4] For similar general reasons it was an argument which could be put forward to silk manufacturers or to shipowners.

But the argument could not have the same applicability in industries which had a clear competitive advantage over foreign rivals: 'Wages are only one element in the cost of production; and it is quite clear that we have not the greatest advantages where we pay the lowest rate of wages, for in many such cases the competition is

[1] *Select Committee on Import Duties*, question 1363.

[2] P. 455. Cf. Ricardo: 'From the effect of the principle of population on the increase of mankind, wages of the lowest kind never continue much above that rate which nature and habit demand for the support of the labourers.'

[3] See *Memoirs*, vol. ii, p. 102. The Political Economy Club, of which Deacon Hume was a member, discussed this question in Mar. 1840, but there is no record of the discussion.

[4] Porter, op. cit., pp. 424–5, describes working conditions in the Saxon hosiery and textile industries. Cf. p. 162 above on the hosiery industry's anxiety to maintain the prohibition on the export of machinery. On the organization of the Leicestershire hosiery industry, see *V.C.H. Leicestershire*, vol. iii, pp. 2 ff.

strongest with foreign countries. Where we produce to the most advantage will frequently be found to be where we pay the highest wages.'

It was accepted that in such industries continental rivals were handicapped by lack of capital.[1] Just as the most efficient spinning firms supported the export of machinery, so they could afford to pay high wages and could, in the propaganda of the Anti-Corn Law League in the eighteen-forties, be indifferent to the thesis that repeal would make possible a reduction of wages.

If Deacon Hume's argument were granted that wages in Britain would be reduced by free trade, the question remained how far could the prices of foodstuffs be reasonably expected to fall. It could be expected in general terms that 'the prices here of the necessaries would assimilate more nearly to those of the Continent',[2] but here, again, neither the officials nor their questioners were satisfied with general answers. As far as corn is concerned, it has been shown that opinions differed widely, and that Porter and Jacob had come, apparently independently, to the conclusion that it would not be much changed.[3] On meat, bacon, and fish, imports of all of which were prohibited, there is no evidence that the Board had collected information. With sugar, however, there was some reason to expect that an abolition of the preferential duty would entail a noticeable drop in price: especially as two trade witnesses, Moore and Saunders, stated that exports from Brazil had increased 'not much of late. In some parts they have diminished, and increased in coffee. . . . Because coffee has been answering better.'[4] This they attributed to the increased consumption of beet sugar in Europe, which was highly protected in France and Germany.

McGregor, Bowring, and Deacon Hume avoided discussion of these questions by postulating the answers in a system of calculation of what they described as the 'taxation' levied by such duties on the people of this country. Any excess in the price of an article, which could be attributed to the operation of a protective duty, was a tax paid into the pocket of the producer of the protected article. The phrase is familiar in anti-corn-law propaganda where the corn law was astutely described as a tax on bread for the benefit of the landlord. It was in their arithmetical illustrations of this 'taxation'

[1] *Select Committee on Import Duties*, questions 815 (Bowring), 1207–8 (Deacon Hume).

[2] Ibid., question 1052.

[3] Cf. pp. 171 ff. above.

[4] *Select Committee on Import Duties*, questions 1809–14.

that they propounded the 'astounding statements' of which McCulloch complained a few years later.[1] Deacon Hume or Bowring assumed figures for the average consumption of meat or corn in this country, and they assumed figures for the amount by which the price of corn in England was raised by the corn law: Bowring thought it was by 5*s*. a quarter and Deacon Hume by 10*s*. a quarter. Then by multiplication they arrived, Deacon Hume at the figure of £36 million, plus an additional £10–20 million produced by the prohibition on the entry of foreign meat and cattle. The preference for colonial sugar produced another £3½ million.[2] These estimates, being striking and easily memorable, had a prominent place in the speeches and articles which gave publicity to the work of this committee, and were widely quoted, thereby diverting attention from the deficiencies of official knowledge.

The Board of Trade's case for a revision of the tariff, except as far as it was concerned with retaliation, rested on the threat to Britain's ability to compete in export markets on equal terms with rivals. But on a question which aroused so much interest and which was of such importance to their general thesis, the evidence that Britain was losing markets to rivals remained vague. It was stated that in cotton hosiery the Saxons had 'taken pretty nearly all the foreign markets from us'. There were also references to Saxon exports of woollen cloth. United States merchants bought these goods extensively, not only for their home market, but also for re-export to Central and South America and the Far East. As well as this there were complaints, which are also recorded in a consular report of 1838, of American competition in cheap cotton cloth in the same markets.[3] The free-traders on the committee, more anxious

[1] *Literature of Political Economy* (London, 1845), p. 340. He was not alone in this criticism: Lord Monteagle, who had been Chancellor of the Exchequer from 1835 to 1839, wrote in Jan. 1841 to McVey Napier of the 'monstrous evidence given (I am sorry to say by official men) before the committee on customs duties. Of these the great delinquent was and is McGregor who ventures the extraordinary assertion . . . that duties and prohibitions impose a charge equal to £100 millions. The printer's devil himself ought to have been able to detect so obvious a statement' (B.M. Add. MSS. 34,621, f. 488).

[2] Their estimates of the 'taxation' imposed by the corn laws varied widely, Bowring assessing it at £11 million, Deacon Hume at £36 million, and J. B. Smith at £90 million, which should have encouraged the public to treat them with some reserve.

[3] *Select Committee on Import Duties*, questions 332, 1672–6, 1716–22, 2000–3; B.T. 1/349, consular report dated 15 Dec. 1838 (Ouseley).

to consider the implications of this situation, did not call for the necessary statements of fact—such, for example, as a comparison of the value of American and British exports of cotton cloth, and of Saxon and British cotton hosiery, to these regions over a period of years. Whether such statistics as were available in the Board could have been broken down in sufficient detail to make these comparisons is not known, but the attempt was not made.[1] The complaints about Saxon competition in the United States may well have been traceable to particular circumstances in 1840. A manufacturer of worsted hosiery from Leicester, Joseph Whetstone, stated that the difficulties of the hosiery trade as a whole had begun in 1837 with the 'entire absence of American demand'.[2] Such circumstances might well have encouraged exaggerated fears of Saxon competition. In the Board of Trade, the only figures of declared values of exports combined cotton hosiery, lace, and small wares, and these showed a slight fall over the decade 1830–40, from an annual average of £1,195,000 in the years 1830–4 to £1,191,000 in the years 1835–9.[3] How far this could be attributed to Saxon competition remained unproven.

While the evidence of damage done so far might be inconclusive, it was possible to speak of an impending danger:

> We place ourselves at the risk of being surpassed by the manufactures in other countries; and as soon as it happens, if ever the day should arrive, that we should be put to a severe trial as to our manufacturing power, I can hardly doubt that the prosperity of the country will recede much faster than it has gone forward. . . . I do not think the advantages [of British capital and skill] are such that we can rely upon them for ever.[4]

[1] After 1834 the imports and exports of Saxony are included in those of the Zollverein as a whole in the official published statistics. In any case they did not separate cotton hosiery from other cotton goods (Dieterici, op. cit.). Porter quotes statistics of the value of total imports and exports of the United States in the *Progress of the Nation* (p. 418), but it is not known whether the Board possessed information about individual commodities.

[2] *Select Committee on Import Duties*, questions 3336, 3388. He said that the Saxons were not yet competing in worsted hosiery. The *Report on the Condition of the Framework Knitters*, *Parliamentary Papers*, 1845, xv, gave two reasons for distress: changes in fashion since 1800, and the increasing popularity, both at home and abroad, of cheap cut-up (unfashioned) hosiery, compared with the old wrought (fashioned) hosiery. As in Spitalfields, foreign competition was not the sole explanation. Cf. pp. 165–6 above.

[3] Porter, op. cit., pp. 368–71.

[4] *Select Committee on Import Duties*, questions 1198, 1203 (evidence of J. D. Hume).

As with the threat of retaliation, it was easier to outline the possible consequences of a policy of high protection than to produce concrete evidence that British trade had yet been damaged.

It remains to consider the attitude of the Board to the various general objections which might have been made to their thesis. Some of these objections were not raised in 1840, and others were not discussed with any thoroughness, but they were all familiar protectionist lines of argument which can be found in pamphlets and parliamentary debates of the eighteen-forties.[1]

There were first, those objections which were grounded in national politics. One of these has already been touched on in the preceding narrative, that is, the argument that imperial preference, even if its effects on the mother country were damaging, should be maintained in the interests of imperial unity if it were necessary to the welfare of the colonies. To a large extent the evidence of the Board side-stepped this argument by holding that both colonies and mother country would gain from the changes which they were proposing. Where the interests of colonies and mother country were admitted to be in conflict, that is over the production problems of free-labour sugar, Deacon Hume was prepared to allow the admissibility of a claim for protection. Neither he nor Porter adopted an anti-colonial position.

In the second place it was frequently argued in the eighteen-forties that protection to agriculture was necessary in the interests of self-sufficiency in time of war. This question was raised once, in the examination of Bowring: he expressed the point of view which later became associated with Cobden that 'you could get no security for peace equal to the extension of our commercial relations'.[2] Elsewhere there is no discussion of the argument: Deacon Hume's article on the corn laws in the *British and Foreign Review* and the H. B. T. *Letters*, both of which deal at length with the expressed claims for protection of the landed interest, both ignore the question, and it may be possible that it was a point of view more commonly expressed in the eighteen-forties than it was earlier.[3]

A second important category of objections related to the value of the tariff as a bargaining weapon in negotiation with foreign

[1] Cf. D. Walker-Smith, *The Protectionist Case in the Eighteen-Forties.*

[2] *Select Committee on Import Duties*, question 874.

[3] J. S. Mill describes this argument as one which was much used in the corn-law controversy (*Principles of Political Economy*, ed. Ashley, London, 1909, p. 920).

countries—an objection which was put forward with particular vigour by Disraeli in the eighteen-forties. Peel also, in his Budget proposals of 1842, explicitly excluded from alteration those duties which might be the subject of bargaining in the commercial negotiations which were about to be undertaken.[1] The same objection might be made to the abandonment of agricultural protection: a country dependent on imported food was in a weak bargaining position. This is also a point of view to which reference has already been made: the officials of the Board were indifferent to such arguments since their experience of negotiation had strengthened their theoretical objections to commercial treaties. Even if there was no question of granting exclusive privileges by either party, such treaties were not good policy: 'I have disliked all treating in the matter: I would take what I wanted, and leave them to find the value of our custom.' Again, Hume said: 'I think it is unwise to do that upon stipulation, upon certain terms, which upon any terms it would be better for you to do yourselves. But my chief objections to treating are, first the risk of refusal, and the repugnance to act after refusal; and next that in the case of compliance, the people of the other country think that their government has been duped into a bad bargain.' Such objections might well have been derived from the experience of commercial negotiation, especially with France, during the eighteen-thirties.[2] A freer admission of imports would in the end lead to an expansion of exports to some quarter.

The theory that protection, while it was damaging in general, was permissible in the case of infant industries, was current in England at this time, and it was put to Bowring by Tufnell.[3] Bowring replied that while protection would undoubtedly enable new industries to establish themselves, it was doubtful whether industries so established would be able to survive without it. The question had little reference to those British industries which had been shown to enjoy a manufacturing superiority, but it was possible to cite the Spitalfields silk industry as one which had been established under the shelter of protection in the eighteenth century and was still

[1] Monypenny and Buckle, *Life of Benjamin Disraeli* (London, 1912), vol. ii, pp. 133–45; Peel, *Speeches*, vol. iii, p. 879.

[2] *Select Committee on Import Duties*, questions 1158, 1173. Cf. pp. 123 and 132 above.

[3] Ibid., questions 709–10. Tufnell was an impartial and official member of the committee; cf. p. 72 above.

claiming protection. The argument had greater applicability in the colonies, notably in the Canadian timber trade, but it was not used in this connexion.[1] It was also relevant in the discussion of manufacturing development on the Continent, where the theory had strong support. The Board of Trade, with their strong convictions of the bad effects of protection on incentives, were at pains to show that the success of manufactures abroad could not be ascribed to protection, though this was a thesis which it was difficult to prove.[2]

Finally there was the objection which was of particular importance at a time when Chartism was emerging as a major political problem, that is, the objection that reduction of the tariff, whether on manufactures or on corn, might create unemployment, at any rate in the short run. The debates on 'distress' of 1829 or 1833 and the investigations of the Board of Trade's statistical department had shown that the Government recognized the political importance of unemployment, although they might be perplexed by its causes. In a letter apparently written in 1832, Deacon Hume had written: 'And yet the people employed in the factories have all along been earning a fair livelihood. Our difficulties are with the *un*employed. . . .'[3] On the effects on employment of the proposed tariff changes in 1840, he agreed that the immediate results might be unemployment in some trades, 'but I feel perfectly confident that the general prosperity of the country should be increased; although, in the earlier stages of the removal of these duties, some few branches might be distressed and some lost'. McGregor spoke in the same way, but added a reference, which was perhaps not seriously intended, to compensation, '. . . it would be the cheapest purchase in the world to pension off all who would actually be injured, such as the always protected, but certainly the most

[1] It might also perhaps have been applied to the growing exports of Australian wool to Britain at this time, which were admitted duty-free, compared with duties of ½*d*. and 1*d*. a pound, according to quality, on foreign wool.

[2] They argued that Switzerland, and before 1834 Saxony, had had low tariffs, and that there had been opposition in Saxony to entry into the Zollverein, but Bowring did not mention that this had come from merchants dealing in foreign goods, and not from textile manufacturers, or that complaints in Britain of Saxon competition had arisen since 1834. Similarly there was now little protection for the French silk industry, but at the time of its establishment under Colbert, imports of foreign silks had been prohibited (*Select Committee on Import Duties*, questions 290 ff., 366 ff., 721).

[3] Badham, op. cit., p. 137.

wretched of all manufacturers that I have ever seen, the Spitalfields silk-weavers'.[1] They held, in general, that new opportunities for employment would take the place of the old, and took a considerable mobility of capital and labour for granted. In this Ricardian context a general discussion of the forces determining the level of employment in the country would not have been expected, but it is surprising that more consideration was not given to the immediate consequences of a process whereby 'some few branches might be distressed and some lost' and 'the export will follow in some form or other'.[2]

In attacking the British tariff, the Board of Trade's position was, politically, a very strong one. They were mostly dealing with problems within the proper scope of their own department: they did not merely have to offer advice to another department. They were speaking on questions on which the public would be prepared to accept their views as authoritative. There can be no doubt of the energy and conviction with which they approached their task.

The difference between their work and that of the modern civil servant is self-evident. The framing of general lines of policy today is the work of the party conference, of party leaders, and political publicists: it is assumed that the Civil Service is non-political. The Civil Service works on a policy once it is laid down by someone else and has received the endorsement of the Cabinet: its job is to find out the facts and limitations in any scheme. Where the modern Civil Service exercises political power is in the way in which it puts schemes into practice and administers them. And, in economic questions, the fact that it has often earlier and fuller information than other people, gives it a position of influence.

The conditions governing the work of Deacon Hume and McGregor were the opposite of this. Neither of the political parties appeared before the electorate with a general programme for economic policy, rather they had loyalties to economic interests which were politically represented. In the absence of a coherent economic programme, put forward by the parties, the task of framing one, and publicizing it, fell to the civil servants: the sweep-

[1] *Select Committee on Import Duties*, question 1081.

[2] There was little parliamentary discussion of this question in 1840–2. Fears of the effect of free trade on employment in England were, however, frequently expressed by the Chartists.

ing generalizations about 'taxation' or about retaliatory tariffs are best understood as part of such a campaign.

It is necessary to make some distinction between the evidence given by the officials of the Board to the committee of 1840, and their views as they were expressed on other occasions. The handling of witnesses by Joseph Hume, Villiers, and Thornely gave every encouragement to exaggeration, and the protectionists, or the neutrals, on the committee were not of the calibre to question such exaggerations effectively. The general tone of the evidence is intelligible in the general political circumstances of 1840. For the ten years since Huskisson had died, Poulett Thomson and his assistants had been battling, on the whole unsuccessfully, in a predominantly hostile environment. In Parliament the groups opposed to change showed themselves to be more effectively organized than those who might have supported it. In international negotiation they had contended, in many countries, with a long-standing fear and suspicion of Britain; and they had been most successful when other countries had been anxious to enlist British diplomatic support. The refusal of the Melbourne Government to inquire into the corn laws, and the strong position of the Radicals, in relation to the Whigs, in 1840 offered an exceptional opportunity. In these circumstances, the officials of the Board grasped the opportunity of appealing directly to the public with a strongly expressed statement of their views: to give evidence before a Select Committee, the proceedings of which were published, was known as a sound means of spreading a point of view.[1]

They had not the administrative powers or the technical knowledge which a modern government department has at its disposal in dealing with such questions. The only example where the Board can be shown to have had the power to develop a policy by administrative action was in the licensing of the export of machinery. They were dependent on parliamentary sanction for the particular measures they took. It is obvious that such major changes as the

[1] On a suggestion that there should be a parliamentary inquiry on British trade in the Levant, Palmerston wrote: 'I see no practical object to be gained by such an inquiry but I do see a great loss of valuable time that would ensue from it to me and the President of the Board of Trade. It might be very amusing to a number of idle gentlemen about Town to come down and speak pamphlets in the Committee in answer to preconcerted questions and thus to have their work printed at the expense of the public, but I should oppose any such inquiry if moved by others and certainly shall not move it myself' (Webster, op. cit., p. 551).

abolition of imperial preference on sugar and timber, or the repeal of the corn laws, could only come through Parliament; but if the history of the tariff question is contrasted with, say, the history of price control in the last war, it is also obvious that many of the things which required legislation then would be handled today by Statutory Rules and Orders. Deacon Hume might have criticized the tariff less had he had the scope of a modern civil servant.

The officials of the Board could not offer the precise information expected of the Civil Service today. They had at many points knowledge and experience which the general public did not share. Nevertheless, it was not enough on which to base the assertions they made; it was not kept systematically up to date, though this might not in any case have been possible. Where they can be criticized is in their unwillingness to state publicly the limitations of their knowledge, and in their failure at times to produce information which did not suit their general thesis. They tended to offer sweeping generalizations accompanied by inadequate information—neither systematic and dispassionate statements of the economic theory on which they were working, nor full summaries of such official information as was known. This was perhaps most clearly shown in the general discussion of the threat of competition from Saxony and its implications for British tariff policy: they had no first-hand knowledge of Saxon industrial conditions, and little of the actual scale of competition in America, but they constructed an elaborate edifice of inferences.[1] In such discussions Bowring and McGregor were the most easily tempted into dogmatism: Deacon Hume was able to produce facts and opinions which did not fit the general argument,[2] and Porter kept consistently to the knowledge at his disposal.

At the other extreme, because of the very limited scale of the committee's inquiries, they had no opportunity of giving adequate evidence on one subject on which from their official experience they were uniquely qualified to speak, that is on the development of British commercial relations with foreign countries. Though there was much reference to retaliation as a reason for tariff reform in Britain, there was no general statement given of the way in

[1] McGregor and Bowring had both paid short visits to Saxony, but had hardly had the opportunity to learn much about wage-rates and the cost of living. A similar criticism may be made of their handling of the question of imperial preference.

[2] Cf. pp. 193, 198 above.

which tariff policies on the Continent, or in America, had developed since 1815, or of the extent to which particular trades in England were affected by them.[1]

The second serious weakness in the evidence which was collected lay in the inadequate attention given to the probable reactions of the affected interests, both in this country and in the colonies. Here again the scale and manner of the committee's inquiries were chiefly to blame: no attempt was made to collect a representative cross-section of witnesses,[2] no sugar-planters or Canadian timber exporters were heard. But the officials of the Board, McGregor in particular, were also to blame in making dogmatic statements about opinion in the industries concerned, when their evidence could not be checked by the questioning of other witnesses, nor supported by clear documentary evidence.

But with these qualifications their evidence remains the fullest discussion of British tariff legislation and its effects, on the eve of Peel's adoption of free-trade measures. It was at its strongest in showing the administrative inconvenience of the existing structure, and in suggesting that it was most likely that the revenue would gain from reduction in the preferential duties on sugar, coffee, and timber. Here, however, by offering estimates of the gain to the revenue, they encouraged the opinion that the annual deficits might be wiped out without recourse to new alternative forms of taxation.[3] They also argued effectively that a number of major industries—coal, iron, pottery, cotton, and wool—were in no need of protection, though to some extent this must be qualified by the evidence collected in the following year on the export of machinery. In dealing with silk, they could show that the industry as a whole had expanded since the time of Huskisson, though it could still be argued that some sections would suffer from further reduction of import duties.[4] On the interests of the landowners, a subject which was not strictly within the scope of this committee but which inevitably underlay the whole discussion, their evidence was perhaps conflicting: Deacon Hume argued that repeal of the corn laws would bring a great reduction in wheat prices and in the area of wheat cultivation, while at other times Porter and Jacob held

[1] Cf. pp. 158 ff. above.

[2] For the selection of witnesses, see p. 73 above.

[3] See pp. 149–52 above.

[4] See pp. 168–70 above.

that repeal would make little difference, and stressed the advantages which would be derived from more regular trading relations with eastern Europe.[1] The Navigation Laws also did not come within the committee's terms of reference, though they presented a related problem: here the Board emphasized that Huskisson's reciprocity treaties had not been the main cause of the shipowners' difficulties in the eighteen-twenties.[2] On the question of imperial preference, they suggested that the timber duties were of importance to one section only of the Canadians, but they agreed that reduction of the sugar duties would be a serious blow to the sugar producers of the West Indies.[3]

On the other hand, in discussing the effects of the tariff on Britain's export trade, they could not make as solid a case as they would have wished. They could point to general tendencies, but they could not show beyond controversy the extent of the damage which was being done.

Their evidence was coloured, not only by an economic theory, but also by their social and official attitudes. They felt it necessary to safeguard the interests of the industrial and commercial middle class to which they belonged, even if the spokesmen of that class were themselves less concerned with them. They showed, in Mallet's words, 'an abhorrence of the aristocracy and landlords and monopolisers of property'.[4] The same middle-class aggressiveness was shown by the leaders of the league in the eighteen-forties, who went far beyond the technicalities of sliding scales and corn imports and attacked all evidences of landlordly power—borough-mongering, tenancies-at-will, the game laws, the condition of rural cottages. Among the officials of the Board of Trade this feeling was further coloured by official experience. Deacon Hume's irritation with the General Shipowners' Society has been mentioned.[5] The same point was made by F. W. Hirst.[6] He described a conversation which he had had at the end of the last century with Sir R. W. Rawson, who had been a clerk at the Board in the thirties and forties. He had vivid memories of the atmosphere at the office at that time, and described how the protests and deputations of the protectionists were considered an intolerable nuisance.

[1] See pp. 171–4 ff. above.
[2] See pp. 177–8 ff. above.
[3] See pp. 187–8, 193 ff. above.
[4] Cf. p. 25 above.
[5] Cf. pp. 174–6 above.
[6] *Gladstone as Financier and Economist* (London, 1931), p. 44.

From a political point of view it is important to establish whether the work of the Select Committee on Import Duties was influential, before the scale of its inquiries is criticized. The evidence which was collected was widely used in propaganda and argument: McCulloch described it as 'a sort of arsenal to which those who wish to declaim on the oppressiveness of English taxation and the ruinous operation of restrictions resort to supply themselves with facts and arguments'.[1] If it can be shown that no other comparable inquiry was undertaken between 1840 and 1842,[2] then its shortcomings are important, and suggest that Peel's Budget of 1842 was more of a leap in the dark than has been supposed.

[1] J. R. McCulloch, *Literature of Political Economy* (London, 1845), p. 340.
[2] See p. 228 below.

13

THE BOARD OF TRADE AND THE BUDGETS OF 1841 AND 1842

IT remains to discuss how far the adoption of free-trade measures, first by the Whigs in the spring of 1841, and then by the Tories in 1842, was influenced by the discussions which have been described in previous chapters. The contents of the Report of the Select Committee on Import Duties may easily be guessed. They pointed out that the British tariff hindered the process of international tariff bargaining, and that it raised prices in England. In this they gave full support and publicity to the wilder statements of the Board of Trade on 'taxation'; which, whatever their limitations might be, were none the less admirable as propaganda. Of equal importance was the argument that a reduction in the rates of duty on foreign sugar, coffee, and timber would probably increase their yield to the revenue, at a time when annual deficits were causing public anxiety.

The report of this committee cannot be considered as a dispassionate assessment of the situation: two of the Conservative members, Sir Charles Douglas and Aaron Chapman, tried to move an amendment that the committee did not 'feel that they should be justified in expressing any opinion founded on the impression it is calculated to create' and that they should be reappointed in the following session, but they were outvoted by a small phalanx of free-traders—Sir Henry Parnell, C. P. Villiers, Thomas Thornely, and Joseph Hume.

The free-trading members of the committee and the witnesses from the Board combined to give as much publicity as possible to their findings. In this they were acting in a manner in no way unusual at this time: Graham Wallas, in his *Life of Francis Place*,[1] gives an account of the way in which the findings of the Select Committee on the Combination Laws were organized and disseminated. The Place papers give a further example of the same

[1] London, 4th ed., 1925, chap. viii.

technique: they contain a correspondence on a publicity campaign for the findings of the Select Committee on Rates of Postage of 1837.[1]

In organizing this campaign they cast their net wide. The officials of the Board themselves produced publications. McGregor brought out a book on the subject, *Commercial and Financial Legislation of Europe and America*, and a pamphlet, *The Preference Interests*.[2] There exists also a pamphlet ascribed to Porter, *The Many sacrificed to the Few*. Deacon Hume's evidence was printed separately, and published, but not until 1842.[3]

Sir Henry Parnell introduced the subject to a different reading public: in September 1840 he sent an article to the *Edinburgh Review*, writing: 'The case is so strong a one, that I think it must lead to some early and useful legislation on the subject: and I am anxious that my article should appear in the January number of the Edinburgh Review so that it may be in the hands of government and of Members of Parliament at the beginning of the Session.' In a later letter he added: 'our uninformed statesmen on these matters learn all they know from reading popular and clearly written essays that bring forward a limited number of strong facts followed by clear and concise reasonings'.[4]

The dissemination of the committee's findings to the press fell to Joseph Hume. Prentice records: 'I published in my paper [the *Manchester Times*] a considerable portion of the evidence, selected for me by Mr. Hume', and he added significantly, 'and even in Manchester, where the bearings of the Corn Law had been carefully studied, few persons took an interest in the investigation'.[5] The *Manchester Guardian* had welcomed the appointment of the Select Committee in May (unlike most papers, which ignored it) but had said nothing about the subject since then. In November 1840 it came out with a long series of articles, which concentrated their attack on the sugar and coffee duties.[6] The greatest effort of

[1] B.M. Add. MSS. 35,151.

[2] This pamphlet is signed M. B. T., a parody of Deacon Hume's more famous H. B. T. *Letters*.

[3] *The Evidence of J. D. Hume before the Select Committee on Import Duties, 1839* [*sic*], Manchester, 1842.

[4] McVey Napier papers, B.M. Add. MSS. 34,621, ff. 287, 640. The publication of *Financial Reform* had been similarly timed—it appeared in the spring of 1830.

[5] Prentice, op. cit., vol. i, p. 164: see *Manchester Times* of 24 Oct. 1840.

[6] *Manchester Guardian*, issues of 18 and 28 Nov., and 2 and 9 Dec. 1840.

Hume and his friends went, however, to the preparation of an article for publication in the *Spectator*, a weekly which supported the Radicals, and particularly the colonial reformers. Hume approached the Manchester Chamber of Commerce asking them if they would share in the printing costs of the article, which appeared on 2 January 1840, and was widely circulated. A copy was sent to Francis Place by Hume, who drew attention to the 'admirable evidence' which had been obtained from the Board of Trade.[1] Four days earlier the Post Office had drawn the Board's attention to the fact that fourteen copies of the *Spectator*, sent out from the Board's office and 'addressed to persons abroad', had been detained as they were not properly franked. One of these is preserved among the papers of the French Ministry of Commerce.[2]

With the meeting of Parliament and the publication of the article in the *Spectator*, the doctrines of the free-traders began to reach a wider public: its substance, or that of Parnell's article, was reproduced in Whig or Radical papers in London and the provinces; in particular the *Morning Chronicle* in March launched a propaganda campaign in favour of tariff reform.[3] On the 20th of February Joseph Hume, Thornely, Villiers, Ewart, and other free-trade Members of Parliament, held a meeting at the Thatched House Tavern, at which they passed resolutions recommending the adoption of the Import Duties' Committee's proposals, and agreed to send these to Lord Melbourne, and to form themselves into a committee for the printing and circulating of their resolutions. At the same time, provincial meetings were held for the same general purpose, but it is noticeable that they were not very many, and were all in or near Manchester—at Salford, Ashton-under-Lyne, and Manchester itself.[4] The Brazilian Association of Liverpool sent in a memorial to the Board of Trade, but else-

[1] J. B. Smith MSS., Hume to Smith, 29 Oct.; Place papers, B.M. Add. MSS. 35,151, f. 291.

[2] B.T. 1/369; Archives nationales, F[12] 6210. In this same bundle there is a copy of the *Mémorial Bordelais*, carrying a closely similar article. It may be guessed that this paper had been sent a copy too.

[3] E. Halévy, *History of the English People* (ed. of 1950), vol. iii, p. 346; *Liverpool Mercury*, 22 Jan., *Manchester Guardian*, 27 Jan., *Leeds Mercury*, 12 June 1841.

[4] Lord Melbourne's letters, Joseph Hume to Melbourne, 24 Apr. 1841. The Members of Parliament on this committee included James Morrison, the partner of John Dillon who had given evidence on import duties. See p. 74 above. *Manchester Guardian*, 17 Feb., 17 Mar., and 24 Apr. 1841.

where it does not seem that the campaign evoked an impressive response.

It has been suggested that the Select Committee on Import Duties was appointed in 1840 as a result of a particular political and economic situation, which gave the parliamentary Radicals exceptional opportunities, and which made their general thesis relevant. The situation of 1840–1 may be compared with that of 1830 with which this study began. In 1830 there had been important sections of opinion in both parties, who were in favour of reimposing an income tax as a means of reducing other taxes, but there had been less agreement about the taxes which it would be most desirable to repeal. But circumstances had not been favourable: there had been opposition from some political leaders in both parties, and neither party, in the Budgets of 1830 or 1831, had been strong enough to tackle the question. Nor was there the kind of demand in the country which would have forced a ministry into a new fiscal policy, for public interest in 1830 and 1831 was focused on parliamentary reform, which the Tories resisted, and which the Whigs were compelled to introduce.

Ten years later the situation had changed. Among the leaders of the Whigs in 1840 it does not appear that the idea of an income tax aroused strong feelings either of desire or of aversion, but they were once again, as a party, too weak to introduce a controversial measure. Among the electorate there was no longer pressure for political reform; on the contrary, the division between middle-class and working-class aims was becoming a familiar political theme. A variety of political or economic agitations occupied the public mind, Chartism, the rights of nonconformists, Ashley's Select Committee on the Factory Acts,[1] the Select Committee on Banks of Issue, and the Anti-Corn Law League. There were thus a number of questions which could be adopted by a political party which was anxious to reinforce its declining popularity.

There can be little doubt that of these the 'free trade movement' had grown in strength between 1839 and 1841, but this movement needs some analysis, and cannot be simply equated with the Anti-Corn Law League. The league itself was growing, but it is clear from its internal history that it did not immediately become a powerful political force.[2] Cobden, for instance, did not enter

[1] This was appointed on 31 Mar. 1840 (*Hansard*, 3rd ser., vol. 52, col. 859).

[2] The letter-book of the Anti-Corn Law League (in Manchester Public

Parliament till 1841, and this was the first year in which its pamphlet literature was really extensive. In February 1841 it tried to run a league candidate, J. B. Smith, against the Whig candidate at a by-election in Walsall. Smith was defeated, but the episode shows an advance in the league's political ambitions.[1] The league, however, did not enlist the support of all friends of a reform of the tariff, and perhaps it did not wish to: both Cobden and Joseph Hume were anxious to keep separate the corn-law movement and the movement against the import duties generally.[2] On the other side, the *Manchester Guardian*, which in the league's view held the right opinion on both these questions, expressed 'a growing disinclination to identify ourselves with the proceedings of the Anti-Corn Law League', in criticism of the league's behaviour at Walsall. Smith complained of the apathy of Manchester merchants in May. There were districts where economic issues other than the corn laws were dominant, and where even the league found progress difficult.[3] But this does not necessarily mean that there was support for industrial protection; rather it suggests indifference to the question.

There is more substantial evidence of the attitude of the working classes, as far as it was expressed in Chartism. As the league grew more powerful, and as Chartism came increasingly under the domination of O'Connor and the *Northern Star*, the two movements came into open conflict. Whereas it had been possible in 1838 or 1839 for people such as Ebenezer Elliott to support both campaigns, it was now necessary for Chartists to establish exactly their point of view, and this was done at countless meetings, whether Chartist meetings, or meetings of the league which were attacked from the floor. The arguments adduced were reported in the *Northern Star*, and were as varied as the different strands in Chartism. But it is noticeable that agricultural protectionism had very little support. Many speakers argued that repeal would be a benefit, but only if it were accompanied by the Charter. A Parliament elected by univer-

Library) shows that in 1839–41 the league had difficulty in supporting its paid lecturers.

[1] Halévy, op. cit., pp. 340–1, discusses this episode.

[2] J. B. Smith MSS., letters from Hume dated 25 Apr. 1840, and from Cobden dated 28 Mar. 1841.

[3] *Manchester Guardian*, 16 Jan. 1841. Cobden and others complained of the response they got in Birmingham, Liverpool, Stockport, and Warrington (Smith MSS.).

sal suffrage alone would protect the working classes against the consequences of free trade, which they feared in the same way as they feared the development of machinery. No one could tell what the consequences would be, but legislation, whether on wages, on factory hours, or on taxation, would be necessary to assure the working class of a share in the benefits of free trade—most Chartist speakers believed that free trade would bring some benefit.

The situation in 1840 differed also from that of 1830 in that a radical change in taxation, which before had been merely desirable, was now an urgent necessity, given the need to balance the Budget every year. The series of deficits which had begun in 1838 continued. In the spring of 1840 a deficit of £1,851,000 was reported. Baring's Budget, introduced on 15 May 1840 (shortly after the appointment of the Select Committee on Import Duties), proposed a 5 per cent. increase in the Customs and Excise duties and a 10 per cent. increase in the Assessed Taxes.[1] This proposal (with a minor alteration of the system whereby it was levied on timber)[2] passed through the Commons without difficulty.

This debate is of some interest, since it was the first Budget for many years to make general increases in import duties. It was attacked strongly by Joseph Hume and by Ewart: both held that bigger death duties on landed property would offer a better way of bridging the gap between revenue and expenditure. Labouchère, in a speech which failed to convince the House, supported the proposals, and held that they would have little effect in checking the consumption of the goods affected. But it is interesting to notice that Peel, who was later to be so scornful of Whig finance, offered no criticism of the increased duties. He stressed again the paramount need to reduce the deficiency, but made no suggestion of better ways of doing this.[3]

During the following year, the situation did not improve. In September Baring wrote despondently to Melbourne:

> The revenue looks ill enough.... As to the Customs there is no remedy but patience. The harvest is good—Trade seems reviving in the manufacturing districts and when the bustle for your foreign affairs blows over I should hope things will be better—but we have had a most

[1] *Hansard*, vol. 54, col. 121.

[2] Ibid., col. 956. The increased duty on timber was changed to a flat rate of 1*s*. 6*d*. per load, in order that the gap between the Baltic and Canadian rates of duty should not be increased.

[3] Ibid., col. 156.

unfortunate year in every way and the wonder is that things are not worse —a bad harvest—money difficulties—America—bustle with France—high price of tea coffee sugar—deficient revenue and new taxes—there is nothing but patience left.[1]

As the year wore on it became clear that there was no hope that the increased duties would fill the gap: in the event the 5 per cent. increase in the Customs and Excise produced less than the increase of 5 per cent. hoped for: the increase in the Assessed Taxes had, however, yielded more than Baring's estimate.[2] In addition, as the result of the introduction of the Penny Post in January 1840, the postage revenue dropped from £1·6 million in 1839 to £0·5 million in 1840. By January 1841, the time of the propaganda campaign which has just been described, the future of the Government's fiscal policy had become an urgent matter.

At the beginning of December 1840 a back-bencher in the Conservative party had reported to Goulburn, on the effects of the Committee on Import Duties, that 'an elaborate Memoir' had been prepared and circulated to the Cabinet.[3] A memorandum which answers to this description, but which is undated and unsigned, survives among Melbourne's papers. This memorandum put the case for a revision of the tariff along the lines which the Committee on Import Duties had recommended: it stressed the theory that the revenue could be increased by a reduction and rearrangement of duties: it spoke of the need to reduce costs of production and export prices. The memorandum proposed drastic reductions of the sugar duties and the timber duties, and enunciated the principle that the British consumer and the British revenue should be considered rather than the interests of the colonies. In all this the similarity with the findings of the Select Committee on Import Duties is obvious. The influence of the committee can be shown by the fact that these views were the opposite of those put forward by Whig Ministers in the Budget debate of the preceding year.

The memorandum also made it clear that the political motives, to which the Tories attributed the Whigs' conversion to free trade in 1841, were in fact prominent in their thoughts. To adopt tariff reform as part of their political programme, and to begin an attack

[1] Lord Melbourne's letters, F. T. Baring to Melbourne, 2 Sept. 1840.
[2] *Hansard*, vol. 60, col. 432.
[3] Peel papers, B.M. Add. MSS. 40,333, f. 427.

on the imperial preferences, would not only perhaps offer a solution to the fiscal problem, but also attract support in the country. Since the passing of the Reform Act, the Whigs had been in need of a programme which would attract the support of the industrial and commercial middle class. Such questions as the reform of the Irish church divided rather than increased their supporters: 'All cards have been played and played in vain and the question of *immediate* victory or defeat sinks into insignificance.'[1] It was not until after their defeat in the Commons on the sugar duties on 18 May that the Whigs decided on a dissolution and general election, but they were nevertheless thinking earlier of their long-term strategy: they should emerge as the party pledged to the support of free trade in order to counteract the revival of the Tory party. A general revision of the tariff, on the principles which had already received publicity, was a more dignified procedure than direct concession to the league. In May Sydenham wrote home from Canada to Russell, giving strong support to the Budget proposals: 'It does *not* meddle with religious prejudices; it does *not* relate to Ireland—it does *not* touch any of the theoretical questions of Government on which parties have been so long divided—it *is* a new Flag to fight under and must prevail eventually, whatever be its success now.'[2] In the spring of 1841 there were signs that Radical support at by-elections was going to Tory candidates,[3] and the adoption of free-trade measures was an attempt to win back their support.

An attack on imperial preference was also supported by Baring, though he 'disclaimed any connection with the agitation which I see is done in our own papers—and more particularly in the last week'. He suggested that there were 'three courses,—a loan—an income tax—an attack on the sugar and timber duties. The deficit and large increases of the estimates . . . will I apprehend render some strong measure necessary and make it impossible to scrape through with a few taxes on small matters.'[4] Saying nothing about the possibility of an income tax, he went on to press Melbourne to force the Cabinet to an early decision on the sugar duties: 'I am fairly entitled to ask whether the Cabinet are prepared to act

[1] Lord Melbourne's letters, loc. cit.

[2] Russell papers, P.R.O. 30/22/4, Sydenham to Russell, 25 May 1841.

[3] B. Kemp, 'The General Election of 1841', in *History*, N.S., vol. 37, June 1952.

[4] Lord Melbourne's letters, Baring to Melbourne, 19 Jan. 1841.

according to the principle which it has been my object to act upon namely to bring up the revenue to the expenditure—or are they determined to leave a revenue deficient even for the last year's expenditure with increased estimates of one million—and to cram the gap up by a loan.'[1]

Baring, who had strongly criticized the irresponsibility of introducing the Penny Post in 1839, was serious in his belief that the gap could be bridged by an attack on the sugar and timber duties—it is not necessary to assume that the Whigs were wholly cynical in their free-trade measures of 1841. In the beginning of February they introduced their first measure, a proposal to equalize the duties on East India and West India rum, into the Commons. This aroused the suspicions of the Conservatives, though it was something which had been brought forward at intervals, by Ewart, since 1833. At the same time a measure, which was never actually introduced, was being prepared to reform and simplify the British tariff, tackling in particular those minor duties which yielded little revenue.[2] On 12 March resolutions dealing with colonial tariffs were introduced by Labouchère. Again they followed the advice offered by Deacon Hume before the Committee on Import Duties: they proposed to reduce import duties and abolish prohibitions in the North American and West Indian colonies. On 5 April they passed without a division,[3] and the way was now open for an attack on colonial preferences in the British market.

This came in the Budget introduced by Baring on 30 April.[4] It attacked not only the sugar and timber duties, as Baring had wished, but also the corn laws, for which a fixed duty of 8*s*. a quarter was proposed. For sugar, revised rates of 36*s*. and 24*s*. were proposed in place of the existing rates of 63*s*. and 24*s*. For timber the rates were to be 50*s*. and 20*s*. in place of the existing 55*s*. and 10*s*.

The similarity between these proposals and those of McGregor the year before are obvious, but it is difficult to guess the precise share which he and his colleagues had in the events leading to the adoption of this free-trade Budget. It has been shown that Baring himself had become converted to the view that the gap between revenue and expenditure could be narrowed, if not bridged, by an

[1] Lord Melbourne's letters, Baring to Melbourne, 19 Jan. 1841.
[2] The same to the same 8 Feb. 1841; *Hansard*, vol. 56, col. 204.
[3] Ibid., vol. 57, cols. 148, 883.
[4] Ibid., col. 1295.

attack on colonial preferences. The question concerned both the Board (in its handling of the East and West India rum duties, and in the reduction of colonial tariffs[1]) and the Treasury. McGregor and Le Marchant, whatever their influence may have been, were fully engaged in the preparation of the scheme, as was Sydenham.[2]

Against the Budget and its accompanying measures a variety of forces was arrayed: Ellice reported to Melbourne that 'in the city every man is for free trade if you will except his own—but that always the variety of monopolies affected by these general measures are a majority of malcontents against the minority of supporters of the Budget'.[3] Parliament received petitions for and against the corn laws. The sugar and timber interests protested: a number of petitions against the change were presented to the House of Lords in May from the West Indies.[4] Sydenham's letters home to Russell record his anxiety about the reactions of the Canadian timber trade: in April, before the Budget, he wrote that 'people will be grievously angry about the timber duties, and I shall have an uphill battle to fight about that. However I shall not shrink from that....' At the end of May he wrote that 'the People have taken the matter much more philosophically than was to be expected, but at Quebec, where the timber merchants reside, they are at boiling point'.[5] Parliament, the Board of Trade, and the Colonial Office, all received protests from both colonies.

In the long debate on the sugar duties of May, the Tory opposition found a further ally in the anti-slavery group: Ellice criticized Baring's failure to come to terms with Lushington and his supporters as one of the main mistakes of his party.[6] The debate hinged on two main subjects—the threat to the anti-slavery movement if any stimulus were given by Britain to the production of slave-grown sugar, which would occur if Brazilian sugar were admitted. On this question the former slave-owners and the anti-slavery members now made common cause. The second subject of debate was the fiscal irresponsibility of a ministry which one year

[1] These questions belonged properly to the Colonial Office, but it was the custom to consult the Board.

[2] Russell papers, P.R.O. 30/22/4, Sydenham to Russell, 25 Feb. 1841: 'Labouchère . . . will have heard from me through Le Marchant and McGregor.'

[3] Lord Melbourne's letters, Ellice to Melbourne, 15 May 1841.

[4] *Hansard*, vol. 58, col. 1.

[5] Russell papers, loc. cit., letters dated 12 Apr. and 25 May.

[6] Lord Melbourne's letters, loc. cit.

proposed to balance its Budget by increasing duties, and next year proposed to do the same thing by reducing them. In the course of this debate the work of the Select Committee on Import Duties came in for considerable criticism. The Tory members, Clerk and Douglas, made belated protests at its partiality: Ashburton described the evidence given by the Board as 'most extravagant, most exaggerated, and absurd'. Even Whigs with official positions, such as Lansdowne and Labouchère, admitted publicly some of these criticisms, though they defended the general doctrines which had been put forward.[1] On 18 May the ministry was defeated by 281 votes to 317. On 4 June it was again defeated, this time by 311 votes to 312.[2] On 23 June Parliament was dissolved.

In the general election which followed, Peel was returned with an undisputed majority, but it would be hard to deduce much from this about public opinion on the questions under discussion. It is certainly true that sugar, timber, corn, and the eleven hundred different rates of duty in the tariff figured largely in electioneering speeches on the Whig side, and that slavery and financial mismanagement were prominent in Tory speeches. But so many other issues, economic or otherwise, or questions of purely local politics or patronage, entered into the conduct of an election that general conclusions from its results are dangerous. But it is worth noticing that the Tories made gains in Lancashire, which was regarded as the centre of the Anti-Corn Law movement, as well as elsewhere. In Manchester the Whig majority dropped from 5,562 in 1837 to 1,483 in 1841. In Liverpool, where two Conservatives were returned in 1837 and in 1841, the Conservative majority was increased. In Wigan, where two Whigs had been returned in 1837, two Conservatives were returned in 1841. There was a conspicuous Conservative victory at Leeds, where in place of Edward Baines and Sir William Molesworth, who had been elected in 1837, two Conservatives were returned.[3] The results of this election would be very difficult to interpret without extended research, but it is clear that, in the centres which were likely to be chiefly affected by tariff changes, the Whig proposals of 1841 had not had a favourable effect on opinion.[4]

[1] *Hansard*, vol. 58, cols. 203, 435; vol. 57, cols. 516–18, 916.

[2] Ibid., vol. 58, cols. 667, 1241.

[3] Dod's *Parliamentary Companion*.

[4] Ibid. It was considered by some of the Anti-Corn Law party that a moderate fixed duty on corn, by removing some of the obvious difficulties of

In the last stage of this narrative, events moved quickly, but the Board of Trade had little direct hand in them. Peel was returned with a majority of 78, and thus had a freer hand to embark on important legislation than the Whigs had had for many years. He had two other assets, the knowledge that he could command support in the Lords, and the fact that most Conservatives, thanks to their fear of civil disorder and to their recognition of the fiscal problem, were disposed to approve of any economic measures he might introduce.[1]

On the other hand the Peel papers contain no indication that Peel, before he was returned to power, had given his attention to the tariff question. In the formation of his ministry there were no free-traders of the type which have been described in previous chapters. Ripon, who was considered to be a protectionist,[2] was made President of the Board of Trade; Gladstone became Vice-President. When he was offered the post he protested that he had no knowledge of trade and finance, and that he had spoken but once on such questions in the House, and once sat on a Select Committee on a trade question.[3] Nevertheless, this was a slight handicap to a person of Gladstone's intellectual power; and he quickly became the effective organizer of the department's work, under Ripon's nominal leadership, in much the same way as Poulett Thomson had been in the early years of the Whig Government. This is clear from the Peel papers: by November 1841 Gladstone was preparing memoranda for Peel on the main lines of the economic policy which he was to present to Parliament in the following session. (Peel's correspondence with Ripon, by contrast, deals more with the departmental problems of the Board, and less with the general strategy of the new ministry.)

Thus the officials of the Board lost the position of initiative which they had possessed since the death of Huskisson. Deacon Hume, who commanded the greatest respect, retired early in 1840 (before the appointment of the Select Committee on Import Duties), and he died in February 1842. Badham, his biographer, claims that in the last months of his life he was consulted by Peel

the existing scale, would make repeal more difficult. They were thus against the Whigs and their Budget (Kemp, op. cit.).

[1] Cf. Thomson's comment on p. 69 above.

[2] Greville, op. cit. vol. iv, p. 423 (19 Nov. 1841).

[3] C. S. Parker, *Sir Robert Peel from his Private Papers* (London, 1899), vol. ii, p. 513; Morley, *Gladstone* (ed. of 1905), vol. i, pp. 240–1; Hyde, op. cit., p. 4.

and Ripon, but there is no evidence of this in the Peel papers; though Peel, when he introduced his Budget in March 1842, and at other times, spoke highly of the value of his opinions.[1] With the general election of 1841 the old group broke up. Le Marchant left the Board, and was created a baronet. Parnell received a peerage in the Dissolution Honours, and died in February 1842. Bowring was elected to Parliament as member for Bolton, though there is in any case little likelihood that the Conservatives would have wished to employ him on statistical investigations.[2] Le Marchant's place at the Board was taken by J. G. Shaw-Lefevre, who was also a utilitarian and a supporter of the Whigs. Porter became head of the newly established Railway Department at the Board.

It is clear, from a number of references in the Peel papers and elsewhere, that the Conservative Ministers viewed the opinions of the Board with misgiving. The long debate on the sugar duties had involved the Board in party controversy. When Ripon arrived at the Board he sent for McGregor, and told him, according to Greville, that after his evidence before the Select Committee on Import Duties, he could have no confidence in him. McGregor stood his ground and refused to resign. In October 1843 Peel wrote in a letter to Graham: 'To tell you the truth Board of Trade accuracy does not stand very high with me just at present.' Another reference, again by Peel, in November 1844, gives the same impression: 'I wish the Board of Trade would write fewer books—and consider instead rather more maturely the bearing of projected alterations in the law.'[3]

The Conservatives then were more reserved and discreet in their relations with the officials of the Board than the Whigs had been. Gladstone himself worked out the effects of the sliding scale of 1828 on the hoarding of corn: the work was not delegated to the Statistical Department. When he asked Porter to prepare for him a memorandum on the provision (other than corn) laws, he took care, as he reported to Peel, not to give him 'any intimation of the

[1] *Hansard*, vol. 60, col. 210. See also p. 193 above.

[2] Bowring's tours had been the subject of a Conservative attack on the Whig ministry in July 1840: during the years 1835–7, when he was member for the Clyde Burghs, he had visited Switzerland and the Near East at the public expense—an office of profit under the Crown. In the course of the debate the value of his reports had been strongly criticized (see p. 108 above).

[3] Greville, op. cit., vol. v, pp. 53–54; Peel papers, B.M. Add. MSS. 40,447, f. 267; 40,450, f. 319.

purpose'.[1] In searching for information on which to base legislation, the Conservatives also acted with much greater circumspection. When they wished to find out first-hand information about the effect on the Continent of the British corn laws and of the laws relating to the import of other provisions, they sent an official who was unconnected with the Board, James Meek of the Victualling Department at the Admiralty: to send Porter or McGregor would, Gladstone believed, attract too much attention.[2]

It is therefore perhaps a paradox that Peel's reorganization of the tariff should have approached so closely to the scheme set forth by McGregor and Deacon Hume in 1840, and the process whereby this may have come about is worth examining.

The circumstances of the Whigs' resignation made it inevitable that commercial and financial policy should be the first questions which Peel should have tackled, and from the beginning the Conservatives were careful to avoid giving any pledges which might involve them in later difficulties—Graham wrote to Peel of the Whigs' hope 'of betraying us into pledges against specifick measures which may embarrass our future policy: but the *Men* rather than their *Measures* are now the just object of attack: we so decided after their defeat on the Sugar Duties'.[3]

At the same time the doctrines put forward by the Select Committee on Import Duties forced themselves on the Conservatives' attention. Peel, in a letter which has been much quoted, wrote as late as December 1841, that he had not read 'a particle of the Report on Import Duties, or of the evidence . . .'.[4] But this shows very little, for by the summer of 1841 the ideas of this committee had been circulated among statesmen, in the manner which Parnell had foretold, when he submitted his article to the *Edinburgh Review*. In particular they were conscious of the views of the *Spectator*. On 4 August Arbuthnot wrote to Graham:

The Duke was very much struck by an article in last week's *Spectator*. It details with great ability, and with a moderation unusual in that paper, what would be the way to make Peel's a strong Government; and after advising a searching investigation into the whole of our Tariff, with a view to improvements in it, the article goes on to declare that if the

[1] Ibid. 40,469, f. 32.
[2] Ibid., f. 29.
[3] Peel papers, 40,318, f. 293.
[4] C. S. Parker, *Sir Robert Peel*, &c., vol. ii, p. 509.

Revenue cannot by such means be sufficiently augmented, recourse must be had to a Property Tax.

I am only quoting the Duke when I say that such must be the first things to do.

Graham replied:

I am a constant reader of the *Spectator*, . . . and I was so much struck with the good sense of the article to which you refer that in writing to Peel I called his particular attention to it.[1]

Graham's letter to Peel is of some importance. He deprecated the idea of delegating any further investigation of the tariff to a Parliamentary committee—this, he thought, was a 'makeshift to gain time'. But he proceeded to outline a programme of reform directly based on the Import Duties Report—alterations in the sugar[2] and coffee duties, repeal of the duty on raw cotton, and then, 'It would also be wise to look narrowly into those 1,100 articles which are subject to duty on importation, and which yield only a net annual revenue of £360,000 while 46 articles produce an income of £22,598,000.'[3] At the same time Graham made it clear that alteration of the tariff must be accompanied by some new form of direct taxation.

Two things are clear about the Conservatives' views on this question. The first is that from the beginning they were prepared to face the introduction of substantial new direct taxation to meet the mounting deficits; in this they differed essentially from the Whigs, and could save themselves from the charge of inconsistency when they went on to adopt Whig measures. Some time in the middle of July, before the election results were fully known, Peel was ventilating the idea of an income tax to Goulburn. Goulburn replied with a letter which set out the advantages and disadvantages of the tax, laying the greater emphasis on the disadvantages: Peel in reply said that the advantages were predominant. The final decision was not taken for some months, however; it was a question on which different Conservative leaders held strong and conflicting opinions. Gladstone showed his life-long objection to the income tax, and proposed instead a revived house tax. Ashburton, whom Peel consulted at some length, favoured an income tax at 5 per

[1] C. S. Parker, *Life and Letters of Sir James Graham* (London, 1907), vol. i, p. 307.

[2] Graham suggested reduction in the rate on colonial rather than foreign sugar.

[3] Peel papers, 40,446, f. 9.

cent. though he held that it would be 'next to insupportable to live in a country where such a tax were permanent'. Graham considered that an income tax was preferable to a house tax (which had proved itself highly unpopular in the thirties). Herries (outside the Government) was strongly in favour also. But all were agreed that the situation demanded something exceptional.[1] By the middle of October Peel seems to have decided in its favour, and in favour of relieving the pressure of taxation on consumption.

This decision, a change of front from his repeatedly expressed criticisms of a revived income tax in the thirties,[2] can be more easily understood than the tariff changes which accompanied it in the Budget of 1842. Some of these changes, such as the new classification of the tariff under twenty heads only, and the drastic reduction of 750 out of the list of 1,200 dutiable articles which already existed, need little explanation; they were primarily of administrative interest. Important changes of principle were involved in the changes in the corn laws, in the timber and coffee duties, and in the discussion on the sugar duties. All these involved political interests which, during their years in opposition, the Conservatives had tended to support. And once the decision to reintroduce the income tax had been taken, there was no longer the same pressing urgency to make any alteration in the tariff which seemed likely to increase the revenue. The influences at work here deserve to be examined.

The explanation seems to lie in the general influence of the propaganda campaign carried out by the group which had organized the Select Committee on Import Duties, for all four duties were under discussion from the beginning: a letter from Ripon at the Board to Peel, written on 17 October 1841, shows that facts and figures were being collected.[3] On 9 February Peel introduced a revised lower sliding scale for corn, which was designed to reduce the incentive to hoard corn, and thus make more steady the supply to Britain. In the Budget introduced on 11 March, important changes of principle were made. The coffee duties were reduced from 6*d*. and 1*s*. 3*d*. per pound for colonial and foreign coffee respectively, to 4*d*. and 8*d*. The duties on square timber were reduced from 10*s*. and 55*s*. to 1*s*. and 25*s*. per load, and there were

[1] Parker, *Sir Robert Peel*, &c., vol. ii, pp. 501–7.
[2] But cf. p. 9 above for Peel's views in 1830.
[3] Parker, op. cit., p. 496.

similar reductions on deals. The import of livestock and provisions which had formerly been prohibited was now permitted. The sugar duties were not altered, but this was due, not only to anxiety about the West Indies, but also to the ministry's hope that alterations in the duty on foreign sugar could be used as a bargaining counter in the impending negotiations for a new commercial treaty with Brazil.[1] Elsewhere the Budget was more conservative: import duties survived without alteration on raw cotton and on wool (which was the subject of criticism in the *Leeds Mercury*); on raw silk there was a reduction, but not an abolition, of the duty. In spite of all that had been said in 1840, there was no reduction in the duties on cotton, woollen, and linen manufactures.[2] The export of machinery was not freed until 1844.

In the end, therefore, the Board's influence was indirect: Peel and his colleagues independently decided to explore this policy. They were distrustful of the people at the Board, and dissatisfied with the information they had at their disposal; on the timber duties, they had to rely on information six or seven years out of date, that collected by the Select Committee of 1835: 'I wish', wrote Peel to Ripon, 'that immediately on our accession to the Government we had sent some experienced and trustworthy person to the North American provinces for the purpose of ascertaining the exact state of the facts with respect to the Canadian timber trade.' On the corn laws they found a similar state of ignorance: Peel complained of the 'very vague notions prevalent on this subject'.[4] But, nevertheless, the foundations of his policy had been laid in the Board of Trade.

Few Budgets in English history can have had so favourable a press as that of 1842. Several papers make it clear that its general outlines came as a complete surprise to the public, but the Budget had something in it to please all parties. Both ministerial and Opposition papers welcomed it, but for different reasons. Whig and Radical papers which had bitterly attacked the revised sliding scale in February as the sort of thing to be expected from a Tory Government, were surprised and pleased at the Customs proposals, but showed their party feeling by attacks of varying strength

[1] Parker, op. cit., p. 498.

[2] *Hansard*, vol. 60, col. 201; vol. 61, col. 458.

[3] Peel papers, B.M. Add. MSS. 40,464, ff. 75, 79.

[4] Ibid., f. 64.

on the new inquisitorial income tax. Many[1] criticized it because it failed to distinguish between incomes from property and incomes from industry and commerce: others, sticking to the Whig proposals of 1841 and to the calculations of McGregor, argued that the tariff changes would themselves have increased the revenue enough to make an income tax unnecessary. The attitude of Tory papers was also significant, for many of them had argued against similar proposals the year before. They praised the income tax as a bold measure to restore national honour, but nearly always they supported the Customs provisions also.[2] Even the *Northern Star*, when it first heard the news, gave strong support to Peel, for having done something to reduce the burden of taxation on the poor, and only regretted that he had not introduced a graduated income tax.[3] In the country at large there were protests, as there were bound to be, from some of the affected interests. The coal owners of Tyneside criticized the reimposition of the coal export duty which had been abolished in 1834; there were objections from colonial timber importers in Liverpool, and from dealers in leather, corks, spelter, and starch. But none of these attracted the strong support, whether in Parliament or with the public, that the silk manufacturers, the shipowners, and the supporters of Attwood had been able to command ten years previously; though 1842 was undoubtedly a year of severe and general depression. There was, in Greville's words, 'a general disposition . . . to acknowledge that Peel is entitled to a fair trial of what must be considered a great political and financial experiment'.[4] The average man, with whom Peel was in harmony, who only two years before had often been indifferent to the doctrine of indirect taxes for revenue only, or suspicious of it, had imperceptibly come to accept it as a piece of economic orthodoxy.

[1] This account is based on a reading of the *Morning Chronicle*, the *Manchester Guardian*, *Gateshead Observer*, *Sheffield Iris*, *Leeds Mercury*, *Hull Rockingham*, *Liverpool Mercury*, and *Aris' Birmingham Gazette*.

[2] This account is based on a reading of the *Standard*, the *Morning Herald*, *Manchester Courier*, *Leeds Intelligencer*, *Birmingham Advertiser*, and *Liverpool Mail*.

[3] *Northern Star*, 26 Mar., 2 and 9 Apr. 1842.

[4] See p. 1 above.

BIBLIOGRAPHY

A. Manuscript Sources

The records of the Board of Trade in the Public Record Office contain three important series:

B.T. 1—in-letters to the Board. These volumes contain letters sent in to the Board with no attempt at classification, other than the date of receipt. They are registered in separate indexes.

B.T. 3—copies of out-letters from the Board. These volumes are indexed.

B.T. 5—minutes of the meetings of the Board.

The miscellaneous series, B.T. 6, also contains a number of important documents.

Foreign Office Records. In addition to the main Foreign Office series (on Austria, Prussia, France, &c.) the series F.O. 97 (miscellaneous) is of importance, as it contains material relating to the activities of Bowring and McGregor.

French sources:

Archives nationales, series F^{12}. This contains information about the activities of Bowring and Villiers in France.

Ministère des affaires étrangères, correspondance commerciale relating to London. This describes some of the Anglo-French commercial negotiations of this period, and contains long French consular reports on economic policy in Britain.

Private manuscript collections used include:

Auckland MSS. (British Museum).
Clarendon MSS. (Bodleian Library).
Gladstone MSS. (British Museum).
Goulburn MSS. (Surrey Record Office).
Granville MSS. (Public Record Office).
McVey Napier MSS. (British Museum).
Melbourne MSS. (Hertford County Record Office).
Peel MSS. (British Museum).
Russell MSS. (Public Record Office).
Smith MSS. (Manchester Public Library).

B. Official Printed Sources

Hansard, Parliamentary Debates.

Parliamentary Papers:

1820, II.	Report from the Select Committee on the Foreign Trade of the Country (Timber).
III.	Report of the Lords' Select Committee on Foreign Trade.
1821, VI.	First Report [*sic*] from the Select Committee on Foreign Trade.
1828, V.	Reports of the Finance Committee of 1828.
1831–2, XIX.	Select Committee on the Silk Duties.
1833, V.	Select Committee on Agriculture.
VI.	Select Committee on Manufactures, Commerce, and Shipping.
XII.	Select Committee on Public Documents.
XLI.	Porter's Tables.
1834, XIX.	First Report of Bowring and Villiers on the Commercial Relations between France and Great Britain.
1835, XII.	Select Committee on Consular Establishments.
XIX.	Select Committee on the Timber Duties.
XXXVI.	Second Report of Bowring and Villiers (Silk and Wine).
XLIX.	Porter's Tables.
1836, VIII.	Select Committee on the State of Agriculture.
XLV.	Report on the Commerce and Manufactures of Switzerland, by John Bowring.
1837, V.	Report of Lords' Committee on the State of Agriculture.
1837–8, XX.	Select Committee on Rates of Postage.
1839, VIII.	Select Committee on Fresh Fruit Trade.
XVI.	Report of the Statistics of Tuscany, Lucca, the Pontifical and the Lombardo-Venetian States, by Dr. Bowring.
XLV.	Porter's Tables.
1840, V.	Select Committee on Import Duties.
XXI.	Dr. Bowring's Reports on the Statistics of Egypt, Syria, and Candia; and on the Prussian Commercial Union. Report on the Commercial Statistics of the Two Sicilies, by J. McGregor.
1841, VII.	Select Committee on the Export of Machinery.
1844, VIII.	Select Committee on Extending the Employment of Shipping.
1845, XV.	Report on the Condition of the Framework Knitters.

C. Other Contemporary Works

BADHAM, CHARLES: *The Life of James Deacon Hume, Secretary of the Board of Trade*, London, 1859.

BAGEHOT, WALTER: *The English Constitution*, London.

BOWRING, SIR JOHN: *Autobiographical Recollections*, ed. Lewin Bowring, London, 1877.

The City; or, the Physiology of London Business, London, 1845.

COBDEN, RICHARD: *Speeches*, ed. J. Bright and Thorold Rogers, London, 1870.

—— *Political Writings*, 4th ed., London, 1903.

DIETERICI, C. F. W.: *Statistische Übersicht der wichtigsten Gegenstände des Verkehrs und Verbrauchs im preußischen Staate und im deutschen Zollverbande*, Berlin, 1838–57.

—— *Handbuch der Statistik des preußischen Staats*, Berlin, 1861.

Enquête relative à diverses prohibitions, Paris, 1834.

Enquête sur les fers, Paris, 1829.

Enquête sur les houilles, Paris, 1833.

GREVILLE, C. C. F.: *Journal of the Reigns of George IV and William IV*, ed. Lytton Strachey and Roger Fulford, London, 1938.

GROTE, HARRIET: *The Philosophical Radicals of 1832*, London (privately printed), 1866.

—— *The Personal Life of George Grote*, London, 1873.

HUME, JAMES DEACON: *Thoughts on the Corn-Laws as connected with Agriculture, Commerce, and Finance*, London, 1815.

—— *The H.B.T. Letters*, London, 1834.

JACOB, WILLIAM: *Considerations on the Protection required by British Agriculture*, London, 1814.

—— *Letter to Samuel Whitbread*, London, 1815 (a sequel to the *Considerations*).

—— *An Inquiry into the Causes of Agricultural Distress*, London, 1816.

—— *A View of the Agriculture, Manufactures, Statistics, and State of Society of Germany and Parts of Holland and France . . . in 1819*, London, 1820.

—— *Report on the Trade in Foreign Corn*, London, 1826.

—— *Report respecting Agriculture and the Trade in Corn in some of the Continental States of Northern Europe*, London, 1828.

KNIGHT, CHARLES: *Passages of a Working Life*, London, 1864.

LE MARCHANT, SIR DENIS, BT.: *Memoir of Viscount Althorp*, London, 1876.

MCCULLAGH, TORRENS: *Memoirs of the Rt. Hon. Richard Lalor Sheil*, London, 1855.

MCCULLOCH, J. R.: *Dictionary of Commerce*, 2nd ed., London, 1835.

—— *Literature of Political Economy*, London, 1845.

MCGREGOR, JOHN: *Commercial and Financial Legislation of Europe and America*, London, 1841.

—— *Commercial Statistics of all Nations*, London, 1844–50.

MOLINARI, GUSTAVE DE: *Histoire du tarif*, Paris, 1847.

NEBENIUS, C. F.: *Der deutsche Zollverein, sein System und seine Zukunft*, Carlsruhe, 1835.

NORTHCOTE, SIR S., BT.: *Twenty Years of Financial Policy*, London, 1862.

PARNELL, SIR H., BT.: *Financial Reform*, London, 1830.

—— *Observations on the Trade between France and Great Britain*, London, 1831 (French translation, Paris, 1832).

PEEL, SIR R., BT.: *Speeches*, London, 1853.

—— *Memoirs*, ed. Mahon and Cardwell, London, 1857.

PORTER, G. R.: *The Effect of Restrictions on the Importation of Corn, considered with Reference to Landowners, Farmers, and Labourers*, London, 1839.

—— *Progress of the Nation in its Various Social and Economical Relations*, ed. of 1847, London.

PRENTICE, ARCHIBALD: *The History of the Anti-Corn Law League*, London, 1853.

RICARDO, DAVID: *Principles of Political Economy*, ed. Sraffa, Cambridge, 1951–5.

SCROPE, G. POULETT: *Memoir of Lord Sydenham*, London, 1843.

TAYLOR, SIR HENRY: *The Statesman*, London, 1836.

TOOKE, THOMAS: *History of Prices and the State of the Circulation*, London, 1838–57.

D. Modern Works

ALBION, R. G.: *Forests and Sea Power*, Cambridge, Mass., 1926.

AMÉ, L.: *Étude sur les tarifs de Douanes*, Paris, 1876.

ASHTON, T. S.: *Economic and Social Investigations in Manchester, 1833–1933*, London, 1934.

ASPINALL, A.: *Three Early Nineteenth-Century Diaries*, London, 1952.

—— *Politics and the Press*, London, 1949.

BARNES, D. G.: *A History of the English Corn Laws from 1660 to 1846*, London, 1930.

BEER, ADOLF: *Die österreichische Handelspolitik im neunzehnten Jahrhundert*, Vienna, 1891.

BENAERTS, PIERRE: *Les Origines de la grande industrie allemande*, Paris, 1933.

BERESFORD, M. W.: *The Leeds Chambers of Commerce*, Leeds, 1951.

BESSBOROUGH, EARL OF (ed.): *Lady Charlotte Guest: Extracts from Her Journal, 1833–1852*, London, 1950.

BRINKMANN, CARL: *Die preußische Handelspolitik vor dem Zollverein*, Berlin and Leipzig, 1922.

—— *Friedrich List*, Berlin and Munich, 1949.

BROCK, W. R.: *Lord Liverpool and Liberal Toryism*, Cambridge, 1941.

BUXTON, SYDNEY: *Finance and Politics, an Historical Study, 1783–1885*, London, 1888.

CHARLÉTY, S.: *La Monarchie de Juillet* (*L'Histoire de France contemporaine*), Paris, 1921.

CLAPHAM, J. H.: *The Economic Development of France and Germany*, Cambridge, 1921.

—— *An Economic History of Modern Britain*, vol. i, Cambridge, 2nd ed., 1930.

CLARK, G. KITSON: *Peel and the Conservative Party, a Study in Party Politics*, London, 1929.

CREIGHTON, D. G.: *The Commercial Empire of the St. Lawrence*, Toronto, 1937.

DONY, J. G.: *The History of the Straw Hat Industry*, Luton, 1942.

DOWELL, STEPHEN: *The History of Taxation and Taxes in England*, London, 1888.

DUNHAM, A. L.: *The Anglo-French Treaty of Commerce of 1860*, Ann Arbor, 1930.

FAY, C. R.: *Huskisson and his Age*, London, 1951.

GASH, N.: *Politics in the Age of Peel*, London, 1953.

GAYER, A. D., ROSTOW, W. W., and SCHWARZ, A.: *The Growth and Fluctuation of the British Economy*, Oxford, 1953.

GREENBERG, M.: *British Trade and the Opening of China, 1800–42*, Cambridge, 1951.

HALÉVY, E.: *A History of the English People in the Nineteenth Century*, London, 2nd ed., 1949–51.

—— *The Growth of Philosophic Radicalism*, London, 1928.

HENDERSON, W. O.: *The Zollverein*, Cambridge, 1939.

—— *Britain and Industrial Europe, 1750–1870*, Liverpool, 1954.

HILL, G. B.: *The Life of Sir Rowland Hill*, London, 1880.

HIRST, F. W.: *Gladstone as Financier and Economist*, London, 1931.

HYDE, F. E.: *Mr. Gladstone at the Board of Trade*, London, 1934.

LAUGHTON, J. K.: *Memoirs of the Life and Correspondence of Henry Reeve*, London, 1898.

LEADER, R. E.: *The Life and Letters of J. Arthur Roebuck*, London, 1897.

LEVASSEUR, E.: *Histoire du commerce de la France*, Paris, 1911–12.

LINDSAY, W. S.: *History of Merchant Shipping*, London, 1876.

LLEWELLYN SMITH, SIR HUBERT: *The Board of Trade* (Whitehall Series), London, 1928.

LOWER, A. R. M.: *The North American Assault on the Canadian Forest*, Toronto, 1938.

MACCOBY, S.: *English Radicalism, 1832–1852*, London, 1935.

MANCHESTER, A. K.: *British Pre-eminence in Brazil*, Chapel Hill, 1933.

MARION, MARCEL: *Histoire financière de la France*, Paris, 1914–18.

MATTHEWS, R. C. O.: *A Study in Trade-cycle History*, Cambridge, 1954.

MORLEY, J.: *Life of W. E. Gladstone*, London, 1903.

—— *Life of Richard Cobden*, London, 1881.

MORRELL, W. P.: *British Colonial Policy in the Age of Peel and Russell*, Oxford, 1930.

NESBITT, G. L.: *Benthamite Reviewing: the First Twelve Years of the Westminster Review, 1824–36*, New York, 1934.

NORTHBROOK, EARL OF: *Journals and Correspondence of Francis Thornhill Baring, Lord Northbrook* (privately printed), 1905.

PARKER, C. S.: *Sir Robert Peel from his Private Papers*, London, 1899.

—— *The Life and Letters of Sir James Graham*, London, 1907.

PHILIPS, C. H.: *The East India Company, 1784–1834*, Manchester, 1940.

POLITICAL ECONOMY CLUB: *Proceedings*, vol. vi, London, 1921.

PRICE, ARNOLD H.: *The Evolution of the Zollverein*, Ann Arbor, 1949.

PURYEAR, V. J.: *International Economics and Diplomacy in the Near East, 1834–1853*, Stanford, California, 1935.

REDFORD, A.: *Manchester Merchants and Foreign Trade, 1794–1858*, Manchester, 1934.

REES, SIR J. F., *A Short Fiscal and Financial History of England, 1815–1918*, London, 1921.

ROBINSON, HOWARD: *The British Post Office, a History*, Princeton, 1948.

ROSTOW, W. W.: *British Economy of the Nineteenth Century*, Oxford, 1948.

ROYAL STATISTICAL SOCIETY: *Annals, 1834–1934*, London, 1934.

SANDERS, L. C.: *Lord Melbourne's Papers*, London, 1889.

SCHLOTE, WERNER: *British Overseas Trade from 1700 to the 1930s*, trans. W. O. Henderson and W. H. Chaloner, Oxford, 1952.

SCHUYLER, R. L.: *Fall of the Old Colonial System*, Oxford, 1945.

SHEHAB, F.: *Progressive Taxation, a Study in the Development of the Progressive Principle in the British Income Tax*, Oxford, 1953.

SMART, WILLIAM: *Economic Annals of the Nineteenth Century*, London, 1910–17.

SOMBART, WERNER: *Deutsche Volkswirtschaft im neunzehnten Jahrhundert*, 7th ed., Berlin, 1927.

TAUSSIG, F. W.: *Tariff History of the United States*, 8th ed., New York, 1931.

TREVELYAN, G. M.: *Life of John Bright*, London, 1913.

VINER, JACOB: *Studies in the Theory of International Trade*, London, 1937.

WAKEFIELD, C. M.: *The Life of Thomas Attwood* (privately printed), 1885.

WALPOLE, SPENCER: *The Life of Lord John Russell*, London, 1889.

WEBSTER, C. K.: *The Foreign Policy of Palmerston, 1830–41*, London, 1951.

WRIGHT, G. H.: *Chronicles of the Birmingham Chamber of Commerce, 1813–1913*, Birmingham, 1913.

INDEX

PRINTED IN
GREAT BRITAIN
AT THE
UNIVERSITY PRESS
OXFORD
BY
CHARLES BATEY
PRINTER
TO THE
UNIVERSITY